RED CAPITALISM

The fragile financial foundation of China's extraordinary rise

RED CAPITALISM
The fragile financial foundation of China's extraordinary rise

Carl E. Walter
and
Fraser J. T. Howie

WILEY

John Wiley & Sons (Asia) Pte. Ltd.

Other Wiley Editorial Offices

John Wiley & Sons, 111 River Street, Hoboken, NJ07030, USA
John Wiley & Sons, The Atrium, Southern Gate, Chichester, West Sussex, P019 8SQ,
  United Kingdom
John Wiley & Sons (Canada) Ltd., 5353 Dundas Street West, Suite 400, Toronto, Ontario, M9B
  6HB, Canada
John Wiley & Sons Australia Ltd, 42 McDougall Street, Milton, Queensland 4064, Australia
Wiley-VCH, Boschstrasse 12, D-69469 Weinheim, Germany

Library of Congress Cataloging-in-Publication Data

ISBN 978-0-470-82586-0 (Hardcover)

ISBN 978-0-470-82894-6 (e-book)

ISBN 978-0-470-82893-9 (e-book)

ISBN 978-0-470-82895-3 (e-book)

Typeset in 11/14pt Times by MPS Limited, a Macmillan Company, Chennai, India.

10 9 8 7 6 5

To John Wilson Lewis

Contents

Preface

After three rounds of *Privatizing China*, our book about China's stock markets, we felt like we wanted to look into something new. Since we took our first look at the stock markets in 1999, we have been interested to note the lack of work on the financial side of China's miracle that gets beyond the macroeconomics of things. We are the first to agree that living and working in the country for 25 years may not qualify us as experts in economics. We do believe, however, that our experience has given us a feel for how China's political elite manages money and the country's economy. Having worked in banks for longer than we care to remember, we wanted to try to understand how China and its ruling class finance themselves and we knew we had to begin with the banks since, in truth, they are China's financial system. Those looking for tales of corruption and princelings with their hands in the till will be disappointed though. We think that the financial side of the story behind a 30-year boom that changed the lives of one billion people is much more interesting; so this is our effort at staking out modern China's political economy "inside the system."

We do not believe in Chinese exceptionalism. China's economy is no different from any other, in spite of the inevitable Chinese characteristics. If there are such things as economic laws, they work just as well in China and for Chinese businesses as they do in other markets. We also do not believe in the recent triumphalism of China's bankers and many of its leaders; this is only a diplomatic ploy. China's banks survived the global financial crisis, as one senior banker has publicly stated, simply because the financial system is closed off from the world. Having seriously studied the collapse of Mexico's peso in 1994, the Asian Financial Crisis of 1997 and those sovereign-debt crises that have followed, China's political elite has no intention of exposing itself to international capital markets. The domestic economy and markets are, and will continue to be, most deliberately closed off. With a non-convertible currency, minimal foreign participation and few overseas assets beyond US Treasuries and commodity investments that will neither be marked-to-market nor sold, why shouldn't the system survive a major international crisis better than open economies? China's financial system is designed so that no one is able to take a position opposite to that of the government.

Of course, the private export-oriented sector suffered massive losses in jobs, earnings and the closure of small companies in 2008 and 2009. But China's banks were not exposed in any material way to this sector. It is a simple fact that China's financial system and its stock, bond and loan markets cater only to the state sector, of which the "National Champions" represent the reddest of the Red. These corporations, the heart of China's state-owned economy, are "inside the system." The private economy, no matter how vibrant, is "outside the system" and, in fact, serves at the will of the system. If nothing else, the events of the fall of 2008 added an additional seal to the Party's determination to sustain a closed, tightly controlled, economy. "Don't show me any failed models," is the refrain of the Chinese officialdom these days. But is China's own financial system a model for the world to study? Can China be thought of as an economic superpower, either now or in the future, with such a system?

With this sort of question in mind, we began to look at the financial history of the People's Republic of China. We were fortunate that 2008 was the thirtieth anniversary of China's highly successful Reform and Opening Policy, so there were many excellent retrospectives prepared by the government agencies. The People's Bank of China, in particular, produced very useful material, some of which took one of us back 30 years to Beijing University where his study of Chinese banks began. We hasten to emphasize that all the information used in writing this book derives from purely public sources. In China, all of the important ministries, corporations and banks maintain excellent websites, so data is just out there in the wind waiting to be downloaded. In particular, China Bond and the National Association of Financial Market Institutional Investors (NAFMII), a sub-set of the People's Bank, have extensive websites providing access to information, in both Chinese and English, on China's fixed-income markets. Data for the stock markets have always been plentiful and, we believe, accurate. Again, Wind Information, China's Bloomberg equivalent, has been a rich source for us. Then, there are the audited financial statements of China's banks, all available online since the respective listings of each bank. Reading these statements has been highly educational. We strongly encourage others, including China's regulators, to do the same.

So the modern age of technology provided all the dots that, linked together, present a picture of the financial sector. How they are connected in this book is purely the authors' collective responsibility: the picture presented, we believe, is accurate to the best of our professional and personal experience. We hope that this book will, like *Privatizing China*, be seen as a constructive outsiders' view of how China's leadership over the years has put together what we believe to be a very fragile financial system.

For all the fragility of the current system, however, one of us is always reminded that his journey in China began in Beijing back in 1979 when the city looked a lot like Pyongyang. With North Korea in the headlines again for all the wrong reasons, it is worth remembering and acknowledging the tremendous benefits the great majority of Chinese have reaped as a result of the changes over the past 30 years. This can never be forgotten, but it should also not be used as an excuse to ignore or downplay the very real weaknesses lying at the heart of the financial system.

We would like to thank those who have helped us think about this big topic, including in no particular order Kjeld Erik Brosdgaard, Peter Nolan, Josh Cheng, Jean Oi, Michael Harris, Arthur Kroeber, Andrew Zhang, Alan Ho, Andy Walder, Sarah Eaton, Elaine La Roche and Victor Shih. Over the years we have grown to greatly appreciate our friends at John Wiley, starting with Nick Wallwork, our publisher who kickstarted our writing career in 2003, Fiona Wong, Jules Yap, Cynthia Mak and Camy Boey. Professionals all, they made working on this book easy and enjoyable. John Owen was an unbelievably quick copyeditor and Celine Tng, our proofreader, gave "detail-oriented" a whole new definition! We thank you all for your strong support. What we have written here, however, remains our sole responsibility and reflects neither the views of our friends and colleagues, nor those of the organizations we work for.

We have dedicated the book to John Wilson Lewis, Professor Emeritus of Political Science at Stanford University. John was the catalyst for Carl's career in China and, indirectly, Fraser's as well. Without his support and encouragement, it is fair to say that this book and anything else we have done over the years in China might never have happened. We both continue to be very much in debt to our wives and families who have continued to at least tolerate our curious interest in Chinese financial matters. We promise to drop the topic for a while now, even though we are well aware that there remains much that needs to be looked at in the financial space, including trust companies and asset-transfer exchanges.May be next time.

Beijing and Singapore
October 2010

List of Abbreviations

ABC	Agricultural Bank of China
AMC	asset-management company
BOC	Bank of China
CBRC	China Banking Regulatory Commission
CDB	China Development Bank
CGB	Chinese government bond
CIC	China Investment Corporation
CP	commercial paper
CSRC	China Securities Regulatory Commission
ICBC	Industrial and Commercial Bank of China
MOF	Ministry of Finance
MOR	Ministry of Railways
MTN	medium-term notes
NAV	net asset value
NDRC	National Development and Reform Commission
NPC	National People's Congress
NPL	non-performing loan
PBOC	People's Bank of China
SAFE	State Administration for Foreign Exchange
SASAC	State-owned Assets Supervision and Administration Commission

CHAPTER

1

Looking Back at the Policy of Reform and Opening

"One short nap took me all the way back to before 1949."

Unknown cadre, Communist Party of China
Summer 2008

It was the summer of 2008 and the great cities of eastern China sparkled in the sun. Visitors from the West had seen nothing like it outside of science fiction movies. In Beijing, the mad rush to put the finishing touches on the Olympic preparations was coming to an end—some 40 million pots of flowers had been laid out along the boulevards overnight. The city was filled with new subway and light-rail lines, an incomparable new airport terminal, the mind-boggling Bird's Nest stadium, glittering office buildings and the CCTV Tower! Superhighways reached out in every direction, and there was even orderly traffic. Bristling in Beijing's shadow, Shanghai appeared to have recovered the level of opulence it had reached in the 1930s and boasted a cafe society unsurpassed anywhere in Asia. Further south, Guangzhou, in the footsteps of Shanghai Pudong, was building a brand new city marked by two 100-storey office, hotel and television towers, a new library, an opera house and, of course, block after block of glass-clad buildings. Everyone, it seemed, was driving a Mercedes Benz or a BMW; the country was awash in cash.

In the summer of 2008, China was in the midst of the hottest growth spurt in its entire history. The people stirred with righteous nationalism as it seemed obvious to all that the twenty-first century did, in fact, belong to the Chinese: just look at the financial mess internationally! Did anyone even remember the Cultural Revolution, Tiananmen, or the Great Leap Forward? In a brief 30 years, China had rejected communism, created its own brand of capitalism and, as all agreed, seemed poised to surpass its great model, the United States of America, the Beautiful Country. Looking around at China's coastal cities bathed in the light of neon signs advertising multinational brands, their streets clogged with Buicks and Benzes, the wonder expressed by the confused Party cadre's comment— "One short nap took me all the way back to before 1949"—can be well understood. In many ways, the past 30 years in China have seen a big rewind of the historical tape-recording to the early twentieth century.

The West, its commentariat and investment-bank analysts all saw this as a miracle because they had never expected it. After all, 30 years ago China was barely able to pull itself off the floor where it had been knocked flat by the Cultural Revolution. Beijing in 1978 was a fully depreciated version of the city in 1949 minus the great city walls, which had all been torn down and turned into workers' shanties and bomb shelters. When the old *Quotations from Chairman Mao* billboards were painted over in 1979, one new one depicted a Chang An Avenue streaming with automobiles: cyclists glanced in passing and pedaled slowly on. Shanghai, the former Pearl of the Orient, was frozen in time and completely dilapidated, with no air-conditioning anywhere and people sleeping on the streets in the torrid summer heat. Shenzhen was a rice paddy and Guangzhou a moldering ruin. There was no beer, much less ice-cold beer, available anywhere; only thick glass bottles of warm orange pop stacked in wooden crates.

THIRTY YEARS OF OPENING UP: 1978–2008

As a counterpoint to the Olympics and 2008, Deng Xiaoping, during his first, brief, political resurrection in 1974, led a large Chinese delegation to a special session of the United Nations. This was a huge step for China in lifting the self-imposed isolation that prevailed during the Cultural Revolution. Just before departing for New York, the entire central government, so the story goes, made a frantic search through all the banks in Beijing for funds to pay for the trip. The cupboard was bare: they could scrape together only US$38,000.[1] This was to be the first time a supreme leader of China, virtually the Last Emperor, had visited America; if he couldn't afford first-class international travel, just where was the money to support China's economic development to come from?

How did it all happen, because it most certainly has happened? How were these brilliant achievements of only one generation paid for? And the corollary to this: what was the price paid? Understanding how China and its Communist Party has built its own version of capitalism is fundamental to understanding the role China will play in the global economy in the next few years. The overall economics of China's current predicament is well understood by international economists, but the institutional arrangements underlying its politics and economics and their implications are far less understood. This book is about how institutions in China's financial sector—its banks, local-government "financing platforms," securities companies and corporations—affect the country's economic choices and development path. Of course, behind these entities lies the Communist Party of China and the book necessarily talks about its role as well.

Prior to the Lehman shock of September 2008, the trajectory China's financial development had been tracing generally followed a well-established path taken by more advanced economies elsewhere in the world. This approach was not easily adopted by a political elite that had been devastated by its own leaders for nearly 20 years and then suffered a further shock in 1989. The general story, however, has become the Great China Development Myth. It begins with the death of Mao in 1976 and the second restoration of Deng Xiaoping two years later. These events freed China to take part in the great financial liberalization that swept the world over the past quarter-century (see Figure 1.1). Looking back, there is no doubt that by the end of the 1980s, China saw the financial model embodied in the American Superhighway to Capital as its road to riches. It had seemed to work well for the Asian Tiger economies; why not for China as well? And so it has proven to be.

In the 1990s, China's domestic reforms followed a path of deregulation blazed by the United States. In Shenzhen, in 1992, Deng Xiaoping resolutely expressed the view that capitalism wasn't just for capitalists.

FIGURE 1.1   Thirty years of reform—trends in regulation

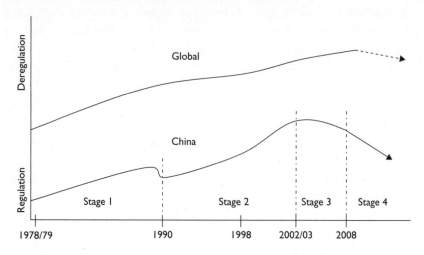

Source: Based on comments made by Peter Nolan, Copenhagen Business School, December 4, 2008

His confidence caused the pace of reform to immediately quicken. China's accession to the World Trade Organization in 2001 perhaps represented the crowning achievement in the unprecedented 13-year run of the Jiang Zemin/Zhu Rongji partnership. When had China's economy ever before been run by its internationalist elite from the great City of Shanghai? Then, in 2003, the new Fourth Generation leaders were ushered in and things began to change. There was a feeling that too few people had gotten too rich too fast. While this may be true, the policy adjustments made have begun to endanger the earlier achievements and have had a significant impact on the government itself. The new leadership's political predisposition, combined with a weak grasp of finance and economics, has led to change through incremental political compromise that has pushed economic reform far from its original path. This policy drift has been hidden by a booming economy and almost-continuous bread and circuses—the Olympics, the Big Parade, the Shanghai World Expo and Guangzhou's Asian Games.

The framework of China's current financial system was set in the early 1990s by Jiang and Zhu. The best symbols of its direction are the Shanghai and Shenzhen stock exchanges, both established in the last days of 1990. Who could ever have thought in the dark days of 1989 that China would roll out the entire panoply of capitalism over the ensuing 10 years? In 1994, various laws were passed that created the basis for an independent central bank and set the biggest state banks—Bank of China (BOC), China Construction Bank (CCB), Industrial and Commercial Bank of China (ICBC) and Agricultural Bank of China (ABC)—on a path to become fully commercialized or, at least, more independent in their risk judgments and with strengthened balance sheets that did not put the economic and political systems at risk.

Reform was strengthened as a result of the lessons learned from the Asian Financial Crisis (AFC) in late 1997. Zhu Rongji, then premier, seized the moment to push a thorough recapitalization and repositioning of banks that the world at the time rightly viewed as more than "technically" bankrupt. He and a team led by Zhou Xiaochuan, then Chairman and CEO of the China Construction Bank, adopted a well-used international technique to thoroughly restructure their balance sheets. Similar to the Resolution Trust Corporation of the US savings-and-loan experience, Zhou advocated the creation of four "bad" banks, one for each of the Big 4 state banks. In 2000 and again in 2003, the government stripped out a total of over US$400 billion in bad loans from bank balance sheets and transferred them to the bad banks. It then recapitalized each bank, and attracted premier global financial institutions as strategic partners. On this solid base, the banks then raised over US$40 billion in new capital by listing their shares in Hong Kong and Shanghai in 2005 and 2006. The process had taken years of determined effort. Without doubt, the triumphant listings of BOC, CCB, and ICBC marked the peak of financial reform, and it seemed for a brief moment that China's banks were on their way to becoming true banking powerhouses that, over time, would compete with the HSBCs and Citibanks of the world.

China at last acceded to the World Trade Organization (WTO) in late 2001 after 15 years of difficult negotiations. Zhu saw membership of the WTO as the guarantee of an unalterable international orientation for a China that in the past had too frequently been given to cycles of isolationism. He believed that the WTO would provide the transformational engine for economic and, to a certain extent, political modernization regardless of who controlled the government. His enthusiasm for engagement with the world paid off as trade with China turned white hot in the years that followed (see Figure 1.2).

FIGURE 1.2   Trends in imports, exports and total trade, 1999–2007

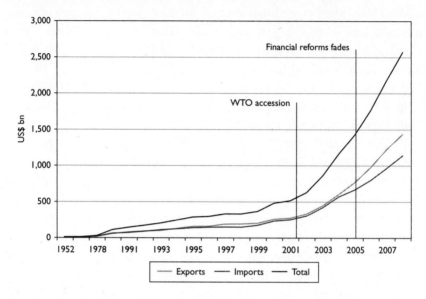

Source: China Statistical Yearbook 2008

It was not just trade; foreign direct investment also poured in, jumping to unheard-of levels of US$60 billion a year and peaking at over US$92 billion in 2008 as the world's corporations committed their manufacturing operations to the Chinese market (see Figure 1.3). Chairmen in boardrooms everywhere believed with Zhu Rongji that China was on a path of economic liberalization that was irreversible.

The commitment of these foreign businessmen was not simply a function of belief. In the early years of the twenty-first century, China's market opened up as it never had before. At the start of economic liberalization in the 1980s, foreign investors had been forced to contend with the practical consequences of the famous "Bird Cage" theory. Trapped in designated economic zones along the eastern seaboard, just as they had been in the Treaty Ports of the Qing Dynasty a hundred years earlier, foreign companies were forced into inefficient joint ventures with unwanted Chinese partners. Then every local government wanted its own zone and its own foreign birds, so that during the 1990s, economic zones proliferated across the country and were eventually no longer "special." Despite this, even as late as 2000, the joint-venture format accounted for over 50 percent of all foreign-invested

FIGURE 1.3 Committed foreign direct investment, 1979–2008

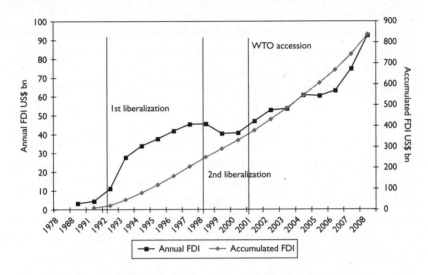

Source: *China Statistical Yearbook* 2009

TABLE 1.1 FDI by investment-vehicle structure, 2000–2008

	Equity JV (%)	Contractual JV (%)	Wholly-owned enterprise (%)	Shareholding (%)	Total FDI (US$ billion)
2000	36.2	16.1	47.4	0.2	40.3
2001	35.1	13.1	50.9	0.9	46.4
2002	28.4	9.7	60.5	1.3	52.4
2003	29.1	7.2	63.1	0.6	52.9
2004	27.1	5.1	66.4	1.3	60.5
2005	24.2	3.0	71.4	1.4	60.3
2006	22.5	4.0	73.4	0.01	65.8
2007	20.9	1.5	76.6	0.01	74.8
2008	18.0	2.0	78.2	0.01	95.3
2009	18.8	2.1	74.8	0.0	91.8

Source: US-China Business Council; as a percent of total utilized FDI

corporate structures. After China's accession to the WTO, this changed rapidly. It seemed that China was open for business after all: by 2008, nearly 80 percent of all foreign investment assumed a wholly-owned enterprise structure (see Table 1.1). At long last, the Treaty Port system seemed a thing of the past, as foreign companies had the choice of where and how to invest.

Over the past few years, they have undeniably committed their technologies and management techniques and learned how to work with China's talented workers to build a world-beating job-creation and export machine. But they have done this in only two areas of China: Guangdong and the Yangzi River Delta comprising Shanghai and southern Jiangsu Province (see Figure 1.4). The economies of these two regions are dominated by foreign-invested and private (*waizi* 外资 and *minying* 民营) companies; there is virtually no state sector remaining. These areas consistently attract 70 percent of total foreign direct investment and contribute over 70 percent of China's exports. They are the machine that has created the huge foreign-exchange reserves for Beijing and they have changed the face of these two regions. It is highly ironic that the old Treaty Ports, which once symbolized its weakness and subservience to foreign colonizers, are now the source of China's rise as a global manufacturing and trading power, becoming in the process the most vibrant and exciting parts of the country and, indeed, of all Asia.

China's economic geography is not simply based on geography. There is a parallel economy that is geographic as well as politically strategic. This is commonly referred to as the economy "inside the system" (*tizhinei* 体制内) and, from the Communist Party's viewpoint, it is the real political economy. All of the state's financial, material and human resources, including the policies that have opened the country to foreign investment, have been and continue to be directed at the "system." Improving and strengthening it has been the goal of every reform effort undertaken by the Party since 1978. It must be remembered that the efforts of Zhu Rongji, perhaps China's greatest reformer, were aimed at strengthening the economy "inside the system," not changing it. In this sense, he is China's Mikhail Gorbachev; he believed in the system's capacity for change as well as the dire need for its reform. Nothing Zhu undertook was ever intended to weaken the state or the Party.

Understood in this context, the foreign and non-state sectors will be supported only as long as they are critical as a source of jobs (and hence, the all-important household savings), technology and foreign exchange. The resemblance of today's commercial sector in China, both foreign and local, to that of merchants in traditional, Confucian China is marked: it

FIGURE 1.4 US$818 billion accumulated FDI by province, 1993–2008

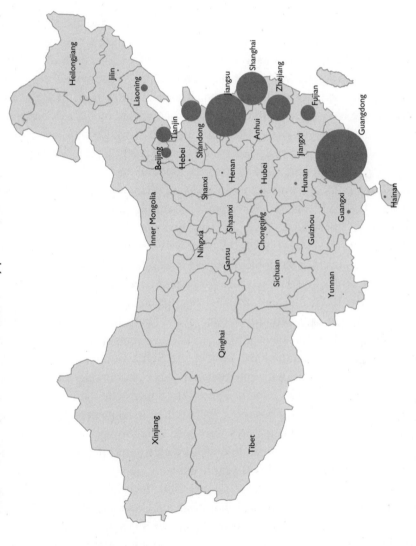

Source: *China Statistical Yearbook*, various

is there to be used tactically by the Party and is not allowed to play a dominant role.

THIRTEEN YEARS OF REFORM: 1992–2005

Foreign investment has enriched certain localities and their populace beyond recognition, but foreign financial services have done far more on behalf of the Party and its system. It is not an exaggeration to say that Goldman Sachs and Morgan Stanley made China's state-owned corporate sector what it is today. Without their financial know-how, SOEs would long since have lapsed into obscurity, out-competed by China's entrepreneurs, as they were in the 1980s. In the 1980s, who could have named a single Chinese company other than Beijing Jeep, a joint venture, and, maybe, Tsingtao Beer, a brand from the colonial past? In Shenzhen, there is a huge billboard with a portrait of Deng Xiaoping located on the spot where he made his famous comments during his historic "Southern Excursion" of January 1992. If Deng had not said that capitalist tools would work in socialist hands, who knows where China would be today? His words provided the political cover for all others who, like Zhu Rongji, wanted China's "system" to move forward into the world.

In early 1993, Zhu took the first big step forward when he accepted the suggestion of the chief executive of the Hong Kong Stock Exchange to open the door for selected SOEs to list on overseas stock markets. He knew and supported the idea that Chinese SOEs would have to undergo restructuring in line with international legal, accounting and financial requirements to achieve their listings. He hoped that foreign regulatory oversight would have a positive effect on their management performance. His expectations in many ways were met. After several years of experimentation, companies began to emerge with true economies of scale for the first time in China's 5,000-year history.

Where did such *Fortune* Global 500 heavy-hitters as Sinopec, PetroChina, China Mobile and Industrial and Commercial Bank of China come from? The answer is simple: American investment bankers created China Mobile out of a poorly managed assortment of provincial post and telecom entities and sold the package to international fund managers as a national telecommunications giant. In October 1997, as the Asian

Financial Crisis was gathering momentum, China Mobile completed a dual listing on the New York and Hong Kong stock exchanges, raising US$4.2 billion. There was no looking back as China's oil companies, banks and insurance companies sold billions of US dollars of shares in initial public offerings (IPOs) that went off like strings of firecrackers in the global capital markets. All of these companies were imagined up, created and listed by American investment bankers.

To symbolize this transformation, the government planned a new target. After China Mobile's successful IPO, Beijing sought as a matter of policy to place as many Chinese companies on the *Fortune* Global 500 list as possible. With the willing help of international investment banks, lawyers, and accounting firms, China has more than achieved this goal. The country is now proudly represented by 44 companies on the list (see Table 1.2).

TABLE 1.2   Chinese companies in the *Fortune* Global 500, FY2009

Rank	Company	Revenues (US$ million)
7	Sinopec	187,518
8	State Grid	184,496
10	China National Petroleum	165,496
77	China Mobile Communications	71,749
87	Industrial & Commercial Bank of China	69,295
116	China Construction Bank	58,361
118	China Life Insurance	57,019
133	China Railway Construction	52,044
137	China Railway Group	50,704
141	Agricultural Bank of China	49,742
143	Bank of China	49,682
156	China Southern Power Grid	45,735
182	Dongfeng Motors	39,402
187	China State Construction Engineering	38,117
203	Sinochem Group	35,577
204	China Telecommunications	35,557
223	Shanghai Automotive	33,629
224	China Communications Construction	33,465
242	Noble Group	31,183
252	China National Offshore Oil	30,680

TABLE 1.2 (Continued)

Rank	Company	Revenues (US$ million)
254	CITIC Group	30,605
258	China FAW Group	30,237
275	China South Industries Group	28,757
276	Baosteel Group	28,591
312	COFCO	26,098
313	China Huaneng Group	26,019
314	Hebei Iron & Steel Group	25,924
315	China Metallurgical Group	25,868
330	Aviation Industry Corporation of China	25,189
332	China Minmetals	24,956
348	China North Industries Group	24,150
352	Sinosteel	24,014
356	Shenhua Group	23,605
368	China United Network Communications	23,183
371	People's Insurance Company of China	23,116
383	Ping An Insurance	22,374
395	China Resources	21,902
397	Huawei Technologies	21,821
412	China Datang Group	21,460
415	Jiangsu Shagang Group	21,419
428	Wuhan Iron & Steel	20,543
436	Aluminum Corporation of China	19,851
440	Bank of Communications	19,568
477	China Guodian	17,871

Source: Fortune, July 26, 2010

Among these companies are five banks, including ICBC, which ranked eighty-seventh by total revenues (as compared to twenty-fifth for JPMorgan Chase). Sinopec and the huge State Grid Corporation ranked seventh and eighth, respectively. The "National Team" was born.

At the start of the 1990s, all Chinese companies had been unformed state-owned enterprises; by the end of the decade, hundreds were listed companies on the Hong Kong, New York, London and Shanghai stock exchanges. In those few short years, bankers, lawyers and accountants had restructured those of the old SOEs that could be restructured into some-thing resembling modern corporations, then sold and listed their shares. In short, China's *Fortune* Global 500 companies were the products of Wall Street; even China's own locally listed version of investment banking, represented by CITIC Securities with a market capitalization of US$26 billion, was built after the American investment-banking model.

China's capital markets, including Hong Kong, are now home to the largest IPOs and are the envy of investment bankers and issuers the world over. With a total market capitalization of RMB24.5 trillion (US$3.6 trillion) and more than 1,800 listed companies, the Shanghai and Shenzhen exchanges have, in the last 10 years, come to rival all exchanges in Asia, including the Tokyo Exchange (see Figure 1.5). If the Hong Kong Stock Exchange is considered Chinese—and it should be, since Chinese companies constitute 48.1 percent[2] of its market capitalization—then China over the past 15 years has given rise to the second-largest equity-capital market in the world after New York. From 1993, when IPOs began, to early 2010, Chinese SOEs have raised US$389 billion on domestic exchanges and a further US$262 billion on international markets, adding

FIGURE 1.5 Comparative market capitalizations, China, the rest of Asia, and the US

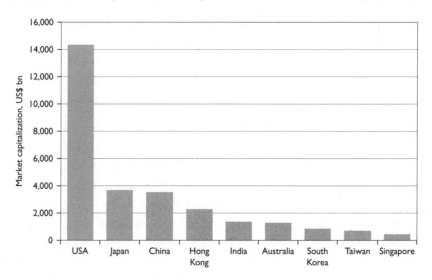

Source: Bloomberg, March 26, 2010

a total of US$651 billion in capital to the US$818 billion contributed by foreign direct investment. Considering that China's GDP in 1985 was US$306 billion, only US$971 billion in 1999 and US$4.9 trillion in 2009, this was big money.

While money is money, there is a difference in the impact these two sources of capital have had on China. FDI created an entirely new economy; the non-state sector. Over the years, the management and production skills, as well as the technologies of foreign-invested companies have been transferred to Chinese entrepreneurs and have given rise to new domestic industries. In contrast, the larger part of the US$651 billion raised on international and domestic capital markets has gone to creating and strengthening companies "inside the system." Beijing had, from the very start in 1993, restricted the privilege of listing shares to state-owned enterprises in the name of SOE reform. The market capitalization in Hong Kong, Shanghai and elsewhere belongs to companies controlled outright by China's Communist Party; only minority stakes have been sold.

All of these—SOE and bank reform, stock markets, international IPOs and, most of all, accession to the WTO—might be described as the core initiatives of the Jiang Zemin/Zhu Rongji program for the transformation of that part of China's economy "inside the system." From 2003 and the accession of the new Party leadership under Hu Jintao and Wen Jiabao, this program began to drift and even came under attack for having created "intolerable" income disparities. The drift ended in 2005 when forward progress on financial reform largely came to a halt long before the collapse of Lehman Brothers in September 2008 killed it stone dead.[3]

THE END OF REFORM: 2005

The year 2005 is fundamental to understanding China's financial markets today—it marks the last great thrust of the Jiang/Zhu era. What remains in place continues to be very visible, providing China with the sheen of modern markets and successful reform. The stock, commodity and bond markets help support Beijing's claim to be a "market economy" under the terms of the WTO. But the failure to complete the reforms begun in 1998 has left China's financial institutions, especially its banks, in a vulnerable position. As the Fourth Generation Leadership took over in early 2003, there were two major initiatives underway. The first was the bank-restructuring program that had begun in 1998 and was just starting on a second round of disposals of problem loans. The second was the ongoing effort to restore a collapsed stock market to health. Zhou Xiaochuan, who had moved from being chairman of the CSRC to governor of the central bank in 2002, was Zhu Rongji's principal architect.

Zhou had necessarily started with the banks since their fragile state in 1998 was a threat to the entire economy. Given China's underdeveloped capital markets, nearly all financial risk was then concentrated in the banks. To create a mechanism to alleviate this stress, Zhou sought to develop a bond market. Such a market would allow corporations to establish direct financial links with end-investors and would also mean greater financial flexibility at times when stock markets were weak or unattractive. At this point in 2003, corporate debt constituted less than 3.5 percent of total issuance in China's bond market (see Figure 1.6).

The market itself provided less than 30 percent of all capital raised, including loans, bonds and equity (see Figure 1.7).

Over the course of 2003 and 2004, Zhou laid the ground work for his future policy initiatives. First, he actively shaped what became the first official government statement in support of China's capital markets since Deng's 1992 comments. In what became known as "The Nine Articles," in early 2004, the Party emphatically affirmed the critical role of capital markets, which were defined to include the bond markets as well as the stock markets.

With this political cover in place, Zhou created the institutional infrastructure he would need to support bank reform. In September 2003, a new Financial Markets Department in the PBOC was established to lead the development of new policies and products for the bond markets. More strategically, on December 6, 2003, the PBOC established a wholly-owned corporate entity known as Central SAFE Investments (more commonly known as "Huijin"), and China Jianyin Investments, a wholly-owned subsidiary of Huijin. These entities became the crucial parts of the effort to restructure and recapitalize the Big 4 banks, channeling new capital to CCB and BOC in 2004. They also became the most fought-over piece of turf in the entire financial system.

Although Zhou's starting point appeared to be banks and the underdeveloped bond markets, his real objective was the stock market. He knew well that bond risk continued to be borne largely by the banks and that only the stock markets truly enabled corporations to raise money directly from

FIGURE 1.6 Bond market issuance by issuer type, 1992–2009

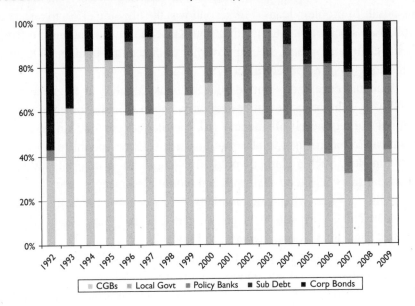

Source: PBOC *Financial Stability Report,* various

FIGURE 1.7 Corporate capital raised in Chinese markets, 1993–1H 2009

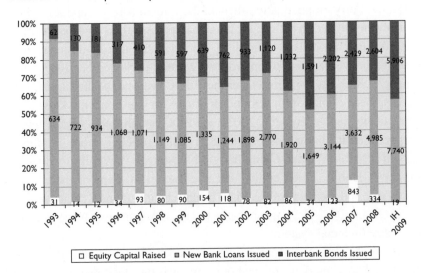

Source: PBOC *Financial Stability Report,* various
Note: Interbank bonds include CGBs, financial bonds and all corporate bonds.

third-party investors outside of the banking system. To drive at a revival of the stock markets, however, was outside the scope of his jurisdiction; he would be stepping on other people's toes. With the strong support of Jiang Zemin, who retained a place as chairman of the key China Military Commission until late 2004, as well as the help of the vice-premier in charge of finance, Huang Ju, Zhou began stepping on toes. Huang was another Shanghai holdover from the previous administration.

From early in 2005, the PBOC, working "closely" with other agencies (see Table 1.3), began implementing its plans for the bond markets, introducing a series of new initiatives one after the other. In February, rules came out permitting international institutions such as the Asian Development Bank to issue RMB bonds ("Panda Bonds") and banks to establish mutual-fund companies as a first step toward a universal bank model. In March came regulations allowing asset-backed securities, and in May forward bond trading and a new corporate-debt product, commercial paper (CP), were introduced.

Functional bond markets without interest rates set by market forces cannot exist and these are to a significant extent related to foreign-exchange policy. Here, too, Zhou was successful. In June 2005, the PBOC was allowed to de-link the RMB from its fixed exchange rate to the US dollar and over the course of the next 18 months, the currency appreciated nearly 20 percent. In addition, in 2007, interest rates were increased in a single step by two percent in what was perceived as an initial step toward market-based

TABLE 1.3 Responsibilities for cross-regulatory financial reform

Reform Initiative	Principal Responsible Entities
Panda Bonds	PBOC, MOF, NDRC
Bank business model: mutual funds subsidiaries	CSRC, CBRC
Asset-backed securities	MOF, PBOC, NDRC
Forward bond trading	PBOC, CBRC
Commercial paper (CP)	NDRC, PBOC
Bank recapitalization	MOF, PBOC
Failed securities company rescues	CSRC, PBOC
Exchange and interest-rate policy	PBOC/SAFE, MOF, Finance Small Group

rates. Taken together, the conditions for an active debt market were put in place. As a package, all these moves represented the most significant effort yet to stimulate the development of a bond market, but they paled in significance with what took place in the banking sector.

In 2004, both CCB and BOC had been recapitalized. Before receiving US$45 billion in new capital from the foreign-exchange reserves, the banks had written off their remaining bad loans. There followed the sale of stakes in both banks to international strategic investors. These investors played two roles. First, their investment confirmed to the international-investor community that the banks had been successfully restructured and now represented an attractive investment opportunity. Secondly, and equally important, these strategic investors were meant to partner with the two banks and upgrade all aspects of corporate governance, risk management and product development. In short, the objective of bank reform was to strengthen banks financially as well as institutionally so that Chinese bankers could offer sound judgment and advice. Instead of their saying "Yes!" and lending floods of money at the Party's behest, Zhu Rongji hoped to create professional institutions that could help the government avoid the mistakes of the past.

In June 2005, Bank of America (BOA) acquired the right to purchase up to a 19.9 percent interest in China Construction Bank and in July, Temasek, one of Singapore's sovereign-wealth funds, a further five percent. As a first step, BOA and Temasek respectively paid US$2.5 billion and US$1.5 billion for nine percent and 5.1 percent interests in CCB. This set off in the Chinese media an ugly bout of political mudslinging at the purported "sell-out" of valuable state banks to foreigners. The accusations derived from the viewpoint that China's banks were now "clean," since all bad loans had reportedly been stripped out. So, the argument went, if foreign investors were to be brought in, they should pay a high price to compensate the state for its losses. Aside from price considerations, even the notion of introducing foreigners itself led to accusations that the nation's financial security was being threatened. This attack from the nationalist left came to encompass the entire bank-reform process. Despite such attacks, the PBOC was able to complete both the CCB and BOC restructurings and public IPOs as planned. But from 2005, the political environment changed and with it the character of the bank-reform initiative.

At the same time the PBOC, again acting through Huijin, had begun buying up bankrupt securities companies in the name of financial stability.[4] In the past, the central bank had provided what it called "coffin money" to compensate retail depositors in collapsed financial-sector entities. This time, however, its approach was different: it bought controlling equity interests in the failed securities companies. Over the course of the summer and fall of 2005, Huijin and its subsidiary, China Jianyin, acquired equity stakes in 17 securities companies—from the huge Galaxy Securities and Guotai Junan securities to smaller entities such as Minzu and Xiangcai. The PBOC's expressed intention was to use a "market-based" approach. This meant that after restoring them to health, the bank hoped to recover its money by selling them off to new investors, and new investors would include foreign banks. From late 2004, the PBOC had put a 51 percent stake in a medium-size, bankrupt securities company up for bid among interested foreign banks. One bank had won the bidding process and a full proposal had been sent to the State Council for approval in the early summer. Zhou's intention was to throw the entire domestic stock market open to direct foreign participation for the first time.

China has been said to have created and perhaps perfected over the millennia the art of bureaucracy. The PBOC and Zhou Xiaochuan, in the course of 2004 and 2005, seemed to have violated every norm of traditional bureaucratic behavior. The bank reforms wiped out Ministry of Finance (MOF) investments in CCB and BOC, and the corporate-debt space of the National Development and Reform Commission (NDRC) was invaded by allowing securities firms and SOEs to issue short-term debt securities. They were trying to blast open the CSRC's territory by selling majority control of a securities company to a foreign bank. In the press, it was beginning to be said of Huijin that it was the "Financial State-owned Assets Supervision and Administration Commission (SASAC)." Even worse, the PBOC was making the case for establishing a Super Regulator that would integrate oversight of the bank, equity, and debt-capital markets under one roof. Suddenly, ugly personal attacks, which clearly emanated out of Beijing, were being made on Zhou Xiaochuan in the Hong Kong press.

A ministry-level entity such as the PBOC can only succeed against a concerted attack from many of its peers in the State Council if it has the full support of the country's top leadership. Jiang Zemin had retired early in the year, and it was unfortunate that in the late summer of 2005, Vice Premier Huang Ju was diagnosed with terminal cancer; a key ally was lost. It was almost inevitable, therefore, that during the October National Day holidays of 2005, the State Council began to cut Zhou Xiaochuan's initiatives down to size, restoring balance across the bureaucracies. After the holiday period, it rapidly became clear that the MOF had recovered influence over the banks, that the CSRC had succeeded in stopping majority-controlled foreign entry into its market, and that the NDRC's authority had been enhanced. Even the heavily pro-PBOC *Caijing* 财经 magazine gave the head of the NDRC a front-page cover story. The results reverberate to this day: an integrated approach to financial reform had ended. What followed has been piecemeal and limited to within the silos of authority belonging to each separate regulator.

From 1998, Zhu Rongji and Zhou Xiaochuan had built up a certain framework to pursue comprehensive reform of the financial markets. This included the creation of bad banks, the strengthening of good banks, a national social-security fund, bond markets with a broader investor base and, last but not least, stock markets open to meaningful foreign participation. In addition, there was a start to currency reform as the RMB was unlocked from its link

FIGURE 1.8   China's foreign-exchange reserves

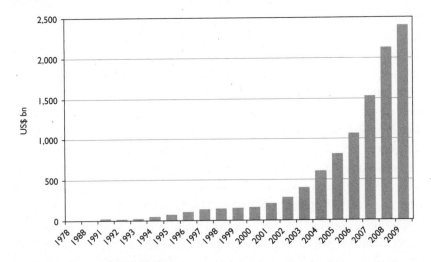

Source: China Statistical Yearbook 2008

to the US dollar. After the PBOC's defeat in 2005, this institutional framework remained incomplete. Worse still, it has been, and continues to be, used to solve problems it was never meant to address. The reason for this is relatively straight forward: with the RMB exchange rate from early 2008 again locked in to the US dollar, interest rates and markets have been frozen in place.[5] The dollars poured in (see Figure 1.8), creating massive amounts of new RMB and huge pressures within the system. Lacking an integrated set of policies, the government addressed these pressures with a plethora of *ad hoc* institutional, administrative and other adjustments reached by consensus decision making and compromise. The result by 2010 is a jerry-built financial structure caught somewhere between its Soviet past and its presumably, but not assuredly, capitalist future.

CHINA IS A FAMILY BUSINESS

What is remarkable about the financial reforms pursued by Zhu Rongji was that they were comprehensive, transformational, and pursued consistently. Failure to follow through may have been inevitable, however, given the fragmented structure of the country's political system in which special-interest groups co-exist within a dominant political entity, the Communist Party of China. What moves this structure is not a market economy and its laws of supply and demand, but a carefully balanced social mechanism built around the particular interests of the revolutionary families who constitute the political elite. China is a family-run business. When ruling groups change, there will be an inevitable change in the balance of interests; but these families have one shared interest above all others: the stability of the system. Social stability allows their pursuit of special interests. This is what is meant by calls for a "Harmonious Society".

In 1998, in the wake of the Asian Financial Crisis and the collapse of Guangdong International Trust & Investment Corporation (GITIC), the families united in crisis. They agreed that financial weakness threatened their system and they supported a thorough bank restructuring inspired by international experience. Now, years later, the appearance of success has been highlighted by the global financial crisis from which their banks and economy were largely insulated. It has made the families supremely confident in their own achievements. How could there be a problem with more than US$2 trillion in reserves and banks at the top of the *Fortune* 500?

Besides, the reforms of the Jiang/Zhu era produced a group of fabulously wealthy National Champions around which many of the families cluster. Family business in China had become Big Business. The US$120 billion and more that was spent on the Beijing Olympics, the Shanghai World Expo and the Guangzhou Asian Games seemed almost immaterial; the hundreds of millions for the Sixtieth Anniversary Parade was nothing. Each of these events was bigger, better, and more expensive than anything any other country has ever managed, but each is little different from individuals being seen driving a Benz 600 or carrying the latest Louis Vuitton bag: they give the appearance of fabulous wealth and, therefore, success; they became a self-fulfilling prophecy. Given the apparent strength of the financial system, where is the need for further reform?

Failing to grasp the impact of unbridled Western-style capitalism on its elite families in a society and culture lacking in legal or ethical counterbalances is to miss the reality of today's China. Greed is the driving force behind the protectionist walls of the "state-owned" economy "inside the system" and money is the language. A clear view over this wall is obscured by a political ideology that disguises the privatization of state assets behind continuing "state" ownership. The oligopolies dominating the domestic landscape are called "National Champions" and the "pillars" of China's "socialist market" economy, but they are controlled by these same families. As the head of an SOE once wisely commented, "It doesn't matter who owns the money, it only matters who gets to use it." In China, everyone wants to use the money and few are willing to be accountable for how it is used.

The Chinese commonly joke that China is now passing through the "primitive stage of capital accumulation" described by Karl Marx. The occasional lurid "corruption" scandal provides a critical insight into what is, in fact, the mainstream privatization process: the struggle between competing factions for incremental economic and political advantage. The state-owned economy, nominally "owned by the whole people", is being carved up by China's rulers, their families, relations and retainers, who are all in business for themselves and only themselves. From the very start of political relaxation in 1978, economic forces were set in motion that have led to the creation of two distinct economies in China—the domestic-oriented state-owned economy and the export-oriented private economy. The first, which many confuse with China, is the state-owned economy operating "inside the system." Sponsored and supported by the full patronage of the state, this economy was, and has always been, the beneficiary of all the largesse that the political elite can provide. It is the foundation of China's post-1979 political structure and the wall behind which the Party seeks to protect itself and sustain its rule.

Over the past 30 years China's state sector has assumed the guise of Western corporations, listed companies on foreign stock exchanges and made use of such related professions as accountants, lawyers, and investment bankers. This camouflages its true nature: that of a patronage system centered on the Party's *nomenklatura*. The huge state corporations have adopted the financial techniques of their international competitors and raised billions of dollars in capital, growing to an economic scale never seen before in all of Chinese history. But these companies are not autonomous corporations; they can hardly be said to be corporations at all. Their senior management and, indeed, the fate of the corporation itself, are completely dependent on their political patrons. China's state-owned economy is a family business and the loyalties of these families are conflicted, stretched tight between the need to preserve political power and the urge to do business. To date, the former has always won out.

Of course the "National Champions" dispose of great wealth and, consequently, interest groups within the Party have formed around what one official once called "these cash machines." But misjudgment forms the character of all human beings; a simple misstep can bring down a powerful wealth machine and the families behind it. The issue then becomes how to remove the political targets while preserving the machine. The "Party"— that is, the winning interest group—can intervene for any convenient reason, changing CEOs, investing in new projects or ordering mergers. Due to these characteristics, the adoption of laws, accounting standards, markets, and other mechanisms of international capitalism are just examples of the formalism that characterizes China today. The names are the same as in the West, but what things are and how they work is hidden beneath the surface. Given the state's scale in critical sectors, together with the enormous power of the government, the influence of this patronage system pervades all aspects of China's economy. It inevitably undermines the very contents of its superficially internationalized institutions.

The 30 years encompassed by the policy of reform and opening have been the most peaceful and economically successful in the past 170 years of China's history, lifting more than 300 million people out of poverty. This achievement must be acknowledged. But the character of China's style of capitalism is marked deeply by how the political elite has coalesced around certain institutions, corporations and economic sectors, how the government and various interest groups have used Western financial knowledge, and the crises the state has met along the way. After all, every country and all economic and political systems experience booms and busts, scandals and wild speculative sprees.The difference lies in how each country manages the aftermath. The aim of this book is to pull back the edge of the Chinese curtain and peer at what is behind, to match the reality of the system's operations with the familiarity of the names it uses to describe them and then to look into the future in the belief that a straight forward look will benefit all.

ENDNOTES

1 See Xing 2007: 739.
2 This figure could be much higher since the market capitalizations of H-share companies listed on the HKSE value *only* the H-shares, excluding all other shares.
3 See Wu 2009.
4 For greater detail, see Walter and Howie 2006: Chapter 9.
5 The PBOC's statement in June 2010 that the yuan is free to float against a basket of currencies remains just that, a statement, and is unlikely to lead to significant change in the currency's value.

CHAPTER

2

China's Fortress Banking System

"[W]e should not bring that American stuff and use it in China. Rather, we should develop around our own needs and build our own banking system."

Chen Yuan, Chairman, China Development Bank
July 2009

In China, the banks are the financial system; nearly all financial risk is concentrated on their balance sheets. China's heroic savers underwrite this risk; they are the only significant source of capital "inside the system" of the Party-controlled domestic economy. This is the weakest point in China's economic and political arrangement, and the country's leaders, in a general way, understand this. This is why over the past 30 years of economic experimentation, they have done everything possible to protect the banks from serious competition and from even the whiff of failure. In spite of the WTO, foreign banks consistently constitute less than two percent of total domestic financial assets: they are simply not important. Beyond the pressures of competition, the Party treats its banks as basic utilities that provide unlimited capital to the cherished state-owned enterprises. With all aspects of banking under the Party's control, risk is thought to be manageable.

Even so, at the end of each of the last three decades, these banks have faced virtual, if not actual, bankruptcy, surviving only because they have had the full, unstinting and costly support of the Party. In the 1980s, the banking system had barely been re-established when uncontrolled lending at the insistence of local governments led to double-digit inflation and near civil war. The Asian Financial Crisis of 1997 drove internationally significant financial institutions such as Guangdong International Trust & Investment Corporation into actual bankruptcy. This compelled the government to undertake a bottom-up reorganization of the banks that it admitted publicly had 40 percent non-performing loan (NPL) levels. The origins of this restructuring can be traced to 1994, when the framework of a system that closely followed international arrangements was sketched out, including an independent central bank, commercial banks, and policy banks. The 1994 effort was stillborn, however, given the priority to bring raging inflation, which peaked at over 20 percent in 1995, under control. In short, China's banking giants of 2010 were under-capitalized, poorly managed and, to all intents, bankrupt just 10 years ago.

A third decade has now gone by during which the banks completed their restructuring and subjected themselves to international governance and risk-management standards. By 2006, three of the four state banks had completed successful international IPOs. After the outbreak of the global financial crisis in 2008, China's banks emerged as apparent world-beaters, besting their peer group in the developed economies in size of market capitalization and even topping the *Fortune* 500 list. They seemed to have weathered the global financial crisis well. But just, at this point, the Party, facing the seeming collapse of China's export-driven economy, reverted to its traditional approach and ordered the banks to lend unstintingly to drive the economy forward. This green light may have erased whatever standards of governance and risk control that bank management had learned over the previous decade.

By the end of 2009, the banks had lent out over RMB9.56 trillion (US$1.4 trillion) and warning lights were flashing as capital-adequacy ratios approached minimum internationally mandated levels. In 2010, these banks are scrambling to arrange huge new capital injections totaling over US$70 billion (if Agricultural Bank of China's IPO is included). Looking forward, the lending binge of 2009 threatens, and will most certainly generate problem loans of sufficient scale to require yet a third recapitalization in the next two to three years. China's major state banks, the National Champions of the financial sector, appear to be heading toward a situation not unlike that of 1998. But their problems will, in fact, be much worse than 1998 since the old problem loans of the 1990s were only swept under the carpet. The "bad" banks, which took on those NPLs, were poorly structured, with the result that the "good" banks have remained liable. The government's penchant for *ad hoc* funding arrangements, an unwillingness to open the problem-loan market to foreign participation, and the belief that it can perpetually put off the realization of losses pose a threat to the financial strength of China's banks long before the NPLs of 2009 arise.

China's banks look strong, but are fragile; in this, they are emblematic of the country itself. The Chinese are masters of the surface and excel at burying the telling detail in the passage of time. Their past experience tells them that this strategy works. But China, perhaps more than at any time in its long history, is now closely enmeshed with the larger world. The collapse of GITIC would never have taken place had it not been caught up in international financial arrangements. China's financial system, similarly, has become increasingly complex; this complexity has begun to erode the effectiveness of the Party's traditional problem-solving approach of simply shifting money from one pocket to another and letting time and fading memory do the rest. Tied up as it is in financial knots, the system's size, scale and access to seemingly-limitless capital cannot forever solve the problems of the banks.

BANKS ARE CHINA'S FINANCIAL SYSTEM

In China, capital begins and ends with the Big 4 banks. The banking system has thousands of entities if the 12 second-tier banks, the urban and rural banks, Postal Savings Bank, and credit cooperatives, are included. But the heart of the system includes just four: Bank of China (BOC), China Construction Bank (CCB), Agricultural Bank of China (ABC) and, the biggest of them all, Industrial and Commercial Bank of China (ICBC). In 2009, state-controlled commercial banks held over US$11 trillion in financial assets, of which the Big 4 banks alone accounted for over 70 percent (see Table 2.1). These four banks controlled 43 percent of China's total financial assets.

Such a concentration of financial assets in the banking system is typical of most low-income economies (see Figure 2.1).[1] What differs in China's

TABLE 2.1 Relative holdings of financial assets in China, FY2009 (RMB trillion)

RMB trillion	2006	2007	2008	2009	2009 US$ trillion
PBOC	12.86	16.91	20.7	22.75	3.32
Banks	43.95	52.6	62.39	79.51	11.61
Securities companies*	1.6	4.98	1.19	2.03	0.30
Insurance companies	1.97	2.9	3.34	4.06	0.59
	60.38	77.39	87.62	108.35	15.82

Source: PBOC *Financial Stability Report* 2010, various.
Note: *includes brokerages and fund-management companies.

FIGURE 2.1 Concentration of banking assets by country income group

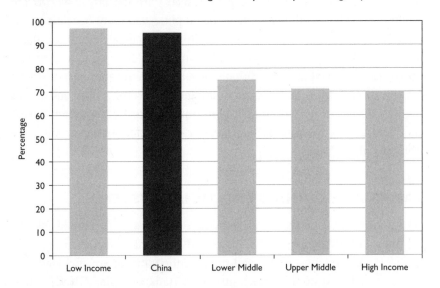

Source: Data from 150 countries; based on Demirguc-Kunt and Levine (2004): 28

case, however, is that the central government has unshakable control of the sector. Foreign banks hold, at best, little more than two percent of total financial assets (and only 1.7 percent after the lending binge of 2009), as compared to nearly 37 percent in the international lower-income group. This will not change anytime soon. A very senior Chinese banker was asked in early 2010 about the government's strategy for foreign banks and where the foreign sector would be in five years. He replied after some thought: "I don't believe anyone has thought much about this; I expect that in five years' time, foreign bank assets will constitute perhaps two or three percent of total bank assets." Despite the undeniable economic opening of the past 30 years and the WTO Agreement notwithstanding, China's financial sector remains overwhelmingly in Beijing's hands. There appears to be little political acceptance of the need to diversify the holders of financial risk.

If one looks at incremental capital raising, it is obvious the stock markets in Hong Kong, Shenzhen and Shanghai are an afterthought. It is bank lending and bond issuance that keep the engine of China's state-owned economy revving at high speed. For example, 2007 was a record year for Chinese equity financing: more than US$123 billion was raised, but in the same year, banks extended new loans totaling US$530 billion and debt issues in the bond market accounted for another US$581 billion. In the past decade, equity as a percentage of total capital raised has been measured in the single digits as compared with loans and debt. Who underwrites and holds all that fixed-income debt? Banks hold over 70 percent of all bonds, including those issued by the MOF (see Chapter 4). Taking this a bit further, in the stock markets as well, the huge deposits placed by institutional investors seeking share allocations in the primary market are also funded by loans from banks. In China, the banks are everything. The Party knows it, and uses them as both its weapon and its shield.

CRISIS: THE STIMULUS TO BANK REFORM, 1988 AND 1998

Today's banking system is the child of the financial crises that began China's 30 years of reform and ended each of its next two decades. At the close of the Cultural Revolution in 1976, there were no banks or any other institutions left functioning. Beijing faced the challenge of institutional design and it was natural that it fell back on traditional Soviet-inspired arrangements. These can be described roughly as a Big Budget, the MOF, and small banks that did little more than lend short-term money. Nor was there an important role for a central bank. Most important of all, the key management of the banks was not centrally controlled by Beijing, but by provincial Party committees (the local Party always needs money). Over the course of the 1980s, this arrangement built up into a lending spree that ended in inflation, corruption and near civil war in 1989. In 1992, the Party, fired up by Deng Xiaoping's words in Shenzhen, took the economy and its banking system straight back to where it had been in 1988. There were spectacular bubbles and busts, most notably the Great Hainan Real Estate Bust of 1993 (outlined later in this chapter).

In line with its decision in 1990 to try out capitalist-inspired stock markets, in 1994, Beijing abandoned the Soviet banking model in favor of one based largely on the experience of the United States. New banking laws and accounting regulations, an independent central bank, and the transformation of the four state banks into commercial banks all followed. Three policy banks were established to hold non-commercial loans. This effort, however, was stillborn, sidetracked by Zhu Rongji's greater priority to bring the country's raging inflation under control. It took the Asian Financial Crisis and the collapse of GITIC in 1998 to catalyze a sustained effort to transform the banks along the lines of the framework adopted in 1994.

China's leaders, no matter who they were or are, know that the country's financial institutions are the source of the greatest threat to financial and social stability. They differ significantly, however, over how to minimize this threat. The traditional impulse of the Party has always been toward crude outright control. For the banking system, this has meant an absence of control and the creation of new crises. Realizing this, Zhu Rongji and his team adopted a more sophisticated approach from 1998. Much as they did in reforming the SOEs, this team sought to create a more independent banking system by adopting international methods of corporate governance and risk management. Once this was in place, the key decision was to submit the whole to the scrutiny of international regulators, auditors, investors and law by listing the banks in Hong Kong rather than in Shanghai. The experience of China's banks in the 1980s and 1990s shows why Zhu would seek such an approach and also sheds light on bank behavior in 2009.

The expansive 1980s

In 1977, China was bankrupt; its commercial and political institutions in tatters. There was no real national economy, only a collection of local fiefdoms held together by a broken Party organization. What strategy could be used to pull it all back together? Looking back to the 1949 revolution, China had sought to create a central planning system with the assistance of Soviet advisors in the 1950s. But, parsing those years between 1950 and the Anti-Rightist Campaign of 1957, only a start had been made. From 1957 to 1962, Mao Zedong threw China into its first prolonged period of disorder and invited all Russians advisors to go home. Pushed aside when the heavy costs of the Great Leap Forward were totaled up, Mao quickly made his comeback and, in 1966, threw the country into chaos for a further 10 years.

Under such chaotic circumstances, how much of a government, much less any planning system, really could have been put in place? Whatever the answer, there was no banking system when the Gang of Four was deposed in 1976; everything had to be rebuilt and the only model anyone knew of was based on blueprints the Soviet advisors had left behind. At the start of the reform era in 1978, there was only one bank, the PBOC, and it was a department buried inside the MOF. From this small group of only 80 staff, a great burst of institution building began.

New banks and non-bank financial entities proliferated wildly in the government's enthusiasm for what it saw then as financial modernization (see Table 2.2). By 1988, there were 20 banking institutions, 745 trust and investment companies, 34 securities companies, 180 pawn shops and an unknowable number of finance companies spread haphazardly across the nation. Every level of government succeeded in establishing its own set of financial entities, just as they have now set up "financing platforms" of every kind. It was as if money could be conjured up simply by hanging up a signboard with "financial" on it.

At such an early stage of revival, and lacking any professional staff, banks could hardly be anything other than an appendage of the Party organization and the Party did not understand how to use the banks. This can be seen in the mission statement devised by the government for banks: "The central bank and the specialized banks should take as their objective economic development, currency stability and increasing social productivity." This statement juxtaposed economic growth with a stable currency, but in the Party's hands, the former will always win out. More critically, there was a basic flaw in institutional design: the banks were organized in line with the government administrative system. Although the PBOC may have been a part of the State Council in Beijing, its key operational

TABLE 2.2 The proliferation of financial institutions in the 1980s

	Type and number of institution	Date founded
1)	20 banking institutions including:	
	People's Bank of China	January 1978
	Bank of China	January 1978
	People's Construction Bank of China	August 1978
	Agricultural Bank of China	March 1979
	Industrial and Commercial Bank of China	January 1984
	China Investment Bank	April 1994
	Xiamen International Bank	December 1985
	Postal Savings	January 1986
	Ka Wah Bank	April 1986
	Urban Credit Cooperatives	July 1986
	Aijian Bank and Trust Co.	August 1986
	Wenzhou Lucheng Urban Credit Cooperative	November 1986
	Bank of Communications	April 1987
	China Merchants Bank	April 1987
	CITIC Industrial Bank	September 1987
	Yantai Housing and Savings Bank	December 1987
	Shenzhen Development Bank	December 1987
	Fengfu Housing and Savings Bank	December 1987
	Fujian Industrial Bank	August 1988
	Guangdong Development Bank	September 1988
2)	745 trust and investment companies including:	
	China International Trust & Investment Corp.	October 1979
	ICBC Trust	April 1986
	Shenyang Municipal Trust & Investment Co.	August 1986
	China Agricultural Trust & Investment Corp.	1988
	Bank of China Trust & Investment Co.	1988
	China Economic Development Trust	1988
	Guangdong International Trust & Investment Co.	December 1980
3)	34 securities companies	1988
4)	180 pawn shops	from 1984
5)	an unknown number of finance companies	from 1984

offices were at the provincial level and here they were subordinate to local Party committees. Throughout the 1980s and into the 1990s, the local Party controlled the appointment of the senior PBOC branch managers as well as those of the other banks. Of course, the preference of the local government will always be for growth and easy access to money. As the consequent raging inflation in the late 1980s attested, combining poorly trained staff with political enthusiasm was tantamount to playing with fire.

Just as in 2009, these institutions loaned out money unstintingly so that by the late 1980s, inflation officially reached nearly 20 percent (see Figure 2.2). As administrative controls were imposed, there began to be runs on local bank branches. Inflation, corruption and lack of leadership experience eventually led to the events of 1989. After the crackdown of 1989 and 1990, the whole thing began again: a few speeches by Deng Xiaoping in Guangdong in early 1992 and the financial system ran out of control. The Great Hainan Real Estate Bust provides an illustration of just what this means.

FIGURE 2.2   Inflation vs. loan growth, 1981–1991

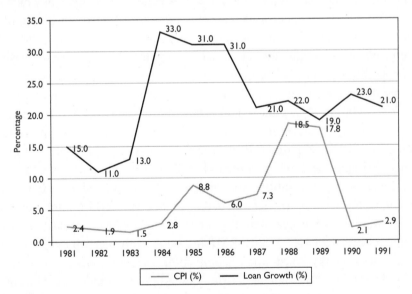

Source: China Statistical Yearbook, various; China Financial Statistics 1949–2005.

The Great Hainan Real Estate Bust

On April 6, 1988, the entire island province of Hainan was made a Special Economic Zone (SEZ). At that time, Hainan was not the home of super five-star resorts and skinny fashion models it has become today. It was a backward tropical island with few natural resources other than its beauty and geographic position near disputed oil and gas fields in the South China Sea. Thanks to Beijing's decision, however, it unexpectedly became, for a brief time, China's version of the Wild West. Hundreds of thousands of enthusiastic young people poured into the boom towns of Haikou and Sanya, attracted by the promise of economic growth that more than 30 favorable investment policies were expected to generate. These policies encouraged the creation of an export industry and this, in turn, was expected to lead to a boom in hotels, entertainment and, of course, real estate.

If Shenzhen was the most westernized SEZ because of its proximity to Hong Kong, then Hainan was the pure Chinese version. In a territory the size of Taiwan, and in a complete financial vacuum, 21 trust companies sprang into existence. In Hainan, the trust companies *were* the banking sector; there was nothing else. Competition was intense in what was the nearest to virgin economic space that China could present. No one thought about any export industry. Everyone understood their opportunity: real estate. In China, it is always real estate. The special status of the trust companies, together with new policies permitting the sale of land-use rights, created explosive profit opportunities. Suddenly, 20,000 real-estate companies materialized—one for every 80 people on the island. Housing prices doubled twice in three years.

The catalyst to Hainan's real-estate craze came from the outside: the Japanese developer Kumagai Gumi, later bankrupted by the Asian Financial Crisis, acquired a 70-year lease on 30 square kilometers of land encompassing the entire port area of Haikou. Imagine *that* deal! Instead of developing port facilities, the company turned to residential development, selling 900 *mu* (about 150 acres) of land at RMB3 million per *mu*. Why would any businessman develop port facilities when industrial land only sold for RMB130,000 to RMB150,000? With such opportunities, it was not an empty boast when people spoke of buying up every inch of land in Haikou. The Hainan get-rich-quick business model soon became the envy of the entire country in 1992, the year Chinese history seemed to come to an end and everything seemed possible.

Then came 1993 and the start of Zhu Rongji's efforts to bring the national economy, and the real-estate sector in particular, under control. The geese and their golden eggs disappeared; speculators fled, leaving some 600 unfinished buildings and RMB30 billion (US$4 billion) in bad debt behind. In this one SEZ alone, *publicized* bad debt totaled nearly 10 percent of the national budget and eight percent of the national total of non-performing property assets! This is what creative local financing in China means. Today in 2010, in every provincial capital across the country, exactly the same kind of real-estate boom has developed and for the same reasons: Party-driven bank lending.

The Hainan debacle led directly to the Party's first effort to develop "good" bank/"bad" bank reforms in 1994. As part of a host of initiatives, three policy banks, including the now-prominent China Development Bank (CDB), were established to hold strategic, but non-commercial, loans. At the same time, the Big 4 banks were meant to become fully commercial institutions. This strategy to modernize the Big 4 banks, however, never gained traction until 1998 when GITIC collapsed.

Guangdong International Trust & Investment Corporation

The Hainan blowout was containable within the Chinese system; the GITIC implosion was not because it and Guangdong were exposed to the global economy. GITIC's financial collapse in 1998 posed a real threat to China that has been all but forgotten. But GITIC, and how it was controlled by the provincial Party, is little different from how today's financial institutions are managed and regulated. After all, as recently as 2008, the mighty Citic Pacific burned up over US$2 billion on a purely speculative and un-hedged foreign-exchange bet (and had to be recapitalized). GITIC came at the time when the entire Asian development model had exploded into the Asia Financial Crisis. Despite the calm face it presented to the outside world, China was severely affected by dramatically decreased export demand channeled through Guangdong Province, which was then, as now, that part of the country most exposed to international trade and investment. At the time, just 10 years ago, China's total foreign-exchange reserves were only US$145 billion, as compared to its international debt of US$139 billion.

GITIC's bankruptcy, still the first and only formal bankruptcy of a major financial entity in China, threw unwanted light on the Party's financial arrangements. It called into question the central government's commitment, if not its capacity, to stand behind its most important financial institutions. GITIC in the 1990s was, after CITIC, the nation's largest and most prominent trust company and acted as the international borrowing "window" for Guangdong, its richest province. In 1993, prior to issuing its first (and only) US$150 million bond in the US, GITIC received the same investment-grade rating from Moody's and Standard & Poor's as the MOF. Its senior managers were well known among foreign bankers for their active participation in cross-border foreign-currency and derivatives markets. One of its subsidiaries was publicly listed in Hong Kong and its chairman had been the subject of a *BusinessWeek* cover story.[2] All foreign bankers were "close" friends with Chairman Huang and all had drunk his premium wines in the club at the top of the company's 60-storey tower in Guangzhou. GITIC was a National Champion before there were National Champions.

The outcome of what started as a familiar story of poor management showed how seriously Premier Zhu Rongji took the issue of moral hazard and the threat posed by a weak financial system. This stands in direct contrast to the government's approach to the banks in 2009, as will be discussed in later sections. The proximate cause of GITIC's collapse was its inability to repay US$120 million to foreign lenders in 1998. Zhu Rongji, outraged that its financial losses were unquantifiable, ordered Wang Qishan, then senior vice-governor of Guangdong, to close GITIC in October 1998. In January 1999, it was declared bankrupt in what was a huge shock to the international financial community's view of China. Rumors rapidly began to spread, both inside and outside the country, that "China's commercial banks are technically bankrupt." These threatening assertions forced Premier Zhu to make the following clarification to reporters at a news conference following the National People's Congress in March 1999:

I think that those [international] banks and a few financial institutions are too pessimistic in their estimates of this problem; that is, they believe that China is already in the midst of a financial crisis and does not have the capacity to support its payments and is not creditworthy. China's economy is rapidly growing;

we have US$147 billion in reserves and balanced international payments. We are completely able to repay our debt. The issue is whether or not the government should repay this kind of debt.[3]

Given the level of international concern and a desire to enforce financial discipline, Zhu ordered GITIC's bankruptcy to proceed in accordance with international standards. A fully transparent process was led by the international accounting firm KPMG acting as the company's liquidator. GITIC was publicly investigated more thoroughly than perhaps any Chinese financial institution before or since. The findings are a matter of public record and should not be forgotten. The scale of its failure was breathtaking. A preliminary KPMG review of its finances as of April 1999 showed total assets of US$2.6 billion set against liabilities of US$4.4 billion. During the four-year liquidation process, 494 creditors registered claims totaling US$5.6 billion, of which US$4.7 billion represented those of 320 foreign creditors.

In the end, GITIC's creditors faced the fact that 90 percent of the company's loans and commitments were unlikely to ever be met. Over 80 percent of its equity investments in some 105 projects spread across the province had also failed and were without value. The recovery rates for GITIC alone was 12.5 percent and for its three principal subsidiaries ranged from 11.5 percent to 28 percent. The picture this presents of the operations of a major financial institution was shocking and continues to be shocking: just where did these billions of dollars go? The answer is that many of the real-estate and infrastructure projects GITIC financed are still there, but are now owned by other arms of the government.

Today, in 2010, bank officials and regulators readily admit that much of the lending in 2009 went to projects without immediate cash flow, such as real estate and high-speed railways. Even so, they continue, in the future such infrastructure will be of great value. What they are describing is the GITIC financing model. The only question is: which entity will end up holding today's bad loans?

In 1998, however, Zhu Rongji did not take such a sanguine view of bad lending. The collapse of GITIC led to the closure of hundreds of trust companies and thousands of urban credit cooperatives across the country. More importantly, it initiated a serious effort to centralize control of the Big 4 banks in Beijing's hands and marked the start of their restructuring.

Zhu Rongji got it: if GITIC was a hyped-up financial fraud, were the state banks any different? The answer was "No" and so began the strong effort to recast China's banking system after that of the United States, which was seen then as the best.

CHINA'S FORTRESS BANKING SYSTEM IN 2009

It is a testimony to the extensive bank restructuring demanded by Zhu Rongji that China's banks have withstood the global financial crisis so well. While many major banks in developed countries were bankrupted by the crisis in 2008, China's banks have emerged seemingly untouched and, some would argue, even strengthened. Listed on the Hong Kong and Shanghai Stock Exchanges, six of these banks now rank highly in the Fortune 500 and one, ICBC, is the largest by market capitalization in the world and the second-largest company overall, behind only ExxonMobile (see Figure 2.3). In contrast, JPMorgan, currently America's strongest bank, comes in at a distant

FIGURE 2.3 *Fortune* 500 ranking of Chinese banks vs. JPMorgan Chase, FY2008

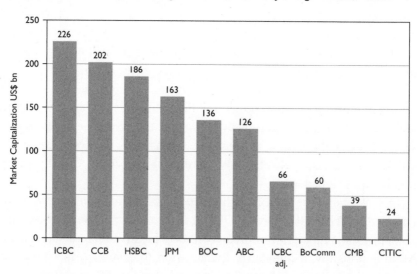

Source: Bloomberg and *Fortune*

nineteenth place. Compared to 1998 when their non-performing loan ratio exceeded 40 percent, China's banks have obviously come a long way.

It is true that China's banks today are stronger and their staff more professional than 10 years ago. Senior management has been quick to learn to "walk the walk" and talk the banker talk and there is a more sophisticated, internationally savvy banking regulator. A closer look, however, suggests that organizational miracles are miracles precisely because they are few and far between. The market-capitalization data shown in Figure 2.3 is a misleading comparison of apples to oranges. Can a JPMorgan, with 100 percent of its shares capable of being traded in the market each day, be compared to banks such as ICBC that have less than 30 percent of their shares tradable (see Figure 2.4)? Market-capitalization figures are based on a traded market price for one share multiplied by the bank's total number of shares. This assumes, as is always true in international markets, that the entirety of a company's shares is listed. The resulting market-cap figure, therefore, represents investors' consensus on the valuation of

FIGURE 2.4 Comparative share floatation of listed banks, FY2008

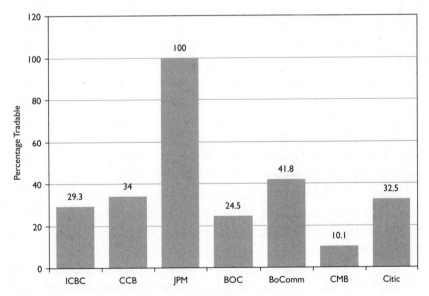

Source: Wind Information

a company's ongoing operations. As has been shown elsewhere,[4] since A-shares, H-shares, and China's famous variety of non-tradable shares all have different valuations, the value of the ICBC's market-cap figure will vary enormously depending on which price is used.

To arrive at the ICBC's market-cap figure, Bloomberg analysts added the value of the bank's Hong Kong-listed shares to that of all the domestic shares. But the domestic shares include A-shares trading on the market in Shanghai and the formerly non-tradable, now locked up, shares held by government agencies. These latter shares are valued at the full tradable A-share price. What would be the value of an ICBC A-share if the government decided to sell even a small part of its 70 percent holdings? The answer has already been provided by the market reaction in June 2001 to the CSRC's plans to do just that: prices collapsed.[5] This share structure and the company valuation problem is the same for all other Chinese banks and companies. There is no good way to arrive at a market-cap figure that is comparable to listed companies in developed markets and private economies.

To illustrate this point further, take the following simplistic calculation: use 30 percent, the amount of its tradable market float, of ICBC's market-cap figure of US$201 billion, or US$60 billion, as a rough proxy for the bank's market value. This approach gives consideration to the dilution effect of the current 70 percent of the bank's shares as if they were available to trade. Despite its crudeness, this result is no less inaccurate than any other. Whatever the number, this serves to highlight the fact that China's banks are worth somewhat less than the number the Bloomberg researchers calculate.

Markets are not simply a valuation mechanism. International stock exchanges are called markets because companies can be bought and sold on them. In China and Hong Kong, given absolute majority government control, shares trade, but companies do not. Major merger and acquisition (M&A) transactions do not take place through the exchanges; they are the result of government amalgamations of state assets at artificial prices. Would that it were possible to gain a controlling interest in a listed Chinese bank or securities company simply by acquiring its listed shares and making a public tender!

One way to make a straightforward comparison between US and Chinese banks is based on their total assets. The fact that many international banks are larger than even the largest Chinese banks is not unreasonable given that the respective GDPs of many developed economies are many times that of China. But as the data in Figure 2.5 illustrate, the Big 4 banks are in the same league as many of their international peers and they tower over Chinese second-tier banks. Asset size gives an idea of significance to the economy but, taken alone, is not a good measure of the strength of these banks; asset quality is.

This gets to the true heart of the issue. Understanding how the Chinese banks were relieved of their problem-loan burdens leads to a clear understanding of their continuing weakness. The data in Figure 2.6 show an impressive and factual reduction in total non-performing commercial bank loans over the seven years through 2008. In 1999, the NPL ratio (simply put, bad loans divided by total loans) of the Big 4 banks was a massive 39 percent just before spinning off the first batch of bad loans totaling US$170 billion in 2000. From 2001 to 2005 ICBC, CCB, and BOC spun off or wrote off a further US$200 billion. In 2007, ABC, the last of the major banks to restructure, spun off another US$112 billion, making a total among the four banks of around US$480 billion.

It is thought that the bulk of these bad loans originated in the late 1980s and early 1990s when bank lending flew out of control, as it did in 2009. If that is the case, this nearly US$480 billion in bad loans was equivalent to about 20 percent of China's GDP for the five-year period from 1988 to 1993, the year Zhu Rongji applied the brakes. A more important point, perhaps, is that the banks silently carried these NPLs for a further five years before anything was about them and another 10 years went by before they were said to be fully worked out (but not written off).

The US savings-and-loan crisis of the 1980s may help put China's NPL experience into some perspective. The Federal Deposit Insurance Corporation (FDIC) has calculated that during the 1986–1999 period in the US, the combined closure of 1,043 thrift institutions holding US$519 billion in assets resulted in a net loss after recoveries to taxpayers and the thrift industry of US$153 billion at the end of the clean-up in 1999.[6] In other words, the recovery rate achieved was over 60 percent. In contrast, the commonly noted rate in China after 10 years of NPL-workout efforts is considered to be around 20 percent.

This vast difference in recovery rates on comparable amounts, together with the dramatic decrease in NPLs shown in Figure2.6, raises a host of

FIGURE 2.5 Selected international and Chinese banks by total assets, FY2008

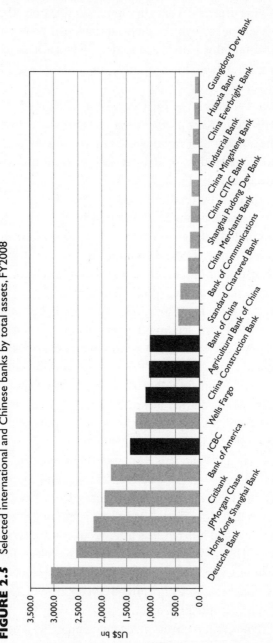

Source: *The Banker* and respective annual reports

FIGURE2.6　Non-performing loan trends in the top 17 Chinese banks, 1999–2008

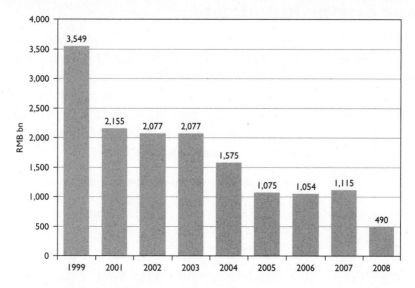

Source: PBOC, *Financial Stability Report,* various; Li Liming, p. 185

questions. If, in fact, the NPL rates of Chinese banks have now improved to such a degree, is it because they are lending to better companies that have the capacity as well as the willingness to repay, or did their original SOE clients simply start to pay again? If the latter is the case, why were the previous problem-loan recovery rates so low? A significant change in client base can be ruled out: Chinese banks overwhelmingly lend to SOEs and always have, largely because they are viewed as reliable, unlike private companies. In retrospect, this attitude seems to be mistaken.

The Party tells the banks to loan to the SOEs, but it seems unable to tell the SOEs to *repay the loans.* This gets at the nub of the issue: the Party *wants* the banks to support the SOEs in all circumstances. If the SOEs fail to repay, the Party won't blame bank management for losing money; it will only blame bankers for not doing what they are told. Simply reforming the banks cannot change SOE behavior or that of the Party itself. Improved NPL ratios over the past 10 years, therefore, suggest a dramatic improvement in the willingness of SOE clients to meet their loan commitments, the selection of investment projects that actually generate real cash flow, or some other arrangement for bad loans.

THE SUDDEN THIRST FOR CAPITAL
AND CASH DIVIDENDS, 2010

If it is true that lending standards have improved significantly, perhaps there is no need to be concerned about the after-effects of the 2009 lending binge; the quality of Chinese bank balance sheets will remain sound and the level of write-offs manageable. The frantic scrambling for more capital from early in 2010, however, suggests otherwise. The CEO of ICBC, Yang Kaisheng, has written a uniquely direct article analyzing the challenges facing China's banks.[7] In it, he describes China's financial system:

> In our country's current level of economic development, we must maintain a level of macroeconomic growth of around eight percent per annum and this will inevitably require a corresponding level of capital investment. Our country's financial system is primarily characterized by indirect financing (via banks); the scale of direct financing (via capital markets) is limited.

This statement of fact says two important things about China's banking system. First, there is an overall economic goal of eight percent growth per year that requires "capital investment." Second, the source of capital in China relies mainly on the banks. In other words, bank lending is the only way to achieve eight percent GDP growth.

With estimates of loan growth, profitability and dividend payout ratios, Yang then states that the Big 3 banks plus the Bank of Communications will, over the next five years, need RMB480 billion (US$70 billion) in new capital.[8] Yang is saying "raised over five years," but these banks are trying to raise this amount in just one year, 2010. Putting aside ABC's proposed US$29 billion IPO goal, by April 2010, the other banks had already announced plans to raise RMB287 billion (US$42.1 billion), as shown in Table 2.3.

This is an astounding amount, coming as it does only four to five years after their huge IPOs in 2005 and 2006 had raised a total of US$44.4 billion. Yang goes on to say that if market risk, operating risk, and increasingly stringent definitions of capital requirements are considered, then the capital required will be even greater. What he doesn't mention, though, is the risk of bad loans. It would seem that Yang's point in citing these facts is that China's current Party-led banking arrangements do not work, in spite of the picture presented to the outside world. It is a defense of the model put forward by Zhu Rongji in 1998.

TABLE 2.3 Reported capital-raising plans by the Big 5 banks, May 2010

	IPO Capital (US$billion)	Post-IPO Core CAR %	3Q 2009 Core CAR (%)	FY2009 Core CAR (%)	Recap Plan	Capital to be Raised (RMB billion)
ICBC	21.9	12.23	9.86	NA	A-share convertible	25
CCB	9.2	11.09	9.57	9.31	A-share rights offering A- + H- share rights offering	45 75
BOC	11.1	11.44	9.37	9.07	H-share rights offering A-share convertible	60 40
BoComm	2.2	NA	NA	7.9	H- + A-share rights offering	42
ABC			8.04	NA	A- and H-share IPO	200
Total	**44.4**					**487**
Total less ABC	**44.4**					**287**
Total (US$ billion)	**44.4**					**71.4**

Source: Annual and interim bank reports, Bloomberg; industry estimates as of May 2010

The experience of the past 30 years shows that China's banks and their business model is extremely capital-intensive. The banks boomed and went bust with regularity at the end of the 1970s, 1980s and 1990s. Now another decade has gone by and the banks have run out of capital again. Even though they appear healthy and have each announced record profits and low problem-loan ratios for 2009, the Tier 1 capital ratios of the Big 3 are rapidly approaching nine percent, down from a strong 11 percent just after their IPOs in 2005 and 2006. Of course, the lending spree of 2009 was the proximate cause. As an analyst at a prominent international bank commented: "The growth model of China banks requires them to come to the capital markets every few years. There's no way out and this will be a long-term overhang on the market."[9] But it is not just the lending of 2009 or even their business model that drives their unending thirst for capital; it is also their dividend policies.

The data in Figure 2.7 show actual cash dividends paid out by the Big 3 banks over the period 2004–2008, during which each was incorporated and then listed in Hong Kong and Shanghai. The figure also shows the funds raised by these banks from domestic and international equity investors in their IPOs. The money paid out in dividends, equivalent to US$42 billion,

FIGURE 2.7 Bank IPOs pre-fund cash dividends paid, 2004–2008

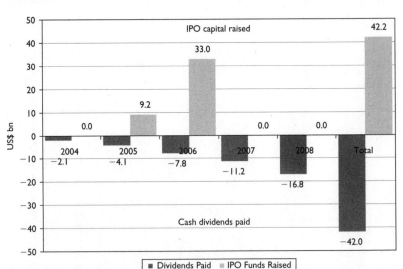

Source: Wind Information for IPO amounts; Statement of cash flows, bank annual reports

matches exactly the money raised in the markets. What does this mean? It means international and domestic investors put cash into the listed Chinese banks simply to pre-fund the dividends paid out by the banks largely to the MOF and Central SAFE Investment. These dividends represented a transfer of real third-party cash from the banks directly to the state's coffers. Why wouldn't international investors keep the cash in the first place?

Investors, as opposed to speculators, put their money in the stocks of companies, including banks, in the expectation that management will create value. But in these three banks, this is not what is happening because the capital did not stay in the banks. Yes, the minority international investors acquired stocks that vary in value in line with market movements. This gives the impression of value creation on their portfolios, but these movements are, in fact, due more to speculation on market movements driven by any number of factors including, for example, overall Chinese economic performance. This should not be confused with value investing: the banks themselves are not putting the money to work to make the investor a capital return. For this reason alone, the market-capitalization rankings are misleading.

As for the Chinese state, which holds the overwhelming majority stake in these banks, such payouts mean the banks will require ongoing capital-market funding after their IPOs. This, in turn, means the government must, in effect, re-contribute the dividends received as a new equity injection just to prevent having its holdings diluted. There can be only one IPO for each bank and one infusion of purely third-party capital.[10] What is the purpose of running a bank that pays dividends to a state that must then turn around and put the same money back again? Why sustain dividend payout ratios at 50 percent or higher? This begins to look very much like some sort of Ponzi scheme, but to whose benefit?

Of course, it is more than that: China's banks are the country's financial system. But, as the analyst said, they operate a business model that requires large chunks of new capital at regular intervals. With high dividend payouts and rapid asset growth, consideration must inevitably be given to the issue of problem loans. How can banks as large as China's grow their balance sheets at a rate of 40 percent a year, as BOC did in 2009, without considering this? Even in normal years, the Big 4 banks increase their assets through lending at nearly 20 percent per annum. Throughout 2009, as the banks lent out huge amounts of money, their senior management emphasized over and again that lending standards were being maintained. How was it, then, that the chief risk officer of a major second-tier bank could exclaim even before 2009: "I just don't understand how these banks can maintain such low bad-loan ratios when I can't?" His astonishment suggests there may be less-than-stringent management of loan standards by the banks' credit departments. This is undoubtedly true.

The most important fact behind the quality of these balance sheets, however, goes beyond common accounting manipulations or even making bad loans. These things are inevitable almost anywhere. It goes back to the financial arrangements made by the Party when weak bank balance sheets were restructured over the years from 1998 to 2007. A close look at how these banks were originally restructured highlights the political compromises made during this decade-long process. These compromises have been papered over by time and weak memories on all sides: it is highly likely, for example, that China's national leaders believe that their banks are world-beaters. In the past, sweeping history under the carpet might have been enough; people would have forgotten. Today, it is far from enough, even for those operating inside the system. The key difference with the past is that the quest to modernize China's banks was made possible by raising new capital from international strategic investors and from subsequent IPOs on international markets. China's major banks are now an important part of international capital markets and subject to greater scrutiny and higher performance standards . . . just as Zhu Rongji had planned.

ENDNOTES

1 See Demirguc-Kuntand Levine 2004: 28.
2 "Inside the world of a red capitalist: Huang Yantian's financial powerhouse is helping to remake China," *BusinessWeek*, May 1994.
3 Li, Liming and Cao, Renxiong, *1979–2006 Zhongguo jinrong dabiange* 中国金融大变革 (*1979–2006 The Great Reform of China's banking system*). Shanghai: Shiji chuban jituan 世纪出版集团: 474.
4 Walter and Howie 2006: 181ff.
5 Ibid., Chapter 9.
6 Curry and Shibut 2000.
7 *21st Century Business Herald 21* 世纪经济报导, April 13, 2010: 10.
8 Yang excludes ABC, which listed its shares later in 2010.
9 "ICBC says China's banks need $70 billion capital," *Bloomberg News*, April 13, 2010.
10 The first round of fund raising via an IPO involves the sale of new shares. This brings new capital into the bank and dilutes the original shareholdings. Thereafter, if the bank sells shares again, the Chinese state must also inject money or have its stake diluted.

CHAPTER

3

The Fragile Fortress

*"Growing big is the best way for Chinese banks to make more money . . .
This model of growth, however, neither assures the long-term sustainable
development of the banking sector nor satisfies the need of a balanced
economic and social structure. Things are very complicated; so will be the
solutions."*

Xiao Gang, Chairman, Bank of China
August 25, 2010[1]

When the Asian Financial Crisis threatened the stability of China's
financial institutions in 1997, Zhu Rongji sponsored a group of
reformers surrounding Zhou Xiaochuan, then chairman of the
CCB, to come up with a plan. The immediate threat to confidence in
the banks was addressed by the MOF injecting new capital into the banks
in 1998. As a second step, Zhou's group proposed a "good bank/bad bank"
approach to strengthen the balance sheets of the Big 4 banks. Modeled
after the Resolution Trust Corporation (RTC) in the US, asset-management
companies (AMCs) would be established for each of the banks. The
AMCs would become the "bad" banks holding the non-performing loans
(NPLs) of the resulting "good" banks. These bad banks would be financed
by the government and be responsible for recovering whatever value
possible from NPLs. The State Council approved the proposal and in 1999
the AMCs were set up. (See appendix for organizational charts of China's
resulting financial system).

In 2000, huge problem-loan portfolios were transferred to the AMCs, freeing the banks of massive burdens and enabling them to attract such blue-chip strategic investors as Bank of America and Goldman Sachs. These international investors were brought in less for their money than for the expertise that the government hoped could be transferred to its banks. But, in a rising crescendo of criticism, conservative and nationalist critics claimed a "sell-out" to foreign interests. Even so, in 2005, CCB enjoyed a wildly successful IPO in Hong Kong, raising billions of dollars in new capital. With this IPO, Zhu and Zhou's efforts achieved a very significant success where, several years before, few had believed such a thing possible for a Chinese bank. Unfortunately, the very success of bank reform fed the fire of conservative criticism which was now amplified by the PBOC's institutional rivals, who wanted to cut Zhou and the central bank down to size. Among these rivals were the NDRC, the CSRC, the CBRC and, most particularly, the MOF. The impact of this concerted criticism affected the financial restructuring process, beginning with ICBC and continuing through to ABC. It also had the effect of ending Zhou's integrated approach to capital-market and regulatory reform.

The practical consequence for the bank reform was the creation of two different approaches to balance-sheet restructuring. Of course, the original plan for all four banks was superficially retained, even after the MOF assumed the leading position in the reform of ICBC and ABC in 2005. No better ideas had been generated as a result of all the criticism, so each of the four banks raised capital through IPOs. But the paths to restructuring differed, as did the manner in which NPL portfolios were disposed of. The major financial liabilities remaining on bank balance sheets arising from the two different approaches are shown in Table 3.1. Information in this table is derived from the banks' financial statements under the footnote "Debt securities classified as receivables." The table illustrates the continuing and material exposure of China's major banks to securities created as a result of their restructuring a decade ago. The simple message of these "receivables" is that the old bad debt has not gone away; it is still on bank balance sheets but has been reclassified, in part, as "receivables" that may never be received.

What is the nature and value of these assets? The various PBOC securities, as well as the 1998 MOF bond, are clear obligations of the

TABLE 3.1   Restructuring "receivables" on bank balance sheets

RMB billion	BOC	CCB	ICBC	ABC
1998 MOF bond	42.5	49.2	85.0	93.3
1999 AMC bonds	160.0	247.0	313.0	0.0
2007 MOF receivable	0.0	0.0	62.3	635.5
2004 PBOC Special Bills	0.8	63.4	434.8	0
2006 PBOC Target Bills	113.5	0.6	0.0	0.0
2007 PBOC bills and bank sub-debt	14.6	57.1	237.1	0
Total receivables	331.4	417.3	1,132.2	728.8
Total Assets	8,748.2	9,623	11,785.1	8,882.6
Total Capital	608.3	492.0	586.4	342.8
Receivables to Total Assets	3.8%	4.3%	9.6%	8.2%
AMC Bonds to Total Capital	**26.3%**	**50.2%**	**53.4%**	**NM**

Source: Bank audited financial statements, December 31, 2009

sovereign. But what value should be assigned to the AMC bonds or, for that matter, the MOF "receivable?" Obviously a receivable due from the MOF is similar to a government bond . . . on the surface. The bond, however, has been approved by the State Council and the NPC as part of the national budget. Such government bonds will be repaid either by state tax revenues or further bond issues. Who has approved the issuance of that IOU? How will it be repaid? These are important questions, given each bank's massive credit exposure to these securities. For example, the total of these restructuring assets is nearly twice ICBC's total capital, with the AMC bonds alone representing 53 percent. The sections below seek to understand how these obligations arose and what they practically represent in order to determine their value and structural implications for the banking system as a whole.

THE PEOPLE'S BANK OF CHINA RESTRUCTURING MODEL

From the viewpoint of strengthening the banks, the original PBOC model was the most effective, providing additional capital to the banks through a combination of more new money and better valuations for problem loans.

In the first step in 1998, bank capital was topped up to minimum levels required by international standards. This was followed by the transfer of US$170 billion of bank NPL portfolios to the AMCs at 100 cents on the dollar. These "bad banks" paid cash, using a combination of PBOC loans and AMC bonds, for the bad-loan portfolios. However, these injections of cash came just at a time when inflation was looming. Consequently, the PBOC sterilized the incremental cash on bank balance sheets by forced purchases of PBOC bills, which could not be used in any further financing transactions. This is the source of the PBOC securities listed in Table 3.1. In 2003, additional bad loans remaining on the balance sheets of CCB and BOC were completely written off up to the amount of the total capital of each bank, a total of RMB92 billion (US$12 billion). Bank capital was then replenished from the country's foreign-exchange reserves and with investments from foreign strategic investors. CCB and BOC were restructured in this way and completed successful IPOs in 2005 and 2006.

The partial recapitalization of the Big 4 banks, 1998

On the collapse of GITIC and amid rumors of bank insolvency, in 1998 Zhu Rongji ordered a rapid recapitalization of the Big 4 banks to at least minimum international standards, which were the only standards available to China. A mountain of bad loans had been created in the late 1980s and early 1990s and ignored for 10 years. This was the typical approach of the bureaucracy toward intractable problems. By 1998, however, it had become obvious to the government that such methods increased systemic risk. At that time, China's banks had never been audited to strict professional standards or, for that matter, to *any* professional standard. As with GITIC, no one could say with confidence how big the problem might be. Given Wang Qishan's experience in having to answer an angry Premier's questions about GITIC's black hole, one can imagine the pressure people at the MOF must have felt as they sought to come up with a figure that would satisfy Premier Zhu.

There was, of course, no time for a real audit, but someone was clever enough to come up with a number purportedly sufficient to raise bank capital adequacy to eight percent of total assets, in line with the Basel Agreement on international banking standards. This figure turned out to be

RMB270 billion (US$35 billion). For China, in 1998, this was a huge sum of money, equivalent to nearly 100 percent of total government bond issuance for the year, 25 percent of foreign reserves and about four percent of GDP. To do this, the MOF nationalized savings deposits largely belonging to the Chinese people (see Table 3.2).

In the first step, the PBOC reduced by fiat the deposit-reserve ratio imposed on the banks, from 13 percent to eight percent. This move freed up RMB270 billion in deposit reserves which were then used on behalf of each bank to acquire a Special Purpose Treasury Bond of the same value issued by the MOF (see Figure 3.1).[2] In the second step, the MOF took the bond proceeds and *lent them* to the banks as capital (see Figure 3.2). This washing of RMB270 billion through the MOF in effect made the banks' depositors—both consumer and corporate—*de facto* shareholders, but without their knowledge or attribution of rights.

TABLE 3.2 Composition of Big 4 bank deposits, 1978–2005

RMB billion	Total	Household	Government	Enterprise	Other
1978	113.5	27.2%	40.3%	32.4%	0.0%
1983	276.4	34.9%	32.6%	31.3%	1.2%
1988	744.9	44.7%	9.2%	39.4%	6.7%
1993	2,324.5	55.7%	5.2%	33.0%	6.1%
1998	6,978.2	57.1%	4.9%	36.2%	1.8%
2003	13,465.0	56.7%	7.9%	30.9%	4.5%
2004	15,355.7	56.6%	8.3%	31.6%	3.5%
2005	18,112.1	55.8%	9.9%	29.5%	4.8%

Source: China Financial Statistics 1949–2005

FIGURE 3.1 Step 1 in recapitalization of the Big 4 Banks, 1998

FIGURE 3.2   Step 2 in recapitalization of the Big 4 Banks, 1998

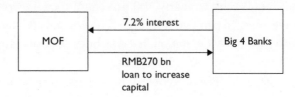

As part of the CCB and BOC restructurings in 2003, these nominally MOF funds totaling RMB93 billion for the two banks were transferred entirely to bad-debt reserves and then used to write off similar amounts of bad loans.[3] This left the Ministry of Finance responsible for repayment. For the banks this was a good deal, as the MOF was now obligated not just to "repay" what was originally the banks' money anyway, but to use its own funds to do so. It is no wonder, therefore, that the bond maturities were extended to 2028, just as it is no wonder that the MOF did not support the PBOC approach to bank restructuring. How could it when, without the approval of State Council and National People's Congress, it had no access to such massive amounts of money?

Bad banks and good banks, 1999

Having shored up the banks by such accounting legerdemain, work began on preparing them for an eventual IPO. Zhou Xiaochuan proposed the international "good bank/bad bank" strategy that had been used successfully in the Scandinavian countries and the US. This involved the establishment of a "bad bank" to hold the problem assets spun off by what then becomes a "good bank." Zhou proposed the creation of one "bad" bank, called an "asset-management company," for each of the four state-owned banks. It was a critical part of the plan that, after the NPL portfolios had been worked out, the AMCs would be closed and their net losses crystallized and written off, a process that was expected to take 10 years. In 1999, the State Council approved the plan and the four AMCs were established.

The MOF capitalized each AMC by purchasing Special AMC Bonds totaling RMB40 billion or roughly US$1 billion each (see Figure 3.3). In line with the plan to close the companies, these bonds had a maturity of 10 years. But RMB40 billion was hardly enough to acquire bank NPL

FIGURE 3.3 AMC capitalization by the MOF and each bank, 1999

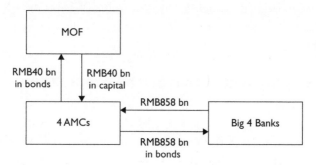

portfolios. More funds were needed and where else to get them but from the banks themselves? The AMCs, therefore, issued 10-year bonds to their respective banks in the amount of RMB858 billion (US$105 billion).

These bonds represent the major flaw in the PBOC plan. The significance of the bonds is that the banks remain heavily exposed to their old problem loans even after they had been nominally "removed" from their balance sheets. The banks had simply exchanged one set of demonstrably non-performing assets for another of highly questionable value. The scale of this exposure was also huge in comparison to bank capital (see Table 3.1). Given the size of the bank recapitalization problem in comparison to China's financial capacity at the time, the government had little choice but to rely on the banks. But this approach was not in line with the international model and did not solve the problem.

In the Scandinavian and US experience, the national treasury had not only capitalized the bad banks, but it had also provided financing to them so that the resulting "good" banks had no remaining exposure to their old bad loans. They had become the problem of the national treasury and ultimately their cost would be paid for from taxes. In China, as long as the government's reliance on the banks to fund the AMCs remained "inside the system," it may not have mattered. A supportive bank regulator could rule that AMC bonds were those of semi-sovereign entities and the question as to their creditworthiness could be avoided. But once these banks became listed on international markets and were subject to scrutiny by other regulators and investors, international auditors would inevitably question the valuation of these bonds. The AMCs were thinly capitalized at about

US$5 billion. The bonds they had issued totaled US$105 billion and the assets they funded had, by definition, little value. What if the AMCs could not achieve sufficient recoveries on the NPL portfolios to repay the bonds due in 2009?

NPL portfolio acquisition by the AMCs, 2000

The first acquisition of bad-loan portfolios by the new AMCs began and was completed in 2000. A total of RMB1.4 trillion (US$170 billion) in NPLs was transferred *at full face value,* dollar-for-dollar, from the banks to the AMCs. This was funded by the bond issues and a further RMB634 billion (US$75 billion) in credit extended by the PBOC (see Figure 3.4). The obvious question that arises is: if these loans were really worth full face value, why were they spun off in the first place? There are a number of possible reasons for this. One is that any write-down by the banks in 2000 would have wiped out all capital injected by the MOF in 1998 and there was, as yet, no consensus on where new capital would come from. Given the amounts involved, there were, after all, limited choices. This is surely part of the answer. Another part is that this transfer was equivalent to an indirect injection of capital since the replacement of bad loans with cash would free up loan-loss reserves (if any). Going forward, it would improve bank profitability and capital by reducing the need for loan-loss provisioning.

The rest of the answer is that the government was unable to reach consensus on the valuation of these "bad" loans. After all, these loans had all been made to SOEs which were, by definition, state-owned.

FIGURE 3.4 AMCs' additional funding from the PBOC, 2000

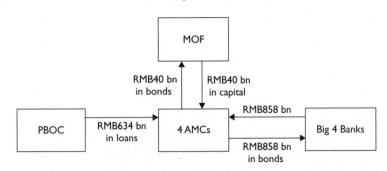

Anything less than full value would suggest that the state was unable to meet its own obligations, a position anathema to Party ideologues. But that was just the point: the state *was* unable to meet these obligations. So instead of bankrupting all SOE borrowers—that is, basically the entire industrial sector—the Party chose to keep the potential losses concentrated on bank balance sheets. Instead of resolutely addressing the problem by writing the loans down, it decided to push the matter off into the future and on to some other politician's agenda. Of course, in 2009, the Party decided to do the same thing, so the AMC obligations were pushed off a further 10 years. This is how things work "inside the system."

PBOC recapitalizes CCB and BOC, 2003

Official data indicate that after this first tranche of bad loans was removed in 2000, the four banks still had RMB2.2 trillion (US$260 billion) more on their books, and this was *before* a stricter international loan-classification system was implemented in 2002. The government took a hard look at bank capital levels, but its own resources remained very limited. Its conservative approach extended to an aversion to increasing the national debt. If the banks were truly to be strengthened, they needed more capital and a lot of it. Zhou's plan had concluded that this could only be provided by international investors. But the problem was how to make bank balance sheets and business prospects strong enough to attract them.

The question boiled down, in part, to how much each bank could afford to actually write off. The PBOC found that of the four banks, only BOC and CCB had sufficient retained earnings and registered capital to make full write-offs of their remaining bad loans while leaving a small but positive capital base. Neither ICBC nor ABC was capable of achieving this in 2003, and both would have ended up with negative capital; that is, they would have been factually bankrupt. But if BOC and CCB's RMB93 billion in capital was to be written down, where could the money be found to build it back up? After much argument, Zhou Xiaochuan proposed the only possible solution: use the foreign-exchange reserves. As the famously outspoken Xie Ping, then director of the PBOC's powerful Financial Stability Bureau, put it: "This time, we did not just play a game with accounting [a direct jab at the MOF's methods in 1998]. Real money went into the banks."

Zhou's plan was approved by the State Council and on the last day of 2003, each bank transferred the value of its capital and retained earnings[4] into bad-debt reserves and wrote it all off. In other words, the MOF's total capital contribution to the two banks—RMB93 billion—was written off, but the MOF remained obligated to repay its 1998 Special Bonds. This fact alone highlights the seriousness of the Party's intention to restructure the banks and is emblematic of the PBOC's ascendancy over the MOF at the time. The two banks each received US$22.5 billion from the country's foreign-exchange reserves by means of the PBOC entity Central SAFE Investment (discussed in greater detail in Chapter 5). Shortly thereafter, in May and June 2004, the banks disposed of an additional total of RMB442 billion in problem assets via a PBOC-sponsored auction process prearranged to create loan recoveries and further additions to their capital accounts. As a result of all these actions, BOC and CCB were in a position to attract foreign strategic investors and ultimately to proceed with IPOs in 2005 (see Table 3.3). But the side effect was to exacerbate the political struggle over bank reform: the PBOC now owned 100 percent of both CCB and BOC.[5]

"Commercial" NPL disposals, 2004–2005

In line with the PBOC blueprint, a second round of NPL acquisition by the AMCs, totaling RMB1.6 trillion (US$198 billion), followed in 2004 and 2005. In addition to a second batch of bad loans of RMB705 billion from ICBC, portfolios also included RMB603 billion from a number of smaller, second-tier banks. For these transactions, the PBOC provided the necessary funding, with estimated credits of up to RMB700 billion (see Figure 3.5 and Table 3.4) But this time, the PBOC had already taken a down payment copied straight out of the MOF's 1998 playbook: in 2004, it had issued compulsory Special Bills totaling RMB567.25 billion (US$70 billion) to BOC, CCB and ICBC. These bills could not be sold into the market and were designed to mature in June 2009 as a part of the unwinding of the entire AMC arrangement.

In issuing the bills, the PBOC accomplished two things. First, it removed the liquidity it had created by financing the NPL spin-offs; and, second, it in effect extracted from the banks a partial pre-payment of about 33 percent of its maximum lending to the AMCs. In essence, this Special Bill

TABLE 3.3 PBOC/Huijin ownership rights in major Chinese banking institutions

%	Date Established	Huijin	Jianyin	MOF	Other State	Foreign Strategic	Public (A+H)
Pre-IPO							
BOC	August 26, 2004	100	-	-	-	-	-
CCB	September 9, 2004	85	10.653	0	4.12	-	-
ICBC	April 2, 2005	50	-	50	-	-	-
ABC	January 15, 2009	50	-	50	-	-	-
CDB	December 16, 2008	48.7	-	51.3	-	-	-
	Date of IPO						
Post-IPO							
CCB	H: October 27, 2005; A: September 25, 2007	59.12	8.85	-	2.03	-	15.92
BOC	H: June 1, 2006; A: July 1, 2006	67.49	-	-	0.85	14.18	31.66
ICBC	H, A: October 27, 2006	35.4	-	35.3	4.6	7.2	17.5
ABC	H, A: July 16, 2010	40.93	-	40.2	3.87	-	15.0

Source: Huijin; bank annual financial reports and ABC offering prospectus

Note: Dates of IPOs include those for both Hong Kong (H) and Shanghai (A) IPOs. "Other State" investors include strategic Chinese investors such as SOEs. For BOC, all NSSF (4.46 percent) and foreign strategic investor shares (13.91 percent) were converted into H-shares at the time of the IPO and are included in the Public number. Jianyin is a 100 percent subsidiary of Huijin.

FIGURE 3.5 PBOC funding for ICBC NPL disposal and commercial loan auctions

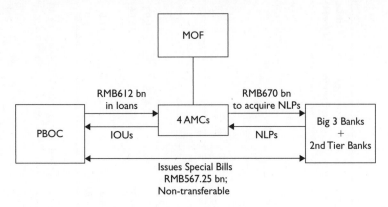

was a predecessor to the mammoth Special Bond issued by the MOF in 2007 to capitalize CIC and it was issued largely for the same reason: to control excess liquidity.

The ICBC and ABC recapitalizations, 2005 and 2007

In contrast to its involvement with BOC and CCB—where its 1998 cash capital contribution had been fully written off but its liability stayed in place—in the case of ICBC, the MOF's original RMB85 billion remained, so that the PBOC/Huijin's contribution was reduced to US$15 billion, equivalent to 50 percent of the bank's equity. Two years later, in 2007, ABC's recapitalization followed the ICBC model, but things appeared to have changed completely. As before, Huijin contributed new capital from exchange reserves to the tune of US$19 billion to ABC, and the MOF's 1998 contribution remained in place. But, as will be discussed in Chapter 5, by this stage, Huijin belonged to the MOF, not to the PBOC.

While, on the surface, things appeared to be consistent with the PBOC approach, in fact the entire structure of bank ownership had reverted to the status quo of the pre-reform era, with the MOF in control. Not only owner-ship was affected; the entire restructuring of problem-loan portfolios was different, as was the government's attitude towards the banks. With the apparently successful rehabilitation of BOC and CCB, the Party was, in effect, telling the banks that they now had to share the burden. From this came the lending binge of 2009; the banks had once again reverted to their role as a simple utility.

THE MINISTRY OF FINANCE RESTRUCTURING MODEL

The MOF, of course, was unhappy with its subordination to the PBOC following the restructuring of the banks up to 2004. Historically, this was almost the first time that their roles had been reversed. However, as described above, from 2005, the MOF was able to exert its influence over the banking system once again, a process that culminated with the establishment of China Investment Corporation (CIC) in late 2007 (see Chapter 5). The principal difference between the MOF's approach and that of the PBOC was that it assumed direct responsibility for the funding and repayment of problem-loan disposals. This, in fact, appeared to nudge things much closer to the international model. The PBOC had succeeded in pushing the MOF away from control of the reform process, but its complex funding arrangements for NPL disposals, although practical given the government's limitations, had never been a good solution. From the start, the AMCs had been thinly capitalized and faced the hopeless task of recovering 100 cents on each dollar of problem loans. How could they really be expected to repay the PBOC, much less the banks?

Looked at closely, however, the MOF's solution also had its weak points. In 2005, when it assumed control of ICBC's ongoing restructuring, the MOF partially replaced AMC bonds with its own paper. That year, a bad-loan portfolio of RMB246 billion was transferred to a "co-managed account" (see Appendix) and ICBC—unlike in the BOC and CCB cases—did not receive cash. Instead, it received what can be called "MOF IOUs" as well as the traditional AMC bonds (see Figure 3.6).

The case of ABC, too, is a pure example of this same MOF approach. Some 80 percent—RMB665.1 billion (US$97.5 billion)—of its NPLs was replaced on a full book-value basis by an unfunded MOF IOU.[6] As with ICBC, the NPL hole on its balance sheet was replaced with a piece of paper conveying the MOF's vague promise to pay "in following years", according to the related footnote in its annual financial statement. For ICBC's receivable, this period is five years; for ABC, it is 15.

On the plus side, this receivable had the advantage of being a direct MOF obligation and relieved the banks of any problem-loan liabilities. Moreover, since ICBC and ABC did not receive cash, excess liquidity did not become a problem. These were the advantages to this approach, but there were also disadvantages.

FIGURE 3.6 NPL restructuring for ICBC and ABC, 2005 and 2007

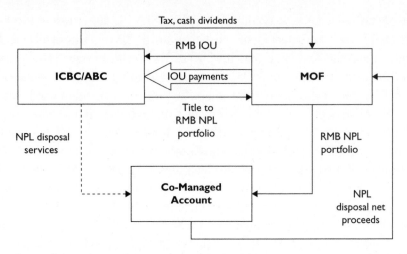

The details of the underlying transactions for the two banks show that this approach is another instance of pushing problems off into the distant future. Actual title to the problem loans was transferred to the "co-managed" account with the MOF. The banks were authorized by the MOF to provide NPL disposal services. But what exactly is this MOF IOU? It may represent the obligation of the Ministry itself, but, notwithstanding the fact that the MOF represents the sovereign in debt issuance, does its IOU represent a direct obligation of the Chinese government? It would have been a far cleaner break had the MOF simply issued a bond, funding the AMCs directly from the proceeds and using cash to acquire the NPLs. There would have been no need for the PBOC to extend credit at all. That was how the United States Department of Treasury funded the Resolution Trust Corporation during the savings-and-loan crisis.

The approach would have cleaned up the banks completely and the liability would have been indisputably with that department with taxing authority. To have done so, however, the MOF would have had to include the required debt issues in its national budget and received the approval of the National People's Congress. An unfunded IOU, in contrast, is entirely "off the balance sheet" (*biaowai* 表外) and would only have been approved as a part of the overall bank-restructuring plan approved by the State Council. Indeed, it is possible that the use of IOUs did not even require State Council approval, as these instruments are purely unfunded contingent liabilities. Contingent liabilities are not included, at least publicly, in the national budget, or anywhere else for that matter.

Then, of course, repayment of its IOUs does not rely on the national budget: it turns out that the banks themselves would be the sole source of cash for funding these payments. Footnotes in the ICBC's audited financial statements and the ABC IPO prospectus indicate that IOU repayment would come from recoveries on problem loans, bank dividends, bank tax receipts and the sale of bank shares. In other words, the banks would be indirectly paying themselves back over "the following years" since it is entirely unlikely that the MOF would sell (or be allowed to sell) any of its holdings in the banks. Since such funding sources represent future payment streams, it appears that the co-managed funds simply hold the two banks' NPLs on a consignment basis; they are a convenient parking lot. Given the experience of the AMCs in problem-loan recovery (see below), there is little likelihood that either bank could do much better. The establishment of the Beijing Financial Asset Exchange in early 2010 is highly suggestive of how the banks will dispose of the bad loans in those co-managed accounts. The shareholders of this new exchange, which is located in the heart of the Beijing financial district, include Cinda Investment, Everbright Bank and the Beijing Equity Exchange. Its stated mission is to dispose of non-performing loans by means of an auction process. Perhaps this exchange will lead the disposal process for the two banks. But what entities have the financial capacity to acquire large NPL portfolios and who will take the inevitable write-down? In the end, the MOF will have to issue a bond to cover the net remainder of both of its IOUs or else extend their maturities. Other than avoiding a discussion with the National People's Congress, it is entirely unclear exactly what is gained by taking this approach.

All of this simply serves to focus the light on the one practical source of repayment: bank dividends. This takes the story right back to bank dividend policies noted in Chapter 2. As will be discussed in regard to CIC in the next chapter, the Ministry of Finance's arrangement has significant disadvantages, even compared with the far-from-perfect PBOC model.

"Bad bank" performance and its implications

By the end of 2006, BOC, CCB and ICBC had all completed their IPOs and the AMCs shortly thereafter had finished their workouts of their

NPL portfolios. Given the weight of the AMCs on each bank's balance sheet, the question must be asked: how well did these bad banks perform their task? As of 2005, even after the second round of spin-offs, the Big 4 and the second-tier banks still had more than RMB1.3 trillion (US$158 billion) of bad loans on their books. The total of the first two rounds at full face value, together with those remaining as of FY2005, amounted to RMB4.3 trillion. The AMCs were funded by obligations totaling RMB2.7 trillion (US$330 billion), as shown in Table 3.4. These liabilities were

TABLE 3.4 AMC funding obligations, 2000–2005

| | AMC Books | | | | |
RMB billion	Face Value	Value (US$ billion)	Book Value	Source	Funding
Tranche 1, 2000 Big 4 bank NPL portfolios	1,393.9	168.3	1,393.9	AMC bonds	857.0
				PBOC loans	634.0
Tranche 2, 2004 PBOC auction of CCB, BOC NPLs	278.9	33.7	90.6		
PBOC auction of BoComm	53.3	6.4	19.5		
Tranche 3, 2005 ICBC disposes to Huarong AMC	246.0	30.1	246.0	PBOC loans	619.5
ICBC auctions to four AMCs	459.0	56.2	121.6		
PBOC auctions second-tier bank NPLs	603.0	73.8	190.5		
Totals 2000–2005	3,034.1	368.5	2,062.1		2,110.5

Source: Caijing 财经, July 25, 2007: 65; PBOC, Financial Stability Reports, various

all designed, even if poorly, to be repaid by cash generated from loan recoveries. Obviously, as the first portfolio of RMB1.4 billion and parts of the second group of portfolios were acquired at face value, repayment was an impossibility from the start. From their first day of operation, the AMCs were technically bankrupt, and practically little different from the "co-managed accounts" now used by the MOF.

At the end of 2006, when more than 80 percent of the first batch of problem loans had been worked out, recovery rates were reportedly around 20 percent—hardly enough to pay back the interest on the various bonds and loans. While recoveries from the second, largely "commercial," batch suggest a higher rate, industry sources suggest that actual recoveries lagged the prices paid. As 2009 approached and passed, the Party was faced with the problem of how to write off losses that may have amounted to 80 percent of AMC asset portfolios, or about RMB1.5 trillion. But losses could easily have been even greater than that and even long-term industry participants are unsure just what this figure might be.

With some 12,000 staff, the AMCs had their own operating expenses, including interest expense on their borrowed funds. An estimate of operating losses *exclusive of any loan write-offs* is shown in Table 3.5. The table uses loan recoveries as a source of operating revenue, an incorrect accounting treatment. But reports indicate that, indeed, the AMCs did use recoveries to make interest payments on their obligations to the PBOC and the banks. Had they not, the banks would have been forced to make provisions against the AMC bonds on their books or the MOF would have had to make the interest payments. There is no indication that this happened. For the sake of arriving at an estimated recovery, figures used in Table 3.5 are assumed to be 20 percent for loans acquired at full face value and 35 percent for loans acquired through an auction, where the AMCs are assumed to have paid 30 percent. Operating expenses are based on 10 percent of NPL disposals, as stipulated by the MOF.

The resulting analysis suggests that the four AMCs lost their RMB40 billion in capital entirely, with estimated write-offs of RMB1.5 trillion (US$176 billion) yet to be taken. This represents a loss rate of around 50 percent. While the profit or loss of the AMCs is only a rough guess, the amount of the write-offs is a more accurate figure and, what is more, they

TABLE 3.5 AMC estimated income statement, 1998–2008

	RMB billion	
1st Round: 1999–2003	**FY2003**	**US$ billion**
Total acquisitions	1,393.9	168.4
Disposals to 2008	1,156.6	139.7
Recovered, assume 20%	231.3	27.9
less:		
Interest expense on PBOC loans/AMC bonds, 1999–2003	190.0	22.9
Operating expense, assume half of MOF target 10% of disposals	57.9	7.0
Total operating expense	247.9	29.9
Pre-tax gain/loss	−16.6	−2.0
Registered capital	40.0	4.8
Retained earnings	−16.6	−2.0
Accumulated write-offs——Round 1	−925.3	−111.8
2nd Round: 2004–2005	**FY2005**	**US$ billion**
Total acquistions—face value	1,639.7	198.1
Total acquistions—auction value, assume 30%	491.1	59.3
NPLs remaining from Round 1	237.9	28.6
Assumed disposals—100%	1,639.7	198.1
Recovered on auction NPLs, assume 35%	171.9	20.8
Recovered, Round 1 remainders, assume 10%	23.7	2.9
Total recoveries	195.6	23.6
less:		
Interest expense on PBOC loans/AMC bonds, 2004–2005	95.0	11.5
Operating expense, assume half of MOF target 10% of disposals	82.0	9.9
Total operating expense	177.0	21.4
Pre-tax gain/loss	18.7	2.3
Registered capital	40.0	4.8
Retained earnings	−2.1	−0.3
Accumulated write-offs—Round 2	−533.2	−64.4
Write-offs – Round 1 + Round 2	−1,458.5	−176.1

Source: Caijing 财经, May 12, 2008; 77–80 and November 24, 2008; 60–62
Note: US dollar values: RMB 8.28/US$1.00

remain on the balance sheets of these four non-public, non-transparent enterprises.

The reason write-downs have not been taken is straightforward. A full or even partial write-off would lead to the outright bankruptcies of the AMCs, confronting the government with a difficult choice: either the banks would suffer significant losses on the AMC bonds or the MOF would have to bear the burden and explain to the NPC. At the outset of the reform process and the creation of the bad banks, their closure and full write-offs, including MOF payment on their bonds, had been part of the plan and explained as such.

Over the years, however, the plan had been changed and the MOF had assumed responsibility as a result of its bureaucratic victory over the PBOC. Now, in 2009, the banks seemed to be performing like world-beaters and the AMCs were noisily talking up their panoply of financial licenses; everyone had deliberately forgotten the history. Why should the MOF rock the boat when it is far easier to defer any decision until a more convenient time?

This is just what happened. In 2009, as their bonds came due, the AMCs were not closed down and their bonds were not repaid. Instead, the State Council approved the extension of bond tenors for a further 10 years. To support their full valuation on bank balance sheets, the MOF provided international auditors written support for the payment of interest and principal. Each bank's annual financial report contains language such as the following from CCB's 2008 report: "According to a notice issued by the MOF, starting from January 1, 2005, the MOF will provide financial support if Cinda is unable to repay the interest in full. The MOF will also provide support for the repayment of bond principal, if necessary." Of course, a "notice" is not quite a guarantee; the MOF would never commit itself in writing to that. It does mean that it will in some way support the repayment of these obligations, unless at some point it is unwilling or unable to do so. Guarantees always come due at inconvenient times, as their extension in 2009 indicates. Until then, CCB, BOC and ICBC continue to carry these bonds at full value. As Table 3.1 shows, a default, or even a write-down of their value, would significantly impair the capital base of these banks and inevitably require yet another recapitalization exercise.

THE "PERPETUAL PUT" OPTION TO THE PBOC

This review of how the asset-management companies were used to resolve the problem-loan crisis in the banks highlights perhaps the most important part of the banking system: the perpetual "put" the PBOC has extended to the AMCs. In fact, this "put" extends beyond the AMCs to the entire financial system and weakens any reform effort that might be undertaken. It is the Party's shield against financial catastrophes. In the name of "financial stability" the Party has required the PBOC to underwrite all financial cleanups, of which there have been many—from the trust-company fiascos of the 1990s, the securities bankruptcies of 2004–05 to the banks—at a publicly estimated (and probably underestimated) cost of over US$300 billion as of year-end 2005 (see Table 3.6).[7] With this option available to them, bank management need care little about loan valuations,

TABLE 3.6 Estimated historical cost to the PBOC of "Financial Stability" to FY2005

Time Period	Amount (RMB billion)	Use
1997–2005	159.9	Re-lending to closed trust cos., urban bank co-ops, and rural agricultural co-ops to repay individual and external debt
1998	604.1	Re-lending to the 4 AMCs for first-round acquisition of bank NPLs
From 2002	30.0	Re-lending to 11 bankrupt securities companies to repay individual debt
2003 and 2005	490.2	Huijin recapitalizes BOC, CCB, and ICBC
2004–2005	1,223.6	Re-lending to 4 AMCs for second-round acquisition of bank NPLs
2005	60.0	Additional lending to bankrupt securities companies to repay individual debt
2005	10.0	Re-lending to Investor Protection Fund
Total	**2,577.8**	
US$ billion	**315.5**	

Source: The Economic Observer 经济观察报, November 14, 2005: 3; PBOC Financial Stability Report 2006: 4; Caijing 财经, July 25, 2005: 67

credit and risk controls. They can simply outsource lending mistakes to the AMCs, perhaps on a so-called negotiated "commercial" basis, and the AMCs will be almost automatically funded by the PBOC.

The new Great Leap Forward Economy

Added to the still unresolved loans of the 1990s, the US$1.4 trillion lending binge of 2009 will inevitably lead to correspondingly large loan losses in the near future (see Figure 3.7). The borrowers and projects are the same as in the previous cycle—infrastructure projects, SOEs and local-government "financing platforms, which will be discussed further in Chapter 5. But this time, their scale of borrowing is much, much larger; the press has even taken to referring to this as "Great Leap Forward Lending," harking back to Mao Zedong's ill-considered Great Leap Forward of 1958–1961. In early 2010, the regulators and Party spokesmen have taken the line that such investments will pay off over time. This is being echoed by brigades of analysts the world over, but the implication is well-understood by the Party itself. As one official put it simply: "In the near term, there will be no cash flow." In other words, a large portion of these loans, over

FIGURE 3.7 Incremental bank lending, 1993–2009

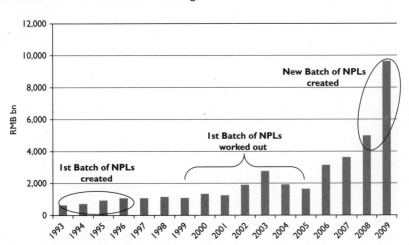

Source: PBOC, *Financial Stability Reports,* various

30 percent of which reportedly went to localities, are already in default. Can the demise of the AMCs as originally called for in 1999 really be expected when their use has proven to be so great? To what extent can the Ministry of Finance continue to issue its IOUs?

Against this background, it is not surprising that questions have been raised about the PBOC's ability to continue to write the check for the Party's profligate management of the country's finances. It is interesting that the PBOC made public its own balance sheet for 2007 and that discussion around a recapitalization was rumored at about the same time (see Table 3.7).[8] This may well explain, at least in part, the use of IOUs written by the MOF for the Agricultural Bank of China restructuring. The 2007 figures show that the central bank is leveraged at nearly 800 times its own capital.

It should not be surprising, therefore, that in August 2005, the PBOC created its own asset-management company designed to take "problems left over from history" off its own balance sheet. Huida Asset Management Company (Huida) was described in its brief appearances in the press as the fifth AMC and its operations since 2005 have remained mysterious since it did not sell its distressed-debt portfolios to outside investors. Huida was meant to operate as the twin to Huijin; Huijin made investments in the financial system that created problem assets while Huida was to collect on unpaid loans associated with such assets when and if they were taken on by the PBOC as part of its operations to maintain financial stability.

Huida, like Huijin, was a creation of the Financial Stability Bureau of the PBOC and all its senior management were staff in the Bureau, just as others were senior staff of Huijin.[9] But unlike Huijin's bank investments, the PBOC wanted to remove problem assets from its own balance sheet. Consequently, the actual equity investor in Huida had to be a third party and, given its close connections with the PBOC, Cinda AMC was the obvious choice (see Figure 3.8).

What were included in such problem assets?[10] On Huida's business license, the targeted assets were related to real-estate loans in Hainan and Guangxi and portfolios assumed as part of the GITIC and the Guangdong Enterprise bankruptcies. Interestingly, these figures are not included in Table 3.6, but can be estimated at around RMB100 billion.[11] Despite such explicitness, financial circles at the time believed that the PBOC's real intention was to put Huida in charge of working out the loans, totaling

TABLE 3.7 PBOC balance sheet, 2007

RMB billion	Q1	Q4	Q4 (US$ bn)	% OF Q4
Foreign assets	9,593.96	12,482.52	1,709.93	73.8%
Claims on central govt	283.93	1,631.77	223.53	9.6%
Claims on depository corporations	652.65	786.28	107.71	4.6%
Claims on other financial corporations	2,190.67	1,297.23	177.70	7.7%
Claims on non-financial corporation	6.63	6.36	0.87	0.0%
Other	1,182.98	709.82	97.24	4.2%
Total assets	13,910.82	16,913.98	2,316.98	100.0%
Currency issuance	2,986.78	3,297.16	451.67	19.5%
Deposits of financial corporations	4,681.70	6,841.59	937.20	40.5%
Deposits of non-financial corporations	30.53	15.80	2.16	0.1%
Bond issuance	3,847.52	3,446.91	472.18	20.4%
Foreign liabilities	92.41	94.73	12.98	0.6%
Government deposits	1,361.00	1,712.12	234.54	10.1%
Other liabilities	888.82	1,483.71	203.25	8.8%
Total liabilities	13,888.76	16,892.02	2,313.98	100.0%
Own capital	21.96	21.96	3.01	0.1%
Total liabilities plus capital	13,910.72	16,913.98	2,316.98	100.0%

Source: PBOC, *Financial Stability Report*, 2008

FIGURE 3.8 The establishment of Huida AMC, 2005

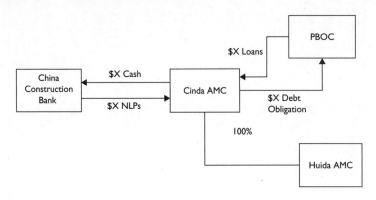

FIGURE 3.9 The transfer of AMC loan portfolios to Huida

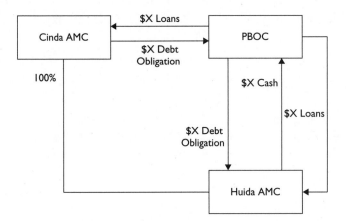

RMB634 billion, the central bank had made to the four asset-management companies in 2000. With a capitalization of just RMB100 million, whether it assumed the old problem assets or any part of the PBOC's more recent AMC loans, Huida was going to be highly leveraged.

Assuming Huida did take on some or all of the PBOC's AMC loans, such a transaction is illustrated in Figure 3.9. As previously described, the PBOC made loans to Cinda AMC in 2000 to enable it to purchase, on a dollar-for-dollar basis, problem-loan portfolios from China Construction Bank. These loans became assets on the balance sheet of the central bank that it then sold to Huida. Huida could only pay for such loan assets, however, if the PBOC lent it money in turn, which appears to have been the case. The net result of such a transaction was that Huida owned the loan assets associated with Cinda, while on its own books, the PBOC now held Huida loan assets.

The only problem with this arrangement is that Huida is a 100 percent subsidiary of Cinda AMC. In other words, Cinda's loan obligations to the PBOC (and ultimately Huida) were being held by itself. If such accounts could be consolidated, then the assets would offset the liabilities and everything would just disappear! None of this makes sense, except from a bureaucratic angle: the PBOC was able to park problem assets off its own balance sheet and Cinda—as a non-listed, and undoubtedly non-audited, entity—had no need to consolidate Huida on its own balance sheet. At best, these loans became a contingent liability: if Huida could not collect, then the PBOC's loan to Huida would not be repaid. As noted previously, contingent liabilities (*biaowai zhaiquan* 表外债券) are not considered to be real in China's financial practice; where in the national budget report are such things mentioned? A look at Cinda AMC's excellent website fails to provide any proof of Huida's existence as a 100 percent subsidiary. One wonders if there is a sixth or even a seventh asset-management company lurking out there in China's financial system.

But this is all just window-dressing compared to the PBOC's huge exposure to foreign currencies, shown as "Foreign Assets" on its balance sheet. Strengthening its capital base, therefore, would appear prudent. By doing so, the government could openly demonstrate its commitment to a strong banking system. Of course, the sovereign, with its vast riches, stands behind the PBOC, but it is not so simple.

China's massive foreign-exchange reserves give a false appearance of wealth: at the time the PBOC acquires these foreign currencies, it has already created renminbi. Under what conditions can these reserves be used again *domestically* without creating even larger monetary pressures? As they are, the reserves are simply assets parked in low-yielding foreign bonds and Beijing's ability to use them is very limited. If the MOF is content to extend the life of the AMCs, consider how much more politically complex the issue of recapitalizing the PBOC would be.

In any event, the government appears to lack the desire to take on such subjects. The pressure to pursue meaningful financial reform has diminished since the struggles of 2005. Drowned in the flood of Party-supported "loans", China's banks in 2009 were back to where they left off before the entire recapitalization program began in 1998: they are financial utilities directed by the Party, just as was the case when the Great Leap Forward began more than 50 years ago. Whatever problems may arise can easily be dealt away to obscure entities that few know or will remember.

CHINA'S LATEST BANKING MODEL

As Chen Yuan remarked, China should not bring "that American stuff over here . . . it should build its own banking system." It is doing just that with the bits and pieces of its old financial system that have been assembled by the asset-management companies. Before the final clean-up of the Agricultural Bank of China and the 2009 loan surge, the fate of the AMCs was actively discussed among the Big 4 banks and the State Council. What should have happened, but apparently will not happen now, was described thus by one of their senior managers:

> For losses stemming from the first package of policy NPLs, the state will bear the burden [an estimated US$112 billion]. The losses on the commercially acquired NPLs [an estimated US$64 billion] are to come from the AMCs' own operating profit after deducting the PBOC re-lending interest. If the price the NPLs were acquired at was not right, then any losses on the PBOC's loans will be made up by AMC capital. In the end, the most likely outcome is that the AMCs will have to wrangle with the state.[12]

This AMC official knew full well that if the AMCs were to take write-offs, they would be bankrupted, forcing the MOF to step in and cover the value of their outstanding bonds and loans from the PBOC. Failing this, the banks would bear losses to their capital that they were (and are) not in any position to bear.

The collapse of Lehman Brothers in September 2008, however, changed this equation completely. The Chinese government acted as if a veil had been removed from its eyes as the international banking system teetered on the verge of collapse. Since at least 1994 and certainly from 1998, bank reform and regulation had been based on the American financial experience. Citibank, Morgan Stanley, Goldman Sachs and Bank of America were seen as the epitome of financial practice and wisdom. This American model and the vigorous efforts of the bank regulator and other market-oriented reformers to channel Chinese financial development within its framework immediately lost all credibility. But there was nothing to take its place. The banks, suddenly without restrictions, not only went on their famous lending binge, but also sought to grab as many new financial licenses as possible. As one senior banker said: "No one knows what the new banking model will be, so in the meantime, it's better to grab all the licenses we can." The easiest place to find a handful of these licenses was the AMCs. How did they come by so many?

In addition to taking on problem-loan portfolios from the banks, the asset-management companies also assumed the debt obligations of a host of bankrupt securities, leasing, finance, and insurance companies and commodities brokers. Of the collapse of this part of China's financial system just five years ago, the world remains ignorant. In many of these cases, the AMCs were meant to restructure debt into equity and then sell it to third parties, including foreign banks and corporations. The proceeds of such sales would have partially or, if well negotiated, fully repaid the old debt. But in the great majority of cases, these zombie companies were never sold, nor were they closed. Ultimately, their names changed and their staff employed, they emerged as AMC subsidiaries. Orient AMC, for example, proudly boasts a group of 11 members, incorporating securities, asset appraisal, financial leasing, credit rating, hotel management, asset management, private equity and real-estate development. Cinda, the largest and most aggressive AMC, has 14, including securities, insurance, trust and fund-management companies. By acquiring the parent AMCs, Chinese banks could in one swoop hold licenses that would, on the surface, catapult them into the league of universal banks.

Of course, the banks were egged on by the AMCs, which did not want to be closed down. There was also an element of vindication: the AMCs were the repositories of unwanted staff who had been spun off as part of bank restructuring. Both began a game of chicken with the government, with the NPL write-offs as the target. By mid-2009, persistent rumors emerged that ICBC and CCB had each submitted concrete plans to the State Council to invest up to US$2 billion for a 49 percent stake in their respective affiliated AMCs. The very idea is astounding: 49 percent of what? But this was no rumor: by late 2009 *Caijing* 财经 magazine reported that the State Council had approved CCB's 49 percent investment in Cinda valued at RMB23.7 billion (US$3.5 billion), with the MOF continuing to hold the balance.[13] The total resulting registered capital of Cinda, including the MOF's original RMB10 billion, was reported to be RMB33.7 billion. This is outrageous because it means not a penny of losses—operating or credit—had been taken by Cinda over its 10 years of operation. This is simply not possible, even if Cinda were the best-managed of the four companies. Or perhaps the operations of its myriad new subsidiaries had offset such losses. Who knew?

Even were it not bankrupt, one wonders at the amazing valuations characterizing the proposed Cinda transaction. Are Cinda and its unknown subsidiary, Huida, any different from those puffed up special-purpose vehicles whose deflation led to the bankruptcy of Enron, not to mention the near collapse of the American financial system in 2008? And there was more to the new arrangements. On the same day the Cinda deal was mooted, the MOF announced that Cinda's RMB247 billion bond owed to CCB was to be extended for a further 10 years. This action undoubtedly represents the first step to extending the institutional life of the other three companies as well.[14]

The year 2009 marked the end of banking reform as advanced since 1998. What will follow is beginning to look like a glossier version of the old Soviet command model of the 1980s and early 1990s. In the end, the Cinda deal could not be done in its proposed form. By mid-2010, however, a new structure for Cinda had been rolled out. Cinda was incorporated, with the MOF as the sole shareholder, and its valueless assets, including the loans it owes the PBOC, were spun off into the now increasingly ubiquitous "co-managed account" in return for more MOF IOUs. This left Cinda and its bevy of financial licenses able to begin the search for a "strategic investor," which, of course, is expected to be CCB. From this continual recycling of debt, it seems that, despite its fantastic riches, the Party—and certainly the MOF—lacks the wisdom and the determination to complete the bank reform begun in 1998.

IMPLICATIONS

The question is often raised: does it matter how the Party manages this machinery for failed financial transactions? China, after all, has the wealth to absorb losses of this scale, if it is determined to do so. The answer to this question must be "Yes." Every day, the press carries stories about China's National Champions and its new sovereign-wealth fund seeking out investment opportunities in international markets. The internationalization of the renminbi has made headlines as China seeks to challenge the dominance of the dollar as the international currency for trade and, perhaps someday, the international reserve currency. But little is heard from China's banks; why?

When in 2008 the Western banking sector was in full disarray and the world was applauding the Chinese for their stimulus package, Merrill Lynch and Morgan Stanley were going for a song. Where were China's banks? A small deal in South Africa and a community bank in California were all there was to show for these proud financial giants. More recently, the head of one of the Big 4 banks dismissed the growth opportunities of developed markets such as the US: tell that to Jamie Dimon![15] One can well imagine how the US Government would have been forced to react had ICBC come to the Department of Treasury in those dark days with a full cash offer for Citigroup, Wachovia, Washington Mutual or Merrill Lynch. For China, the whole shopping basket would have been cheap. Opportunities forgone in a period such as the world has just passed through may never present themselves again. In contrast, China's corporates, the China Development Bank, and its sovereign-wealth fund have actively sought international investments: why haven't the banks?

Put another way: if market valuations for Chinese banks are real and the banks are in such great shape, why hasn't China's banking model been exported? As US and European regulators and governments look for a way to prevent the next financial crisis, why is China's model—with its asset-management companies, outright state ownership and central bank lending—not invoked? If, as some predict, China seeks to replace the US at the center of the global economy at some time in the near future, one would expect it to export not just capital, but also intellectual property. It is nowhere to be seen, nor is it expected.

The story of the past 10 years suggests that China's banks, despite their *Fortune* 500 rankings, are not even close to becoming internationally competitive. They simply do not operate like banks as understood in the developed world. Their years of protective isolation within the "system" have produced institutions wholly reliant on government-orchestrated instruction and support. When the Organization Department determines a bank CEO's future, what can be expected? Despite the prolonged effort to reform the corporate-governance mechanism of the banks, can anyone believe that a bank's board of directors is more representative of its controlling shareholder than its Party Committee? These banks are undeniably big, as they always were, but they are neither creative nor innovative. Their market capitalizations are the result of clever manipulation of valuation methodologies, not representative of their potential for value creation. In 2010, as one Chinese bank after another announced multi-billion-dollar capital-raising plans, one wonders what happened to the huge amounts of capital each had raised just three or four short years ago. Despite apparently outstanding profits, they have not grown their capital fast enough and that is even without considering any mark-to-market valuation of the now perpetual AMC bonds or their huge exposures to the domestic bond markets. The fact is they are now, and were even after their IPOs, undercapitalized for the risks they carry on their balance sheets, and this accounts for their outstanding return-on-equity ratios.

China's banks are at the mercy of domestic political disputes and this emphasizes their passive role in the economy. As others have noted, China's banks have traditionally operated like public utilities. Zhu Rongji's effort to push the banks toward an international model has been stopped and the banks have reverted to their traditional role. Without question, in 2010, they are again huge deposit-taking institutions, extending loans as directed by their Party leaders. Whatever degree of influence their boards of directors and senior management may have gained over the past decade, from 2009, they are no longer much more than window-dressing, as is the previously well-regarded bank regulator. If banks are about measuring and valuing risk, these entities, having begun to learn, have now quickly forgotten.

Any argument that they have no need to study "that American stuff" since the bulk of their "lending" is to state enterprises is demonstrably specious: SOEs don't repay their loans. Banks know that it does not matter whether or not such loans are repaid. First, the Party has taken all responsibility and management cannot be blamed for following orders. Second, as this chapter has shown, there is already a well-proven infrastructure in place to hide bad loans. The future development of the AMCs, as well as the almost-virtual "co-managed account," now seems assured. Careers can be lost only if managers fail to heed the Party's rallying cry. It is the Party, and not the market, that runs China and its capital-allocation process.

In the absence of public scrutiny, few have called into question the quality of bank balance sheets and earnings. This is understandable domestically, where the media is subject to the Party's "guidance," but it is also the case outside of China. International stock markets and brigades of young equity analysts have lent the credibility of their institutions to the idea that banks in China are just that, banks, and have value, if not as individual institutions, then as proxies of the country's economy. That is just the point: they are indeed proxies of the economy "inside the system." In this economy, the Party makes what organizational arrangements it likes, a prime example being the bank buy-back of the un-restructured AMCs. The public line supporting this idea as put forth by an analyst at a major American bank goes: "The asset managers will have the largest capitalized banks in the world behind them which are interested in their expanded business, so there are valid business reasons why this [investment in the AMCs] should happen." Other foreign analysts at major institutions have eagerly echoed this thought.

Such unthinking commentary does China no service. It would be even more dangerous if the Chinese government were lulled into believing that the Big 4 banks are in fact world class and proceeded to encourage them to expand internationally. What effect would the consequent scrutiny by Western regulators and media have? Having seen what constant media focus on sub-prime debt and securitization vehicles caused in the US in 2008, however, no one should be sanguine. Bear Stearns and Lehman Brothers, it should be remembered, disappeared over a weekend. China's political elite has surely learned a lesson from this experience, just as it has from other international financial crises.

In China, political imperatives make significant internationalization of the banks unlikely. The Big 4 banks form the very core of the Party's political power; they work in a closed system with risk and valuation managed by political fiat. True, China's banks have taken on an international guise by public listings, advertising campaigns and consumer lending. As 2009 has shown, however, such change is superficial: true reform of their business model remains a goal that will be the more difficult to reach the closer it is made to seem. These banks will always be closely guarded and directly controlled domestic institutions. Leaders of major international banks in recent years have spoken of creating "fortress balance sheets" able to withstand significant economic stress. In China, there is also the drive to create a fortress, but it is one that seeks to insulate the banks from all external and internal sources of change in the belief that risk should remain under the Party's control.

In 2009, China's banks extended a tidal wave of loans exceeding RMB10 trillion. If in the next few years, these loans do not give rise to a significant volume of NPLs and continue to be carried on balance sheets at full face value, the banking system by definition must continue to be closed. On the other hand, if risk classifications based on international standards are applied consistently, a repeat of the 1990s experience is in the making, with huge volumes of unpaid loans and the banks again in need of a massive recapitalization. Already, the tsunami of lending and high dividend payouts have stretched bank capital-adequacy ratios and forced the need for more capital, which comes largely from the state itself. It is somewhat ironic that the demand for capital can also be mitigated by reducing loan assets, ensuring that the AMCs will continue to play a central role.

There is a further important aspect to this arrangement. Over the past several years, China's banks have enthusiastically entered consumer businesses; credit and debit cards, auto loans and mortgages have become common in the country's rich coastal areas. From 2008, the collapse in exports has revealed a great weakness in China's export-dependent economic model; experts from all sides have urged the government to develop a domestic consumption model similar to that of the US (always the US model!). Pushing in the same direction is China's ageing demographic. If the government does seek to replace export demand with domestic consumption, this suggests that the domestic savings rate will decline, as will household deposits. What will happen to the banks then? Today's financial system is almost wholly reliant on the heroic savings rates of the Chinese people; they are the only source of non-state money in the game. The AMC/PBOC arrangement works for now because everyone saves and liquidity is rampant. What happens to bank funding if the Chinese people learn to borrow and spend with the same enthusiasm as their American friends? From this viewpoint, a profusion of new investment and consumer-lending products appears unlikely. Similarly, this view suggests that full funding for social security is a reform whose time will not come.

Finally, there is the foreign banking presence. International banks were very active in the negotiations leading to China's accession to the World

Trade Organization, producing a detailed schedule that opened China's domestic banking markets. China has largely abided by the agreement and, over the past eight years, foreign banks have invested heavily in developing networks and new banking products. With a focus primarily on domestic consumers, new branch networks and the brand advertising of the major American and European banks have become common in China's major cities and media. Foreign banks have also been quick to engage in the development of a market for local-currency risk-management products.

These banks understand that China and its financial system are in transition and most are prepared to persist in the expectation that at some time in the not-too-distant future, the market will be open fully to them. This was the commonly held position prior to 2008. But the conclusions about the global financial crisis now being drawn by the Chinese government suggest that opening and reform along the lines of the now apparently discredited international financial model will no longer continue. This is not to say there is another model . . . except for the prolongation of the status quo, and this is the direction to which recent events point. What future, then, is there for foreign banks in China?

In summary, China's banks operate within a comfortable cocoon woven by the Party and produce vast, artificially induced, profits that redound handsomely to the same Party. As demonstrated by the 2008 Olympics or the wild celebrations of the country's sixtieth anniversary, the Party excels in managing the symbolism of economic reform and modernization. Ironically, however, if the Asian Financial Crisis in 1997 caused one set of Chinese leaders to see the need for true transformational reform of the financial system, the global crisis of 2008 has had the opposite effect on the current generation of leadership. Their call for a massive stimulus package reliant on bank loans may have washed away for good the fruits of the previous 10 years of reform. Even more ironic, while the "good" banks have been weakened, the "bad" banks created for the earlier reform effort are being strengthened, perhaps in preparation for the next inevitable wave of "reform." If emerging markets are so defined because their institutions are always "in play," buffeted by the prevailing political needs of the government, then real change depends on the next major crisis and a Party leadership willing to accept that today's symbols do not reflect underlying reality and that the true needs of China's economy are not being met.

ENDNOTES

1   *China Daily*, August 25, 2010: 9.

2   The bonds originally had a 10-year maturity, but this, as well as the coupon, changed in 2005. The new coupon is a more manageable 2.25 percent despite its much longer tenor, which was extended to 2028.

3   In ABC's case, this bond was just replaced by an MOF IOU.

4   The RMB93 billion noted is the amount injected into the two banks in 1998 by the MOF's arrangements as part of the RMB270 billion Special Bond. As the total NPL ratio for the banks stood at 40 percent at that time, it cannot be the case that any of the banks had any real retained earnings.

5   In fact, the PBOC slightly diversified CCB's shareholders by allowing a number of central SOEs, as well as the National Social Security Fund, to hold shares. Hence, the PBOC held only a little more than 95 percent of CCB at this point.

6   The original AMC bond,totaling RMB138 billion, owed to ABC from 1999 was replaced by the IOU; RMB150.6 billion in NPL assets was used to offset a PBOC loan of the same amount.

7   See *The Economic Observer* 经济观察报, December 26, 2005: 34. This number may be even larger. The PBOC, in its Financial Stability Report 2005, has also reported a figure of RMB3.24 trillion or US$390 billion.

8   Keith Bradsher, "Main Bank of China is in Need of Capital," *New York Times*, September 5, 2008.

9   Yu Ning, "*Huida deng chang* 汇达登场 (Huida takes the stage)," *Caijing* 财经, July 25, 2005: 65.

10 See "*Huida zichan tuoguan fuchu shuimian Zhan Hanqiao huoren rending shizhang* 汇达资产托管浮出水面：张汉桥获任认定事长 (Huida Asset Management surfaces; Zhang Hanqiao likely appointed as Chairman)," *China Business News* 第一财经日报, August 3, 2005: 1.

11 The absence of the Hainan and Guangdong figures makes one wonder about the fate of the huge amounts of "triangle debt" Zhu Rongji untangled in the early 1990s that were left over from the 1980s banking debacle.

12 *Caijing* 财经, May 12, 2008: 79.

13 www.caijing.com.cn/2009-09-23/110258742.html

14 The bond owed to Bank of China by its related AMC, Orient, was also extended as it came due in 2010; without question the similar Huarong bond held by ICBC can also be expected to see its life extended later in 2010.

15 CEO and Chairman of JPMorgan Chase & Co.

CHAPTER

4

China's Captive Bond Market

"Compared with other financial instruments and against the backdrop of a high savings rate and high ratio of M2 to GDP, China's corporate bond market has been developing very slowly and its role in economic growth has been rather limited. Such lack of development has also distorted the financing structure and produced considerable implicit risks, whose consequences may be grave for social and economic development."

Zhou Xiaochuan
Speech at China Bond Market Development Summit
October 20, 2005

The demand from corporations and other issuers for cheaper capital than banks were willing or able to provide gave rise to the debt-capital markets in the developed economies. The basic assumption of issuers is that banks do not have a monopoly on understanding and valuing risk; large institutional investors, such as insurance companies and pension funds, also have the capacity to make investment judgments independently. So why rely only on banks for capital if you can get money more cheaply from other investors? Why not use markets to press the banks for cheaper funds? In China, over the past several years, a similar process appears to be happening. Its bond markets have enjoyed record issuance volumes, developed standardized underwriting procedures and allowed some foreign participation. Is it possible that in the not-distant future, investors in this market will compete with banks for corporate issuers and so take some of the credit- and market-risk burden from them, as has been one of the explicit reform objectives of the central bank?

In China, nothing is as it appears; words similar to those used internationally can have different meanings. Here, the markets were created by the same group of reformers who promoted bank reform. Beginning in 2005, with the aim of reducing excessive risk concentration in the banking system, they took over the largely moribund inter-bank market for government debt and introduced products modeled after those available to corporations internationally. On the surface, their efforts appear to have paid off. But huge issuance volumes, thousands of market participants and a growing product range do not alter the fact that China's debt markets remain at a very primitive stage—an assessment with which no market participant in China would disagree, as Zhou Xiaochuan's comments above attest. China's debt markets are captive both to a controlled interest-rate framework on the one hand, and, on the other, to investors that, in the end, are predominantly banks. To understand why China's bond markets are moribund requires digging into the technical details. But seeing how these markets are controlled is a key part of understanding how the Party manages China's financial system: the symbols of a modern market are there, but the market itself is not.

Normally, the word "primitive" is used to indicate that the necessary market infrastructure is missing, but in China, all such infrastructure is in place. Like highways, new airport terminals or CCTV's ultra-modern office building in Beijing, it exists because the Party believes bond markets are a necessary symbol of economic modernity. So there are ratings agencies (five), regulators (at least seven) and industry associations (at least two) with overlapping authorities and little respect for one another. There are now many of the same products that can be found in more developed markets, including government bonds, commercial paper (CP), medium-term notes (MTN), corporate bonds, bank-subordinated and straight debt, some asset-backed securities, and so on. These products are traded for cash, repo-ed[1] out, or sold forward, and interest risk is hedged through swaps: all as might be expected.

What makes China's bond markets "primitive," however, is their lack of the engine that drives all major international markets. That engine is risk and the market's ability to measure and price different levels of it.

Risk, in market terms, means price; like everything else, capital has a price attached to it. In China, however, the Party has made sure that it alone, and not a market-driven yield curve, provides the definitive measure of risk-free cost of capital and this measure is based ultimately on the funding cost for bank loans, the one-year deposit rate. Consequently, in the primary (issuing) market for corporate debt, it is common practice that underwriting fees and bond prices are set with reference to bank loans, and not to true demand. Artificially low prices are then compensated for by the issuer's agreement to an exchange of additional value outside of the market through, for example, conducting a certain amount of foreign-exchange transactions. In other words, bond-price setting is bundled with other business not in the market and the underwriter then holds the bond to maturity. Why? In the secondary (trading) market, investor demand is free to price capital, but the low issuing prices in the primary market mean that the bond underwriter will take a loss if he sells. Thus, the number of Chinese government bonds (CGB) and other bonds traded daily is in the hundreds at best. To the extent that bonds change hands, they do so at prices reflecting the premium that holders must pay to buyers to unload the security. If there is no active trading, there can be no accurate market pricing standards, only a price that might be called a "liquidity premium."

There is an additional, historical, reason explaining the weakness of China's bond markets. China is a country where the state—that is, the Party—owns everything and there is no tradition of private property. It might be expected, therefore, that the debt markets would have grown into the most developed market for capital. Unlike stock, debt does not touch directly on the sensitive issue of ownership. As even the most casual observer cannot help but note, however, everyone in China—from retail mom-and-pop investors to provincial governors and Communist Party leaders—is infatuated with stock markets. This has been true since the early 1980s when shares were "discovered" and is one of the main explanations for why observers believe that China is evolving along the path traced by developed economies.

So why not debt? The reason is simple: the government and SOE bosses quickly figured out that stock markets provide enterprises with "free" capital in the sense that it need not be repaid. In contrast, like a loan, bond principal must be paid back at some point and in the past, this often has proved to be "inconvenient." Even better, a public listing provides an SOE with a "modern" corporate veneer (plus higher compensation levels for senior staff if the company is listed overseas) that issuing debt does not. Again, it's the great attraction of symbols. Selling shares is a game-changer in these and many other ways, while issuing more debt is just business as usual. No Chinese CEO was ever lauded in the financial press for borrowing money from a bank.

China's beautiful market infrastructure is necessary, but insufficient to raise the bond market above its primitive stage. As a result of manipulated pricing, corporate issuers are indifferent to the choice of debt instruments; bonds or loans are the same to them. More importantly, underwriters and investors are also indifferent to this market because they cannot make money. This chapter explains why this is so. Caught up in guidelines left over from the Soviet central-planning era, interest rates do not reflect true market forces, so debt valuations are distorted. But this is how the "system" likes it; the Party's urge is to control. Party leaders believe they are better positioned than any market to value and price risk. The near-collapse of the international banking system in 2008 has only confirmed them in this belief.

What does bond market "development" mean, however, if not establishing over time a finely tuned understanding of the price of risk? Part of the notion of risk is that of change. But China's debt-capital markets have from their inception been founded on the expectation that there will be no change, whether in the quality of issuer or in supply and demand as understood by developed markets. Zhou Xiaochuan's remarks, therefore, are an almost-unique public indication that at least some senior officials are aware of the real systemic dangers being created by this suppression of risk. Given his expertise, his remarks on the consequences for social and economic development are not entirely surprising. If all this is true—that the market is creating risk—why does China need a bond market or, in any case, the one it has currently?

WHY DOES CHINA HAVE A BOND MARKET?

The fact that banks hold over 70 percent of all bonds highlights the importance of this question. For the group of market reformers surrounding Zhu Rongji and Zhou Xiaochuan, developing the bond market was a basic part of the bank-reform process that began in 1998. A strong bond market would encourage institutions other than banks to hold corporate debt, and risk could be diversified. But if the markets are not wholly opened to the participation of investors not controlled by the state, this cannot happen. The reality is that China's bond markets has evolved over the past 30 years because the national budget needs to be financed; however, its tax-collecting capacity was, and remains, too weak. If corporate investors could rely on bank lending, the MOF cannot, not if it follows in the model of state treasuries elsewhere in the world. What would a minister of finance be if he could not issue government bonds? What would a modern economy be if it didn't have a government-bond yield curve to measure risk? The MOF's growing demand for funds from the early 1980s led to the creation of a narrow market, which reformers 20 years later would seek to broaden.

In the early 1980s, markets for securities of any kind did not exist in China. The last bond the country had issued was in 1959 and all knowledge associated with it had long since been lost to the Cultural Revolution. But ambitious national budgets in the early 1980s began to create small deficits (see Figure 4.1). Confronting the question of how to deal with increasing

FIGURE 4.1   National budget deficits vs. MOF issuance, 1978–1991

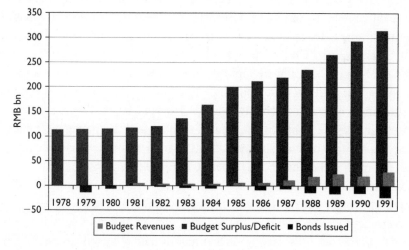

Source: China Statistical Yearbook; Wang Nianyong, p. 53
Note: Includes central and local government budgets; excludes maturing bonds rolled over in 1989–1991.

amounts of red ink, the idea of issuing bonds was voiced by a courageous person at the MOF. This raised questions about the identity of the investor base and what price to pay them. At the start, only SOEs had money (of course, all borrowed from the banks), so by default, they were compelled to fund the government budget as a political duty. As for price, bond interest was set administratively with reference to the one-year bank-deposit rate set by central bank fiat to which was added a small spread. As the data in Table 4.1 indicate, individuals received a higher interest rate than SOEs, which reflected both the MOF's need for third-party funding as well as the demand of retail investors for a reasonable yield. This was a real market situation and the MOF had yet to find a way to minimize its funding costs. As for a secondary market for debt, there was none. SOE investors were forbidden to sell bonds based on logic relating to the MOF's "face": selling a bond was seen as a lack of confidence in the state's creditworthiness.

Over the course of the 1980s, successful agricultural reforms and the growth of small enterprises in the cities rapidly enriched the general population. By 1988, nearly two-thirds of all bonds were sold directly to household investors. Then, from 1987, the real market turned as inflation boomed and banks were ordered to stop lending. SOEs and individuals, strapped for cash and seeing yields turning negative, discovered they could sell off their bond portfolios, although at deep discounts, to "speculators". Suddenly a wholly unregulated over-the-counter (OTC) secondary market sprang into existence just as the craze for shares hit its peak in 1989 and 1990. Here were China's first (and still only) true markets for equity and debt capital! They were rapidly closed down.

When the political dust from June 4 had settled, China in 1991 had the beginnings of regularized bond and stock markets, but they were ensconced safely inside the walls of the new Shanghai and Shenzhen exchanges. The new infrastructure suggested that market reformers had prevailed, but the truth is they had been forced to compromise away the heart of the markets. The two exchanges existed only to provide controlled trading environments where prices and investors could be managed to suit the government's own interests. For its part, the MOF had also realized by this time that its fund-raising difficulties in part reflected investors' fear of locking up their cash with no legal way to recover it until their bonds matured. To expand its own funding sources, therefore, from the early 1990s, the MOF began to develop a secondary market on the exchanges.

TABLE 4.1 Composition of national savings and sales of bonds, 1978–1989

Year	% National Savings			Issued in RMb br	% Sold to		Coupon SOEs	Coupon Individuals	% Inflations
	State	SOEs	Individuals		Institutions	Individuals			
1978	41%	32%	13%	-	-	-	-	-	-
1979	43%	34%	23%	-	-	-	-	-	-
1980	22%	16%	20%	-	-	-	-	-	-
1981	-	-	-	4.87	99.8	0.2	4.0	-	2.4
1982	17%	27%	29%	4.38	55.0	45.0	4.0	8.0	1.9
1983	-	-	-	4.16	50.5	49.5	4.0	8.0	1.5
1984	20%	24%	39%	4.25	48.1	51.9	4.0	8.0	2.8
1985	19%	3%	50%	6.10	36.0	64.0	5.0	9.0	8.8
1986	19%	21%	60%	6.25	36.6	63.4	6.0	10.0	6.0
1987	13%	26%	61%	11.69	35.9	64.1	6.0	10.0	7.3
1988	7%	30%	63%	18.88	37.8	62.2	7.5	-	18.5
1989	0%	34%	66%	22.39	0.0	100.0	-	15.0	17.8

Source: Gao Jian: 47–9; *China Statistical Yearbook*, various
Note: All coupons for maturities of minimum 5 years

FIGURE 4.2 Debt issuance by issuer type, 1992–2008

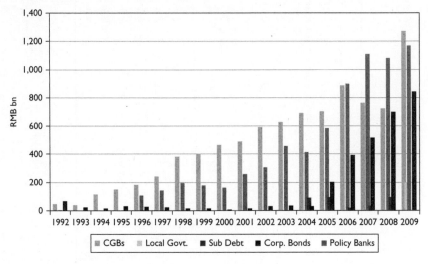

Source: PBOC *Financial Stability Report*, various; China Bond
Note: The 2007 government bond number excludes the RMB1.55 trillion Special Treasury Bond used indirectly to capitalize China Investment Corporation.

Proper pricing of the bonds remained a problem, however, and it wasn't until 1994 that the MOF stumbled on a workable combination of underwriting structures and market-based bidding within the strictures of PBOC interest rates that allowed CGB issue amounts to increase (see Figure 4.2). The innovator at the MOF, Gao Jian, loves to recount the story of how he created a Dutch auction-based bidding system for a loose group of primary dealers using a Red Tower Mountain cigarette carton to hold their bids.[2] Someone's smoking habit and an equitable way to distribute the obligation to underwrite government debt largely solved the MOF's fund-raising difficulties and created the market infrastructure that could be used a decade later.

RISK MANAGEMENT

In spite of the success of Gao's cigarette carton and Dutch auctions, underwriting CGBs, as well as corporate and bank debt, has remained very much a political duty, just as it had been from the beginning. This can be seen from the simple fact that the market did not, and still does not, trade. What is a market without trading? The reason for the lack of liquidity is straightforward: bond prices in the primary market are set below levels that reflect actual demand. Despite its surfaces—record issuance, improved underwriting procedures and issuer disclosure, and even a grudging openness to foreign participation in some areas—it is less a market to raise new capital at competitive prices than a thinly disguised loan market.

This reality is highlighted by the fact that of the primary dealer group of 24 entities, all but two are banks.[3] With the sole exception of the NDRC's recondite enterprise bonds (*qiyezhai* 企业债) that are underwritten by securities companies, banks are the dominant underwriters of all bonds including CGBs, PBOC notes and policy-bank bonds. They underwrite and hold the bonds in their investment accounts until maturity, just like loans. Due to the skewed pricing mechanism in the primary market, banks, like their cousins, the securities companies have not developed the skills to value capital at risk. They do not need to: the PBOC does it for them by fixing the official CGB trading prices in the market as well as the even-more-important one-year bank-deposit rate.

PBOC's perfect yield curves

To fully appreciate why there is no "market" in China's bond markets requires delving into the meaning and practice of bond "yield curves." These curves show the relative level of interest rates payable on similar securities of different maturities (see Figure 4.3 for examples) and "cost" means what investors demand for a given level of risk. The interest rates payable by government, or sovereign, issuers are used as the basis of bond-underwriting decisions in all developed markets. This is founded on the theory that countries do not go bankrupt (which is clearly disputable) and that, therefore, they represent the risk-free standard in a given nation's domestic bond market. In China, the MOF represents the sovereign issuer, the highest credit possible, and the Chinese credit-ratings agencies place the MOF as a unique risk category a level above the AAA (Triple-A) rating represented by, for example, PetroChina. It sounds much better to be a "Quadruple A" than the "Triple A" of, for example, the US Department of Treasury, which one Chinese agency has cheekily assigned it in the Chinese system. Figure 4.3 shows the PBOC-mandated minimum credit

FIGURE 4.3 Mandated minimum spreads over MOF by tenor and credit rating

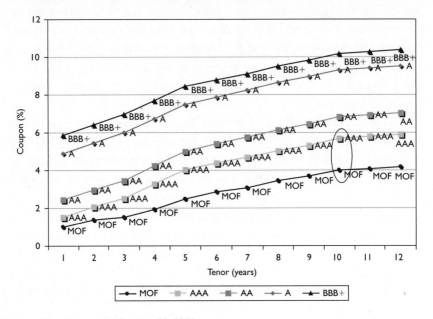

Source: China Bond, as of October 20, 2009

spreads for a variety of enterprise-bond credit ratings over the cost to the MOF. These curves show an ideal world that does not exist: why?

As in other international markets, the curves are based on the underlying MOF yield curve; for example, the minimum 10-year AAA-to-MOF spread is circled.[4] The trouble in China, however, is that the MOF yield curve is disregarded in favor of the PBOC's bank interest rates on loans. It is disregarded because it does not truly exist, as is explained below. The PBOC-mandated one-year loan and deposit rates used by banks are shown in Figure 4.4.

The regulated spread between the cost of funds on deposits and minimum bank lending rates is deliberately set to provide lenders a minimum guaranteed 300 basis point (three percent) profit.[5] When a bank underwrites a bond, therefore, it will, among other things, compare its potential return with that of a loan of a similar maturity to a similar borrower. The issuing company will, of course, consider the same thing. To the extent that this comparison to loan rates influences the underwriting decision, bond

FIGURE 4.4 One-year PBOC RMB bank deposit vs. lending rates, 2002–2008

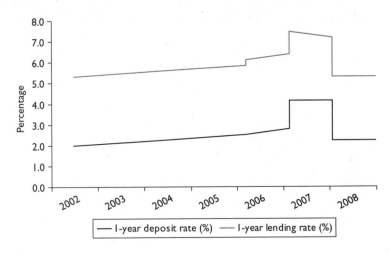

Source: China Bond

pricing does not reliably reference the MOF yield curve. In actual practice, the MOF curve is frequently disregarded and corporate and financial bonds are priced lower than the curve would indicate. This is because banks are motivated by compensation from the issuer via other supplemental businesses. But they also know full well that, as mentioned, the MOF yield curve is a fiction.

Fictional curves from fictional trading

Figure 4.5 shows an actual picture of a single day's corporate-bond trading on December 8, 2009. The yield curves presented look like something created by random machine-gun bursts against a wall. What the figure represents can be understood by examining the two highlighted AAA transactions, both for bonds with tenors of around five years. As can be seen, the trades were completed at wildly different levels—a low of less than two percent and a high of close to five percent. These are not unique transactions; the chart abounds in such examples. Why was there such a differential between two seemingly similar securities?

The absence of active market trading explains this strange data. On December 8, 2009, for example, the *entire* China inter-bank market for

FIGURE 4.5 Actual enterprise-bond yield-curve data, by credit rating

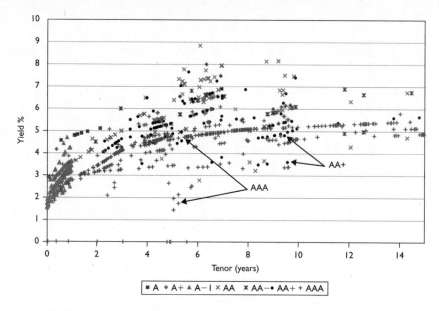

Source: Wind Information, December 7, 2009; excludes MOF, CDB, and financial bonds

corporate bonds recorded only 1,550 trades—this in a market comprising over 9,000 members and RMB1.3 trillion (US$190 billion) in bond value. In contrast, the US Treasury market each day averages 600,000 trades comprising US$565 billion in value. If market participants do not actively trade, how can the price of a bond be determined and serve as a meaningful measure of value?

The true character of China's bond market becomes even clearer when the focus is put on only MOF and CDB bond trades, as shown in Figure 4.6. On December 7, 2009, the number of trades totaled 52 for MOF bonds and 108 for CDB. These numbers could, in all likelihood, be halved since market-makers create volume (as they are required to do) by, among other actions, selling a bond to a counterparty in the morning and buying it back in the afternoon. With trading volume so light, whatever yield curves that can be drawn are almost arbitrary. How then can the MOF curve be considered a meaningful pricing benchmark for corporate-debt underwriters or, indeed, corporate treasurers?

FIGURE 4.6 MOF and China Development Bank bond trades

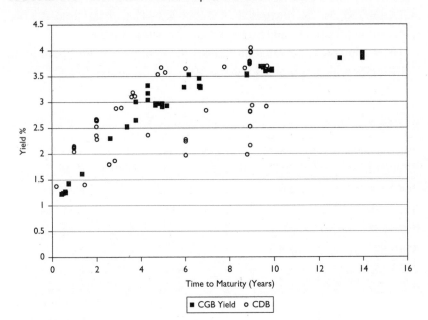

Source: Wind Information, December 8, 2009

Fixing a yield curve

The data raise a question regarding the basic quality of the MOF curve represented in Figure 4.3. China uses what are called in the financial industry "daily price fixings" for its debt securities. This means that there is an "official price" set for traded products such as foreign exchange or securities. Usually, this is done by the central bank or market regulator in consultation with a number of market participants and is necessary because the given product did not trade or traded too few times for the market to establish a price.

Official price setting is not an uncommon practice: there are fixings even for such actively traded products as the Japanese yen, as well as such partially convertible currencies as the Indian rupee and, of course, the Chinese renminbi. In China, since October 2007, this official "fixing" for bonds has been done by the China Government Securities Depository Trust and Clearing Corporation, a nominally "independent" entity owned by the PBOC and the depository for all bonds traded in the inter-bank market. Bloomberg carries the China Bond daily fixing table for CGBs and CDB bonds, as illustrated in Table 4.2. The *actual* traded price information for each bond traded on that day is also shown.

The trading data show that on January 4, 2010, there were a total of 32 CGB trades with a combined value RMB5.57 billion and 55 CDB trades

TABLE 4.2 China Bond price-fixing data, January 4, 2010

Issuer/Coupon/ Maturity Date	Reference Number	Maturity (years)	Fixed Price	Yield %	Trading Record
MOF / 3.56 / 04/11	80004	1	102.47	1.58	No Trade
MOF / 1.55 / 05/12	90009	2	98.5	2.20	No Trade
MOF / 2.51 / 02/13	60001	3	100.31	2.40	No Trade
MOF / 1.77 / 12/13	80026	4	95.64	2.95	No Trade
MOF / 2.90 / 12/14	90031	5	99.6	2.99	No Trade
MOF / 2.71 / 11/15	80022	6	96.64	3.29	3 trades @ 96.327, 96.6794, 96.7298
MOF / 3.22 / 12/16	90032	7	99.34	3.33	1 trade @ 99.7776
MOF / 3.68 / 11/19	90027	10	100.19	3.66	1 trade @ 100.3244
CDB / 2.04 / 12/10	90223	1	99.93	2.12	2 trades @ 99.8945, 99.895
CDB / 2.21 / 12/11	80221	2	99.15	2.67	4 trades @ 99.1316 2 @ 99.113 & 99.0066
CDB / 3.39 / 02/13	30201	3	100.94	3.07	No Trade
CDB / 4.81 / 09/13	80215	4	104.91	3.36	1 trade @ 105.6118
CDB / 3.75 / 11/14	90220	5	100.41	3.65	1 trade @ 99.944
CDB / 3.42 / 08/15	50214	6	98.31	3.76	No Trade
CDB / 3.50 /04/16	90202	6	98.10	3.84	No Trade
CDB / 4.01 / 07/19	90207	10	100.20	4.01	No Trade

Source: Bloomberg, China Bond, and Wind Information. All fixed-rate bonds

with a combined value of RMB29.53 billion. The actual trades used in the daily fixing table were extracted from this voluminous activity and illustrate precisely why Chinese sovereign yield curves are more fiction than fact. For the one-year to five-year section of the CGB yield curve, not one of these bonds traded, not even once! This official yield curve, built out of nothing but assumptions, did dovetail nicely, however, with the six-, seven- and 10-year bonds, which traded a grand total of five times that day.

Data for the MOF and CDB bonds shown in Table 4.2 have been charted in Figure 4.7. Together, they describe a smooth, upward-sloping yield curve. Against this background, what reliance should market participants put on CGB yield curves or, in the case of the CDB bonds, to a notional spread over treasuries? It is not surprising, therefore, that the absence of trading for what should be the most liquid products characterizes the market as a whole as well.

Also on January 4, the entire inter-bank market saw only 615 trades (see Table 4.3), among which CGBs incredibly traded the least of all and represented only 3.3 percent of the total value traded. In contrast to the US$25

FIGURE 4.7 MOF and CDB "fixed" yield curves, January 4, 2010

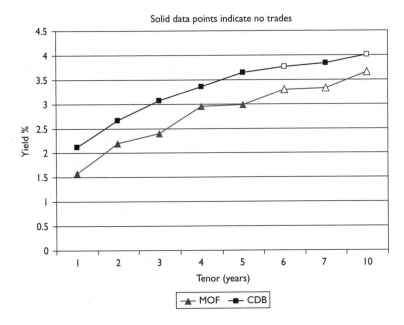

Source: Wind Information, January 4, 2010

TABLE 4.3 Inter-bank bond trading summary, January 4, 2010

	Value Traded (RMB million)	No. of Trades	% Value Traded
MTNs	31,050	149	18.3
Enterprise bonds	10,909	97	6.4
CGBs	5,570	32	3.3
PBOC notes	31,550	74	18.6
CP	15,220	144	9.0
Financial bonds	75,390	119	44.4
Total	169,689	615	100%

Source: Wind Information

billion in bond value traded that day in China, the average daily trading volume in the US debt markets is US$565 billion, a figure itself far in excess of the average total daily *global* equity trading of US$420 billion.[6] These US trades result on average in over US$1 trillion in bond value moving between accounts *each day* on the US Federal Reserve Bank's electronic settlement system.

If the price points, "fixed" or not, on Figures 4.5 and 4.6 measure anything, it is the liquidity premium paid by investors to sell their bonds into a saturated market. This accounts for the widely scattered price points around faint yield curves. The story is summed up in Figure 4.8, which illustrates the fundamental illiquidity of CGBs, corporate and financial bonds. In all of 2008, for example, MOF bond turnover was only RMB3.5 trillion or about 10 percent of all outstanding CGBs. The most liquid securities are the shortest in tenor—MTNs, CP and PBOC notes—but even these turned over less than one time during the entire year.

In sum, the absence of active market trading limits the price-discovery function of China's bond markets. In turn, unreliable prices mean that the market participants cannot value risk accurately. A simple question such as how much a AA issuer would have to pay investors to buy its 10-year bonds cannot be answered with any certainty. On the other hand, China's market investors don't really care. Why should they when the majority of bonds offer "riskless" yields well over the one-year bank-deposit rate

FIGURE 4.8 Inter-bank market trading volume and turnover, FY2008

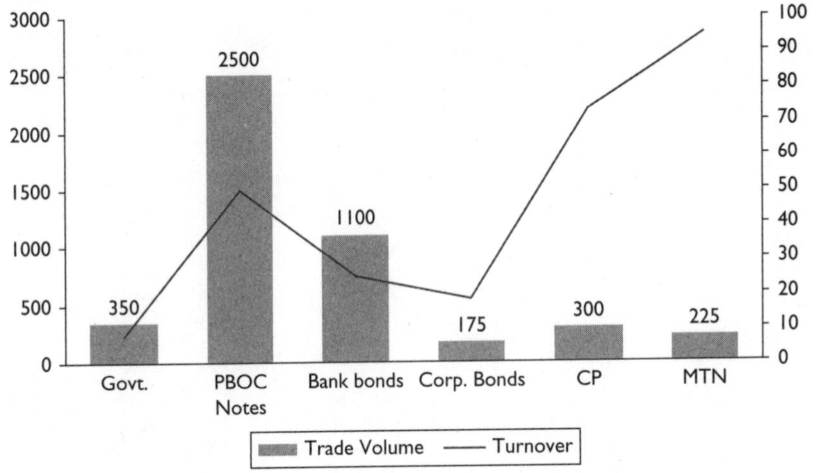

Source: PBOC

of 2.25 percent but, at the same time, well under demand in the secondary market? As long as inflation remains under control, why shouldn't banks be happy to hold the bulk of these securities to maturity, just as they do their loan portfolios?

Cash vs. repo markets

China's repo markets illustrate just what liquidity means in a bond market. Figure 4.9 shows the seven-day repo interest rate for 2008. Contrast the active trading in interest rates here with the anemic yield curves traced by the CGBs and CDB bonds shown in Figure 4.6. Clearly the cost of capital is being driven by supply and demand. What accounts for such trading? The wildly speculative bidding on shares offered in Shanghai IPOs forces investors to put together the largest amount of funding possible to secure an allotment in the share lottery. In IPO subscription lotteries, massive amounts of capital—often equivalent to tens of billions of dollars—are frozen to secure allocations of shares. A large portion of these funds is raised by repo transactions. This market, however, is much more akin to the pure short-term inter-bank loan market than to the long-term capital-allocation function of bond markets. The point, however, is that demand drives the price of capital here, but not in the bond market.

FIGURE 4.9 Seven-day repo volumes, interest rates vs. capital frozen in IPO lotteries

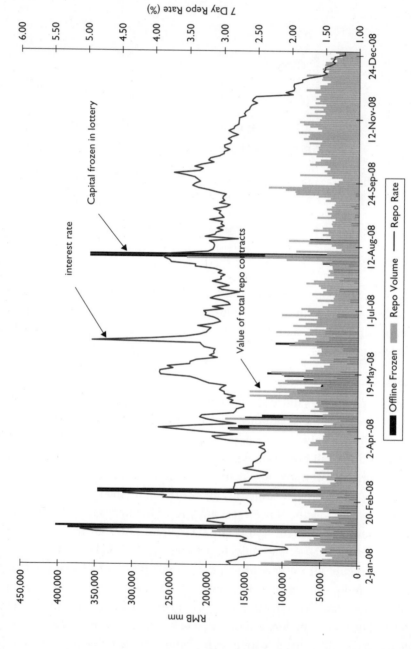

Source: Wind Information

Note: "Offline Frozen" indicates amount of capital used in bids for shares in the institutional "offline" IPO lottery.

As is obvious to even infrequent observers of China's economy, speculation is a fact of life. This largely stems from the artificially fixed returns on bank deposits, loans and bonds, the only available investment alternatives outside of real estate, shares and luxury goods. Set at levels unreflective of the true demand for capital, the managed rates for these products create a stillborn fixed-income market and force investors to speculate. Capital gains, which are untaxed, are the main play for investors in China, whether retail or institutional, and none can be found in the debt-capital markets.

The "327" Bond Futures Scandal

If any one incident highlights why the government seeks to strictly control markets, it must be the bond futures scandal of 1995. This story is already ancient history, but it explains why there is still no financial-future product of any kind in China's capital markets.[7] At its simplest, the scandal was a struggle between a major local broker backed by the Shanghai government, and the MOF; in other words, between local and central government interests. Wanguo Securities, owned by the Shanghai government, received inside information that the MOF planned to issue 50 percent more bonds in 1995 than it had the previous year. Expecting this larger volume to offset any gains from declining inflation, Wanguo's traders, in contrast to the overall market view, expected bond prices to remain low. Over the early part of 1995, they accumulated a huge (and illegal) short position in bond futures contracts, in particular, the March 27 contract (which gave the scandal its name). News of this leaked out (nothing in China remains secret for long) and other market participants began to accumulate long positions, expecting prices to be higher in the future. This trend increased when other brokers learned that the MOF had determined to significantly reduce its issuance plans. Somehow, Wanguo remained ignorant of this and continued to build its short position in an effort to corner the market.

Acting through its wholly-owned China Economic Development Trust and Investment (China Development Trust; Zhongjingkai), the MOF took a corresponding long position. As the head of the China Development Trust was Zhu Fulin, the former Director of the Treasury Bonds Department of the MOF, this was never going to be a fair fight. When the MOF at last announced its much-reduced issuance plans and bond prices remained high, Wanguo frantically sought to square its position during the last eight minutes of market trading. Market volumes soared to unprecedented levels. By the end of the day, Wanguo's actions had driven prices down but at the cost of a market collapse and the technical bankruptcy of many other brokerages. That evening, the Shanghai exchange, facing the reality that the futures market had collapsed, canceled all trades that had taken place in the last 10 minutes of trading and closed the market for three days so that contracts could be unwound and renegotiated. This meant that Wanguo itself faced being bankrupted.

An investigation ensued and Wanguo's chairman, a respected founder of the Shanghai exchange, was arrested and later sentenced to 17 years in prison. The fallout continued when Wanguo itself was merged with Shenyin Securities, then Shanghai's second-largest firm, to become today's giant Shenyin Wanguo. The very reformist chairman of the CSRC, Liu Hongru, took responsibility, although he had no direct control over the exchange at this time, and the financial-futures product was eliminated and remains so. Soon thereafter, Beijing took over control of both securities exchanges. Shanghai was most definitely the loser in this battle.

In this zero-sum game, someone had to be the winner and, of course, it was the MOF. China Development Trust was rated the top broker on the Shanghai exchange for 1995 "due to its massive trades in treasury bond futures . . . accounting for 6.8 percent of total annual exchange turnover."[8] Politically astute, China Development Trust seems not to have booked for itself what must have been massive profits. Rather, it allowed its "clients," who no doubt included the MOF, to do so. In the following years, this powerful company became a major institutional market manipulator, whose actions could be seen in some of the most outrageous cases of stock ramping and corporate collapse. However, given its MOF background, Zhongjingkai escaped censure and closure until Zhou Xiaochuan finally closed it in 2001. It was not the only such institutional player with a central government background.

Ironically, one month before the 327 Incident, Vice Premier Zhu Rongji, who was then responsible for the financial sector, had fiercely criticized the rampant speculation in the bond futures market "by a number of huge interest groups, taking funds of the state, the local governments and the enterprises to seek profits." Zhu had identified a growing problem but was apparently unable to do anything about it. He could, however, eliminate the futures product. Given the political cost associated with this scandal, it should not be surprising that the Party prefers an orderly, controlled bond market, even if this is, after all, moribund. But by refusing to reform the market, the Party simply promotes the forces of speculation which, as China has become more prosperous, become all the stronger.

THE BASE OF THE PYRAMID: "PROTECTING" HOUSEHOLD DEPOSITORS

At the base of China's bond and loan markets are China's household savers. Today, banks hold more than 70 percent of all bonds in value terms, but this was not always the case. In the earliest days of the market in the 1980s, individuals became the dominant investors, annually snapping up 62 percent of all bond purchases. By 2009, however, they had nearly disappeared from the field, accounting for only one percent in outstanding bond value (see Figure 4.10). Foreign banks account for another seven percent, which means that state-controlled entities hold 92 percent of total bond investment. What's more, many of these same state entities are the only issuers in the market.[9]

This fact has profound implications for China's financial system. If the markets today simply function as clearing houses that move money from one pocket of the state to another, then they have developed away

FIGURE 4.10   Change in types of bond investors, 1988 and 2009

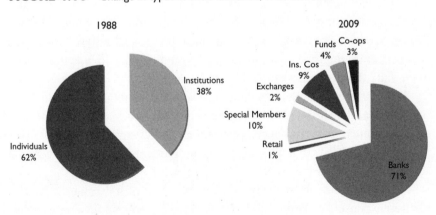

Source: 1988, Gao Jian: 49–51; 2009, China Bond

from their more diverse origins in the 1980s into something resembling a pyramid scheme. This is exactly why Zhou Xiaochuan has described them as "distorted" and filled with "implicit risk." Why has the role of the critically important non-state investor become so diminished?

As part of its effort to develop greater market capacity, in 1991 and 1992, the MOF experimented with different underwriting methods. Its own experience had clearly highlighted the problems limiting large-scale bond issuance. First of all, there was the pricing problem. But, secondly, the over-reliance on the retail market created major difficulties. As individuals purchased bonds in small amounts, simple logistics limited the total amount of bond issuance and offering periods were often up to six months before an issue could be closed. Even to access these investors, the MOF found itself having to pay close to market prices. The retail market also tended to buy and hold until maturity, thus inhibiting the emergence of a secondary market. Finally, maturities tended to be short as a result of both inflation and retail preference. Small issue sizes, high cost, shorter maturities and the fact that there was no secondary market prevented the development of benchmark interest rates and, ultimately, meaningful yield curves. All of these are legitimate reasons to seek to develop an institutional investor base.

The MOF had sought early on to develop institutional investors by seeking support from banks and non-bank financial institutions. However, banks in the 1980s had little excess liquidity and, therefore, little capacity to invest. Even if the State Council had allowed the MOF to develop a market-based pricing method, the retail nature of the investor base may have limited its ability to raise funds in line with its needs. It was at this point that the story of stock markets and bond markets came together. Having created stock exchanges to manage the "social unrest" associated with street trading, the government also brought bonds "inside the walls," especially those of the Shanghai Stock Exchange.

The exchanges enabled demand to be sourced from both individual and institutional investors; all were members of the new markets. The banks also had much deeper pockets given rapidly growing retail deposits (see Table 4.4) and it was not long before the government began to lean on them for support as they discovered an interesting fact.

Accessing funds from the banks had the effect of lowering the MOF's interest expense. The Party could urge banks to buy bonds at levels just above the one-year rate they were paying retail depositors, while retail investors

TABLE 4.4 Composition of Big 4 bank deposits, 1978–2005

RMB billion	Total	Government	Enterprise	Retail	Other
1978	113.5	40.3%	32.4%	27.2%	0.0%
1983	276.4	32.6	31.3	34.9	1.2
1988	744.9	9.2	39.4	44.7	6.7
1993	2,324.5	5.2	33.0	55.7	6.1
1998	6,978.2	4.9	36.2	57.1	1.8
2003	13,465.0	7.9	30.9	56.7	4.5
2004	15,355.7	8.3	31.6	56.6	3.5
2005	18,112.1	9.9	29.5	55.8	4.8

Source: China Financial Statistics 1949–2005

using the same bank deposits to buy bonds would require far higher returns. In other words, the banks provided the government with direct access to household deposits at government-imposed interest rates without even having to ask the depositor for permission: the banks simply disintermediated them. Unlike unruly retail investors seeking to maximize returns, banks had the pleasing aspect that their senior management (Party members) did as they were told. The Party was now easily able to direct funds where it wanted and in the amount it wanted without the need for excessive cajoling or paying market rates. Meanwhile, it could persuade itself that this was the right thing to do since it "protected" the household depositor from undue credit risk.

At first, there was no conflict of interest: individuals were crazy about shares, not bonds, and banks could not buy shares. But as China emerged from the major inflation of the mid-1990s, bonds suddenly offered a very attractive return in comparison to a collapsing stock index. The problem was that retail investors were unable to get their hands on them. In just a brief period of time, China's banks had monopolized bond trading on the Shanghai exchange. The story goes that a feisty Shanghainese housewife complained about this *de facto* government-bond monopoly and her anger reached all the way to Zhu Rongji. Characteristically, Zhu took decisive action and in June 1997, he summarily kicked the banks and the bulk of government bond issuing and trading out of the exchanges and into what was then a small and inactive inter-bank market.[10] Since then, individual investors have been limited to buying savings bonds through the retail

TABLE 4.5 Number of investors, October 31, 2009

Member type	Number
Special members (PBOC, and other government agencies)	16
Commercial banks	382
Credit cooperatives	830
Non-bank financial institutions	163
Securities companies	122
Insurance organizations	131
Funds	1,502
Non-financial organizations	5,908
Total inter-bank market members	**9,054**
Individuals (not members of the inter-bank market)	7,334,832

Source: China Bond
Note: Members include individual branches in the case of institutions.

bank networks and institutional investors have been largely limited to the inter-bank markets.[11]

This significant structural change meant that although the market continued to rely overwhelmingly on the state-owned banks, all other state-owned entities that could qualify as members could also participate (see Table 4.5).

In short, bonds returned to their earliest stage, when the state was its own investor. But the principal difference was that banks and all other non-bank financial institutions replaced SOEs, which meant that household savings would be channeled directly by the Party. This explains how the banks came to hold over 70 percent of all fixed-income securities in China, including 50 percent of all CGBs, 70 percent of policy-bank bonds, and nearly 50 percent of commercial paper and medium-term notes issued (see Figure 4.11). Only in the case of the NDRC's enterprise bonds do insurance companies (NBFI) displace the banks as the principal investors, holding some 46 percent of these securities.

In the international markets, banks also dominate underwriting and trading, but investors and their beneficial owners are, of course, far more diverse, with large roles being played by mutual and pension funds as well as insurance companies. In China, such diversity is beside the point since all institutional investors, whether banks or non-banks, are controlled by

FIGURE 4.11 Investor holdings of debt securities, by issuer, October 31, 2009

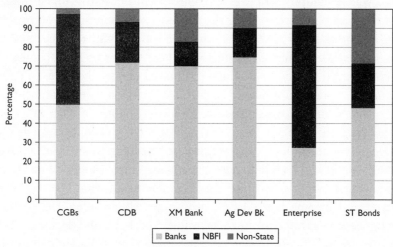

Source: China Bond
Note: Non-state investors include foreign banks, mutual funds, and individuals.

the state. In such circumstances credit and market risk cannot be diversified. This is why China's markets remain primitive and why there is the "implicit risk" alluded to by Zhou Xiaochuan.

In late 2009, the CBRC suddenly became aware of this inevitable reality when it stopped all issuance of bank-subordinated debt. Why had it been oblivious to this risk from the beginning? If the state owns China's major banks outright, as it does, what is the significance of Bank of China issuing subordinated debt to investors that are largely other state banks? The state is simply fooling itself by subordinating its own capital to its own capital. The level of risk in the system has not changed one bit, even if the financial landscape seems the richer for adding this new product.

All of this raises the question of why it has been so difficult for foreign banks and other financial institutions to become involved in this market. Over the past 15 years, China's leaders have witnessed the Mexican debt crisis of 1994, Argentina's peso crisis of 1999 and the ongoing sovereign-debt crises of Greece and Spain. They have seen the huge ramp-up of their own stock index in 2007 and its collapse in 2008. Local newspapers and other media commentary are rife with talk of hedge funds, hot money and unscrupulous investment bankers. An inherently conservative political class, whose natural instinct is to control, will not easily invite those it cannot easily control to participate actively in its domestic debt markets. But, as appearances have to be preserved, there will always be slight movements toward market opening. But there will be no true opening.

What would happen to bank and insurance company holdings of CGBs or other corporate and financial bonds in an inflationary environment? As mentioned, China's central bank manages interest rates in order to contain change because change is risk. No matter that these state institutions hold fixed-income securities as long-term investments to avoid marking their value to market, in an inflationary environment their value will inevitably decrease as funding costs rise. The inevitable result would be a growing drag on bank income even if valuation reserves are not taken. This problem can be seen clearly in bank financial statements. For example, the auditors for ICBC's 2009 financial statements usefully show separately the yields on the bank's loan, investment-bond, and restructuring-bond portfolios (see Table 4.6).

The restructuring bonds yield on average almost exactly the one-year bank-deposit rate and are fixed. In other words, in a low-inflation environment, they will nearly break even, whereas the bonds held as investments yield 3.34 percent, around 1.1 percent over the one-year deposit rate. This is somewhat better, but raises the question: why hold such huge bonds portfolios when loans yield on average nearly seven percent? Banks hold these portfolios partly for liquidity reasons, but largely

TABLE 4.6 Yields on loans, investment and restructuring bonds, 2008–2009

	2008			2009		
	Loans	Bonds	Bonds from restructuring	Loans	Bonds	Bonds from restructuring
CCB	7.16	3.64*	2.01	5.35	3.11*	2.13
BOC	6.12	3.63*	2.1	4.44	2.73*	2.25
ICBC	7.07	3.88	2.23	5.21	3.38	2.19

Source: Bank FY2008 financial statements
Note: * CCB and BOC bond rates are calculated on portfolios that include the restructuring securities; hence returns are pulled down. ICBC rates have been separately calculated.

FIGURE 4.12 Composition of total assets of Big 4 banks, FY2009

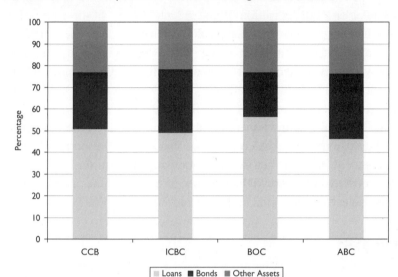

Source: Bank 2009 annual reports

because they are required to do so by the Party. If the ultimate objective of bank management were to maximize profit, would such low-yielding bonds make up 20–30 percent of their total assets (see Figure 4.12)?

Interest-rate risk holds true for all bonds, but corporate bonds also have a credit aspect. In the event of their inability to pay interest, banks will experience a drag on income and, sooner or later, would be compelled to re-categorize their internal credit ratings and make provisions as the bond becomes, in effect, a problem loan. Even if the bank could sell the bond into the market under such circumstances, it would be forced to take an outright loss. China's major financial institutions, banks and insurance companies are all listed on overseas exchanges and audited by international firms. The need to take reserves should be unavoidable in such circumstances. China has not been, and will not be, exempt from such circumstances.

In short, China's banks face severe challenges on three fronts. In addition to their structural exposures to the old NPL portfolios of the 1990s, there will inevitably be new NPLs arising out of their lending spree of 2009. Thirdly, the banks are fully exposed to both interest rate-related and credit-induced write-downs in the value of their fixed-income securities portfolios. In 2009, securities investments constituted 30 percent of the total assets of China's Big 4 banks, or RMB7.2 trillion. While the interest risk of these portfolios can now be hedged somewhat as a result of the very recent emergence of a local-currency interest-rate swap market, for the state, it is a zero-sum game: BOC may effectively hedge, but its counterparty will almost inevitably be another state-owned bank. The effect of mark-downs, credit losses or even simply negative yields on bank capital would obviously be significant. From the viewpoint of the issuer, too, they seem to make little difference. In the international markets, corporations can source cheaper funds from other classes of investor; but in China, the banks remain the investor and the all-in cost to the issuer will be the same as a loan. So the question again presents itself: why did China build its fixed-income market?

ENDNOTES

1   A "repo" or "repossession" contract is a kind of financing transaction in which a party holding, most commonly, government bonds provides the bond as collateral to a second party who then lends money to the first party. This is a cheap way of funding a large bond portfolio.

2   For the only authoritative history of China's government bond markets, see Jian Gao 2007.

3   This group is not the same as the primary-dealer group authorized by the MOF for CGB underwriting. The two non-banks are CITIC Securities and China International Capital Corporation. In late 2009, some foreign banks received licenses to underwrite financial bonds only to be told that "circumstances are not yet mature" for their active participation.

4   Of course, underwriters are free to set higher interest rates (known as coupons) on enterprise bonds if their issuer clients agree.

5   From January 2004, the cap on maximum interest rates on loans was eliminated, but banks are still subject to a minimum rate charged, which is 90 percent of the PBOC set rate for the relevant tenor.

6   Figures from US Department of Treasury, Office of Debt Management, June 2008.

7   There is, however, now a stock index future product.

8   Foo Choy Peng, "China Economic Rated Top Broker," Bloomberg, January 13, 1996.

9   The Asian Development Bank and the International Financial Corporation, a part of the World Bank, have been the only foreign issuers in the domestic bond market to date.

10   The inter-bank market in China was established in 1986 as a funding mechanism for banks in which those with surplus funds place them with others needing additional funding in order to balance their books.

11   A small number of bonds remained listed on the Shanghai exchange to enable securities firms to finance themselves through repo transactions. Until recently, banks were excluded from this market. Their reintroduction is largely an effort to merge what has become two separate markets: the exchange-based and the inter-bank.

The Struggle over China's Bond Markets

"If it doesn't have access to a stable and sufficient source of capital, the China Development Bank will be unable to operate normally."

Unnamed staff member,
Treasury Department, China Development Bank
January 11, 2010[1]

The combination of bank restructuring and the stock market's collapse from mid-2001 catalyzed dynamic growth in China's bond markets. This period began with the appointment of Zhou Xiaochuan to the governorship of the PBOC in early 2002. That year, a total of RMB933 billion (US$113 billion) in bonds, largely Chinese government bonds (CGB) and policy-bank bonds, was issued. By 2009 new issuance had nearly tripled, to RMB2.8 trillion (US$350 billion), and included a large chunk of corporate and bank bonds. As of year-end 2009, the total value of China's outstanding stock of debt securities had reached RMB 17.5 trillion (US$2.6 trillion),with a mix of products that included government bonds (US$841.8 billion), PBOC notes (US$620.6 billion), bank bonds (US$747.1 billion) and a variety of corporate debt (US$354.1 billion) being traded between more than 9,000 institutional investors.

Many issuers struggled to get a piece of this market, none more significant than the China Development Bank (CDB). As the trends in

Figure 4.2 illustrate, the CDB has begun to challenge for the dominant position, becoming, in effect, the country's second Ministry of Finance. The bank's RMB620 billion (US$912 billion) in issuance in 2009 was nearly on a par with the MOF's RMB666.5 billion (excluding savings bonds) and represented nearly 30 percent of the total market. Equally significant, driven by the need to finance the stimulus package, Beijing at last recognized the legitimate funding needs of local governments and allowed certain poor provinces to issue bonds. In addition, all levels of local government made aggressive use of the bond markets, raising RMB423 billion (US$62 billion) via their own enterprises on top of massive levels of bank borrowing.

Far surpassing the CDB and the localities were the PBOC's efforts to sterilize the creation of new RMB generated by China's huge inflows of foreign currency. From 2003, as China's trade surplus began to widen and foreign investors flocked to invest, the PBOC began to issue ever-increasing amounts of short-term notes (and sometimes long-term notes, as we saw in Chapter 3) to control the domestic money supply. This use of a market-based tool to manage the macro-economy was a first in China, but pressures on the PBOC grew to the point that its institutional rival, the MOF, was able to step in and "help out." A complex series of trans-actions relating to the establishment of China's second sovereign-wealth fund revealed a triumphant MOF in control of the very lynchpin of the domestic financial system, once again bringing the story back to the bank dividend policies described earlier.

THE CDB, THE MOF AND THE BIG 4 BANKS

The rapid growth in the China Development Bank's funding and lending activities coincides with the ascension of the new Party and government leadership in 2003 and the start of a continuing debate about China's economic development model. During this time, the CDB became the darling of those supporting a return to both a more state-planned economy domestically and a natural-resource-based foreign policy internationally. But understanding the CDB's position is complicated by the fact that, on the one hand, it represented a challenge to the prevailing banking model sponsored by Zhou while, on the other, it depended on the PBOC for approval of its annual bond-issuance plan. The dramatic increase in its bond issuance during this period may be the result of the PBOC's antipathy toward the MOF; but the MOF also had its own tactics.

Chen Yuan, the bank's very ambitious founding chairman, positioned the CDB deliberately as an alternative model to the Big 4 banks. The Big 4, under Zhou Xiaochuan's reform program, followed a path modeled after their international counterparts, including the deliberate introduction of international banks as strategic investors. As we saw earlier, Chen Yuan was opposed to what he referred to as "that American stuff." Instead, he proposed to "develop around our own needs and build our own banking system" which, he said, "must provide the capital to meet the needs of our high-growth economy, resolve the various financial bottlenecks of our enterprises and provide a channel for capital for various types of enterprise."[2]

The bank's investment projects, once included in the national budget, are now independent of it; the CDB can, to a certain extent, determine on its own "commercial" principles what projects to invest in and what not. Nonetheless, its projects are state projects and its obligations are state obligations. The CDB, unlike the Big 4 banks, was established as a ministerial-level entity with quasi-sovereign status reporting directly to the State Council. It is a typical example of an organization, not an institution, built around one man, the son of a powerful revolutionary-era personage. Chen's father, Chen Yun, was the planner whose famous "Bird Cage" theory provided the ideological foundation for the Special Economic Zones in the 1980s. Political conservatives were able to accept the idea of foreign investment as long as it was "caged" inside these special zones. This powerful political concept has now morphed and provides the inspiration for the distinction between "inside" and "outside" the system. Unless there are bounds imposed by a determined Party leader, as was the case during Zhu Rongji's era,[3] "princelings" such as Chen Yuan can drive the political and economic process in ways contrary to the national interest, as we will see further in the next chapter. In Chen's case, the goal has long been to add both an investment bank and a securities company to the CDB portfolio and become China's first universal bank (and this in spite of his avowed aversion to "American stuff"). If the CDB can be a universal bank, is it any wonder that the Big 4 banks have reacted defensively by wanting to acquire the licenses held by their respective AMCs?

If it had succeeded, the strategy Chen marked out for the CDB would have marked a return of China's banking system to the pre-reform era and the People's Construction Bank of China (PCBC). Essentially a division of the MOF, the PCBC provided exactly the same kinds of long-term capital services for the economy as Chen's CDB. The difference, however, is that the CDB possesses a modern corporate veneer and polished public-relations expertise, as evidenced by its website on which Chen's old-fashioned sloganeering is pushed into the background. That, however, is not the most important difference. The PCBC was funded by the national budget and it channeled, on behalf of the MOF, the disbursement of interest-free investment funds to SOEs and special infrastructure projects contained in the state plan. But the CDB does not rely on the national budget for funding.

This fact and Chen's own ambitions created a trap for the CDB. As a policy bank, the CDB funds itself through debt issuance in the markets, and China's bond markets are fully reliant on the commercial banks and the PBOC for support. Some 72 percent of the CDB's funding comes from those very banks Chen holds in such low esteem. As Figure 5.1 illustrates, beginning in 2005, CDB bond issues began to grow rapidly. This growth

FIGURE 5.1   MOF vs. policy bank bond issuance, 2001–2009

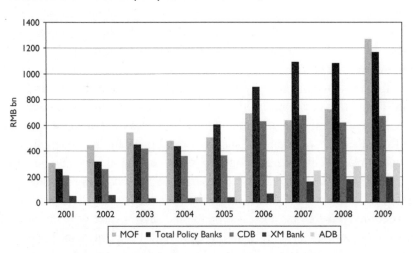

Source: China Bond
Note: 2007 MOF issuance excludes the CIC Special Bond of RMB 1.55 trillion; 2009 MOF issuance excludes RMB200 billion local government bonds.

was approved by the PBOC, whose own position was being challenged by the MOF.

Since banks are the source of all funds, if this situation had continued, market saturation could have been reached and, from that point, the CDB would have begun to squeeze out the MOF, as Figure 5.1 indicates. Can one man fight the MOF as well as the Big 4 Banks? The answer is "No" and this is where ambition led Chen Yuan astray.

In addition to pursuing greater business scale, Chen appears to have envied the superficial modernity of the commercial banks. This led him to seek to create China's first universal bank and to become publicly listed. He was clearly encouraged to pursue this goal and on December 11, 2008, the CDB became a joint-stock corporation, the first step in preparing for an IPO. But why in the world would the State Council seek to make a policy bank— which had been designed to make and hold non-commercial investments in state-designated infrastructure projects—into a commercial entity and then to list it? Chen's argument was that "commercialization" would not change the bank's strategy as a development bank:

> The lesson we can take is that a first-class bank should not take even the very best Western bank as a standard. We should have an objective international standard . . . expressed as having high-quality assets, the trust of market investors, and an objective, fair and deep understanding of society's needs and to work to resolve those social needs in order to receive society's approval.[4]

The CDB model, with its emphasis on social-justice issues, threatens the last 15 years of profit-oriented banking reform in China and has already erased the policy-bank reforms of 1994. While Chen's words and vision may have resonated among the country's people and top leadership in the wake of the global financial crisis, they found no such resonance in the bond market.[5] The reason for this is simple: the banking regulator had been less than precise in defining the CDB's new status. After its incorporation, is the CDB still a semi-sovereign policy bank or is it now a commercial bank? From this definition flows the valuation of its outstanding bonds, as well as the pricing for future bond issues. Market pricing will differ depending on the answer and there is as yet no clear answer. It is not just about pricing: if the CDB is a commercial entity, other banks and insurance companies will only be able to invest up to a regulation-imposed limit and the CDB's days of cheaply funded expansion will rapidly come to an end.

The uncertainty as to the CDB's exact status is what accounts for its bonds being more actively traded than those of the MOF. Uncertainty is risk and the risk created by Chen's ambition is by no means small for his investors, the commercial banks. They currently hold an estimated RMB3.2 trillion (US$460 billion) of his old bonds on their balance sheets and even a small 0.5 percent drop in value for them would mean mark-to-market losses of RMB16 billion (US$2.3 billion). Even though they hold CDB debt as investments, the loss of value on such a scale might ultimately require their international auditors to recommend loss provisions and a hit to their income.

In early 2010 as the party reflected on the massive lending binge of 2009, the accepted line became: "We know these projects do not produce cash flow today, but they will prove very useful to China's development later on." This describes perfectly the function of lending by policy banks. On the other hand, policy loans in commercial banks are, by definition, NPLs. This was recognized in 1994 when the CDB was established and the Big 4 banks embarked on commercialization. It is now beyond irony that just as China's hard-built commercial banks have turned themselves into policy banks, the China Development Bank is striding in the opposite direction.

Without question, this market-based outcome has marked a defeat for Chen Yuan's ambitions for the CDB and represents a major victory for the MOF, which in all probability encouraged his listing ambitions. As discussed below, when China Investment Corporation (CIC) acquired Central Huijin in 2007, it acquired a full 100 percent interest in the CDB. The tables were now turned on Chen Yuan. In the greatest of political ironies, the CDB has now returned to its roots—as a mere sub-department of the MOF—but at what cost to the system?

The People's Bank of China and the National Development and Reform Commission

In contrast to the CDB's aspirations and the MOF's bloodless revenge, the now discredited market-oriented model espoused by reformers is far less eloquently described.[6] It involved the development of direct, market-based, enterprise-financing capabilities based on the decisions of enterprise management. In other words, corporations were to be given a choice between banks and debt markets. Not only that, they were to take responsibility for their decisions for both shareholders and bond investors; in short, the full international capital-markets model. To create this possibility, in 2005, in the midst of collapsed domestic stock markets, the PBOC leveraged a regulatory loop hole defining "corporate bonds"[7] as those with maturities above one year. It used this definition to create a short-term debt product, commercial paper (CP; *duanqi rongziquan* 短期融资券), that quickly became the debt product of choice among SOEs.

In 1993, the PBOC had ceded the corporate-debt product to the State Planning Commission (SPC) primarily because issuers would not take responsibility for repayment of bonds on maturity. This created huge difficulties at the time and largely caused the product to be terminated. But in 2005, corporate bonds were a hot product again due to both bank reform and the weak equity markets. Unfortunately, the "enterprise bond" (*qiyezhai* 企业债) market belonged to the SPC's grandchild, the National Development and Reform Commission (NDRC), with underwriting done only by securities companies regulated by the CSRC. As the volume of issuance in the years up to 2005 illustrate (see Figure 5.2), neither

FIGURE 5.2   Issue volume by product type, 1992–2009

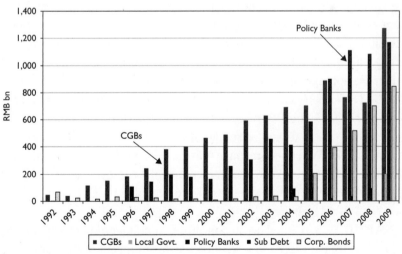

Source: PBOC, *Financial Stability Report*, various
Note: 2007 CGB issuance excludes the RMB1.55 trillion Special Bond

agency gave much thought to developing this product. From the NDRC's perspective, a bond was an afterthought. The few projects contained in its planning documents were funded by the national or local budgets or the banks and it could see no need to develop the bond product. From the CSRC's perspective, bonds represented a zero-sum game with equity products, and the regulator's avenue to achievement was not fixed-income products or markets.

Zhou Xiaochuan provided a detailed analysis of the corporate market's resultant inadequacies in his famous October 2005 speech excerpted at the start of this chapter.[8] He rightly pointed out that the root cause of the market's failure to develop was found in the command-economy mentality of the "early days of the transition when the economy was more planned than market-driven." This comment, historically couched as it was, pointed straight at the NDRC, but the fact is that previous central bank administrations had also done little to promote the bond markets, leaving them to the MOF.

With the support of the Party's "Nine Articles," which explicitly called for the development of bond markets, the PBOC drove through this "one year and above" loop hole and created a CP market out of thin air. In 2005, its first year, more than RMB142 billion (US$17 billion) in CP was issued by presumably capital-starved SOEs. This amount tripled in 2008, with growth being driven by a unique ease of issuance: no regulatory approvals were required, only registration. PBOC reformers modeled this process after that used in the US wherein issuers are required to have a credit rating (this takes about three weeks in China), an underwriter (banks, which are not regulated by the CSRC), a prospectus, and a filing with the PBOC. To further ease the government out of any role in the market, in September 2007, the PBOC sponsored the establishment of an industry association—the National Association of Financial Markets Institutional Investors (NAFMII)—to manage things. In contrast to the opaqueness of China's equity markets, the universe of debt issuers, their financials, approval documents and prospectuses are available for all to see online on the China Bond website.

NAFMII is registered as a non-profit, non-government organization authorized by the PBOC to advise on the development of the debt-capital market, to sponsor new policies and regulations, and to review debt issues.

When establishing NAFMII, the PBOC was astute enough to create a governing board including the Who's Who of China's banking industry. In its brief existence, the agency has become the regulator in charge of the most rapidly growing segments of the inter-bank debt market, including local-currency risk-management products. Its scope of authority would, of course, exclude the NDRC's enterprise bonds (*qiyezhai* 企业债), as well as financial bonds and subordinated bank debt which, given their direct impact on the sensitive banking sector, remain directly with the PBOC.

If the commercial paper ploy did not upset the NDRC, the PBOC's next move did. In April 2008, the PBOC, working through NAFMII, created a three–to–five-year medium-term note (*zhongqi piaoju* 中期票据). Unlike bonds, which are issued once and remain outstanding until redemption or maturity, MTNs are issued like CP as part of a "program" that allows the issuer, depending on his funding needs, to issue more or less of the securities within a certain overall limit. Perhaps a bit sarcastically, the NAFMII called these securities "non-financial enterprise financing instruments" (*feijinrong qiye rongzi gongju* 非金融企业融资工具) in order to clearly demarcate them from the NDRC's "enterprise" bonds and the CSRC's "company" bonds. MTNs, like CP, only require registration with NAFMII.

The NDRC, however, did not find the wordplay funny and sought to stop the PBOC and its MTNs by claiming control over the notes which, after all, had tenors of more than one year. The State Council accepted the case, delaying the product's debut for four months. Later in the year, however, a consensus developed that more debt in the right hands would bolster the swooning stock markets and MTNs were given the go-ahead. In just three months, enterprises raised RMB174 billion (US$26 billion), in new capital and, in 2009, the market grew explosively. By year-end, some RMB608 billion(US$ 89 billion) in new MTNs had been issued. Together with CP, these new instruments accounted for 22 percent of the total capital raised in the fixed-income markets in 2009.

With the defeat of its approach to financial reform in 2005, the PBOC could only push the development of new products in its own space as part of the infrastructure for the future. As Figure 4.10 shows, CP and MTNs with their shorter maturities brought in new non-state investors, mutual funds and foreign banks. For the first time in China's bond markets, such investors played a significant role, accounting for 30 percent of short-term corporate-debt holdings. Such small victories can, over time, add up to something important when circumstances change.

LOCAL GOVERNMENTS UNLEASHED

The PBOC's product innovations provided a solution to financing problems for all sorts of Chinese corporations and not just those commonly thought of as SOEs. It has been 15 years since the last serious reform of China's system of taxation created a clear split between those taxes belonging to the center and those to the localities. Since that time, SOE reform, the closures of hundreds of failed local financial institutions and the centralization of bank management have greatly reduced the financial resources available to local governments. The shortfall between revenues and expenditures has widened significantly.

In its 2009 budget report to the National People's Congress (NPC), the MOF confirmed that, overall, local governments ran major fiscal deficits. The report stated that total local revenues amounted to RMB5.9 trillion (US$865 billion), of which RMB2.89 trillion (US$423 billion) derived from tax-transfer payments from the central government. Set against this, local-government expenditures were RMB6.13 trillion (US$900 billion). The life of a provincial governor or city mayor is dominated by a scramble to raise capital in support of local development and new jobs. Previously, SOE reform—selling off poorly performing SOEs outright or listing the shares of good ones—and attracting large amounts of foreign investment had shown the way forward for the most commercially sophisticated provinces. But there are few provinces that share the commercial attractions of China's coastal areas. There are only so many SOEs that can be publicly listed, even on supportive Chinese exchanges. After the Asian Financial Crisis, the poorly performing SOEs had been privatized or closed entirely to preserve local resources. As a result, to increase their budgets and service their debt, local governments rely on cash flow from projects and land auctions, which reportedly contribute over one-third of local extra-budgetary revenue.

The global financial crisis of 2009 posed the greatest challenge yet to localities: Beijing's RMB4 trillion (US$486 billion) stimulus package required local governments to identify projects and come up with financing for two-thirds of project spending. For some time before the crisis, local governments had been leveraging their utilities, roads, construction brigades and asset-management bureaus by incorporating them into limited-liability companies. Under this legal guise, they could borrow money from banks and, taking advantage of bond-market reform, issue debt. According to the CBRC, by June 2009, there were 8,221 fund-raising platforms operating at provincial, regional, county and municipal government levels, of which the majority (4,907) were owned by county governments. Many of these entities had been established simply to take advantage of the government's free-for-all lending boom. After all, if they could come up with the capital to meet Beijing's demands, why not raise more to finance their own economic incentive programs? It is common wisdom in China that once the window of opportunity is open, it is open for only the briefest of moments and the wise person will grab all that is possible of whatever opportunity is on offer. It is also common wisdom that when the Party takes the responsibility, the regulators will sit silently on the sidelines. Thus, in 2009, conditions were perfect for local governments to do all in their power to raise funds, with little possibility of their being blamed for financial excess.

"Financing platforms"

In those easy days of 2009, local governments and their "financing platforms" (*rongzi pingtai* 融资平台) had almost-unprecedented access to credit. After a long discussion in 2008, Beijing decided that local governments would be officially permitted to run fiscal deficits. The symbol of this new thinking was the RMB200 billion (US$30 billion) in bonds issued in early 2009 by the MOF as agent for the localities. Even more important, however, locally incorporated investment companies and utilities were allowed to issue NDRC-approved enterprise bonds (*qiyezhai* 企业债) and to these were added the new short-term PBOC securities, CP and MTNs. With the window wide open, local Party secretaries rapidly expanded their fund-raising platforms beyond simple "Municipal (or County) Investment Companies" to the incorporation of various entities such as water, highway, and energy utilities. China's muni bond market was born.

Among the many new issuers in the inter-bank market were some 140 local-government incorporated entities (see Table 5.1). With such names

TABLE 5.1 Local "financing platform" debt issuance, June 30, 2009

Region	# Issuers	Total RMB billion	% Total Local Gov't
1 Greater Shanghai			
Shanghai	10	76.13	19.4
Zhejiang	19	54.1	13.8
Jiangsu	13	46.2	11.8
Anhui	10	14.2	3.6
Jiangxi	5	10.5	2.7
sub-total	57	201.1	51.3
2 Greater Beijing			
Beijing	10	35.4	9.0
Tianjin	6	20.1	5.1
Hebei	2	4.2	1.1
sub-total	18	59.7	15.2
3 Greater Guangdong			
Guangdong	9	25.8	6.6
Fujian	4	7.7	2.0
Hunan	3	2.8	0.7
Guangxi	2	2.1	0.5
sub-total	18	38.4	9.8
4 The Southwest			
Chongqing	8	19.6	5.0
Yunnan	2	6	1.5
Sichuan	3	4	1.0
sub-total	13	29.6	7.5
5 Central			
Henan	4	12.1	3.1
Hubei	4	7	1.8
Shaanxi	3	5	1.3
sub-total	11	24.1	6.2
6 The West			
Inner Mongolia	5	8.4	2.1
Gansu	2	2.3	0.6
Xinjiang	2	2.2	0.6

TABLE 5.1   (Continued)

Region	# Issuers	Total *RMB* billion	% Total Local Gov't
Qinghai	1	2	0.5
Ningxia	1	0.8	0.2
sub-total	11	15.7	4.0
7 The Northeast			
Jilin	2	5.2	1.3
Liaoning	2	4.2	1.1
Heilongjiang	1	4	1.0
sub-total	5	13.4	3.4
8 Various	7	10	2.6
Total	**140**	**392**	**100.0**

Source: Wind Information; bonds include CP, MTNs and enterprise bonds; issuers do not include local manufacturing SOEs

as Shanghai Municipal Construction Investment and Development Co. Ltd., Wuhan Waterworks Group Co. Ltd. and Nanjing Public Utility Holdings Co. Ltd., these entities are similar to municipal-bond issuers in the US, but with one difference. In addition to issuing long-term bonds to match the maturity of long-term investment projects, these entities also eagerly issued short-term commercial paper and MTNs. In fact, it seems they have issued every sort of debt security for which they could obtain approval.

In 2009, the amount of capital raised in the bond markets by these provincial, municipal and county entities totaled nearly RMB650 billion (US$95 billion), accounting for over 50 percent of enterprise bonds issued and 48 percent of total CP and MTN issues. The overall explosion in CP and MTN issuance in 2009 is explained by the lack of complex approval procedures and of the requirement of a bank guarantee; issues had only to be registered with NAFMII. Making it even more attractive, MTN underwriting fees and interest expenses were lower than for the NDRC's bonds or even bank loans. Truly, 2009 was a bonanza for some local governments. Looked at carefully, the geographical distribution of these local issuers is quite limited; fully 66 percent of local government issuers and 76 percent of all money raised came from China's richest locations: Greater Shanghai,

Beijing and Guangdong. What can explain why Zhejiang, China's richest provincial economy, has 19 local-government issuers down to even the county level, while Henan, China's most populous province, only four? In discussion with market participants, it seems the answer is simply that money begets money.

So the other 8,000 less-fortunate localities depended, as has been the case historically, on their partnerships with local bank branches for debt financing. How do they borrow if their resources are so constrained? Figure 5.3 shows that one of the ways local governments capitalize their financing platforms is by contributing land and tax subsidies. The land, in turn, may be used as collateral for a bond issue or a bank loan.

The more valuable the land, the stronger is the platform's capacity for borrowing. The mortgaged land might be used as part of a large development for houses, office space or shopping centers. The stronger a local economy, the greater the potential profit of such a development and the greater the interest other investors may have in participating in the equity of the platform through wealth-management products developed by trust companies and sold to the banks' high-net-worth customers (see Figure 5.4).

In China's many poorer localities, these sorts of opportunities do not exist. They simply cannot meet the minimum standards of the bond markets, so they borrow from banks, as they have always done. To do so, they cut corners. For example, Figure 5.5 illustrates how a local government may borrow from another local government and use the money to inject as capital in its financing platform. Once the capital is registered and

FIGURE 5.3 Local-government funding alternatives

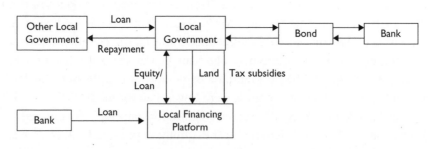

Source: Based on FinanceAsia, June 2009: 32

FIGURE 5.4 Trust-based financing for local financing platforms

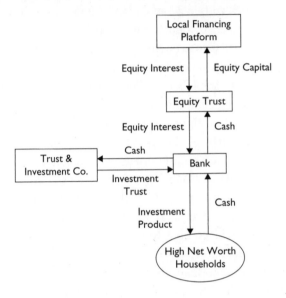

FIGURE 5.5 The temporary debt-based equity capitalization of a local financing platform

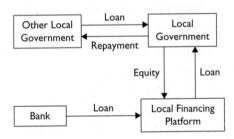

the company is established, the local government takes back the money and repays the other local government. The financing platform exists, has nominal registered capital and business licenses and is fully able to borrow money from other banks.

PBOC and CBRC surveys found such local platforms had borrowed some RMB6 trillion (US$880 billion) by the end of September 2009, with nearly 90 percent of stimulus projects tied to bank loans.[9] These same surveys also noted that these loans amounted to 240 percent of local government revenues and, in 13 of China's 29 provinces and autonomous zones, liabilities exceeded total fiscal revenues. These local borrowings were found by the CBRC to account for 14 percent of total lending in 2009 and, for some banks, as much as 40 percent of total new credit issued. By year-end 2009, Beijing was publicly admitting to RMB7.8 trillion (US$1.14 trillion) in outstanding local-government bank debt.

If this widely reported figure is accurate, then local governments and their agencies have borrowed the equivalent of 23 percent of the country's annual GDP. Analysts at China International Capital Corporation (CICC) put current debt levels at RMB7.2 trillion (US$1.1 trillion), peaking at RMB9.8 trillion (US$1.4 trillion) in 2011. But the report provides an even greater service when it states: "If the financing chain for the platforms is not broken, they will be able to dissolve potential credit risks in the course of current economic development trends." [10] In other words, as long as banks continue to lend, there will be no repayment problems. As will be discussed in this book's conclusion, rolling outstanding debt when it matures—that is, re-issuing new debt to repay the old—is a principal characteristic of China's financial system.

Provincial government semi-sovereign debt

As noted earlier, in March 2009, the MOF announced the issue of RMB200 billion (US$30 billion) of local-government bonds. These were rolled out rapidly, before a regulatory framework could be developed or the philosophy behind their credit ratings could be thought out. The thinking behind this seemed to be that as provincial governments are equivalent to ministries in the Chinese bureaucratic hierarchy, and thus represent the state, they would attract similar ratings. But most people know full well that Qinghai is different from Shanghai.

However, a spokesman for the MOF explained that although the debt would be issued in the name of the provincial governments and approved as a part of their budgets, the MOF would act as their agent. More importantly, given this, the coupon on, and the risk of, the bonds would approach that of sovereign debt. In essence, the spokesman was attempting to sell the idea that provincial issues carried risk equivalent to the country itself. While this may be true in theory, in practice, it is not and many market participants did not accept the idea. Moreover, this was not the picture presented in the MOF's own rules governing local debt issues. These stated explicitly that if the locality could not make repayment, the debt would be rolled forward over a period of one to five years, with the original principal amount being repaid in installments the local government could afford. In short, the original three-year bond might, in fact, have a tenor of eight years or longer.

Clearly, this was not central government debt. Despite widespread questioning in the market, the bonds were priced closely to MOF bonds of a similar maturity by the friendly primary-dealer syndicate. What might have happened to prices in the secondary market is unknown because there has been no secondary market. The fact is, these bonds have disappeared onto the balance sheets of the MOF's primary-dealer group, that is, China's banks.

CHINA INVESTMENT CORPORATION: LYNCHPIN OF CHINA'S FINANCIAL SYSTEM

If the inter-bank market somewhat resembles a pyramid scheme, it nonetheless plays an extremely important role in the PBOC's effort to manage inflation through control of the money supply. In 2002, a policy disagreement blew up over how to cool inflation that was threatening at that point. This disagreement evolved over four years into a struggle over how to manage the inflationary impulse caused by China's huge trade surpluses. Driven by enthusiasm over China's joining the WTO, fixed-asset investment exploded from 2002, increasing on an annual basis by 31 percent, the highest level seen since Zhu Rongji's heyday began in 1993 (see Figure 5.6). Memories of mid-1990s double-digit inflation caused the PBOC to issue short-term notes continuously into the market for the first time in China's post-1949 banking history. From an initial issue equivalent to US$26 billion in 2002, this rose over the following years until 2007, when the PBOC soaked up nearly US$600 billion from the banks. The central bank also adjusted upward bank-deposit reserve ratios nine times and raised interest rates five times. These aggressive measures were effective temporarily, but by 2007, the explosion in foreign reserves and the consequent creation of new renminbi posed an almost insurmountable challenge.

FIGURE 5.6   Investment, FX reserves and money supply, FY2001–2008

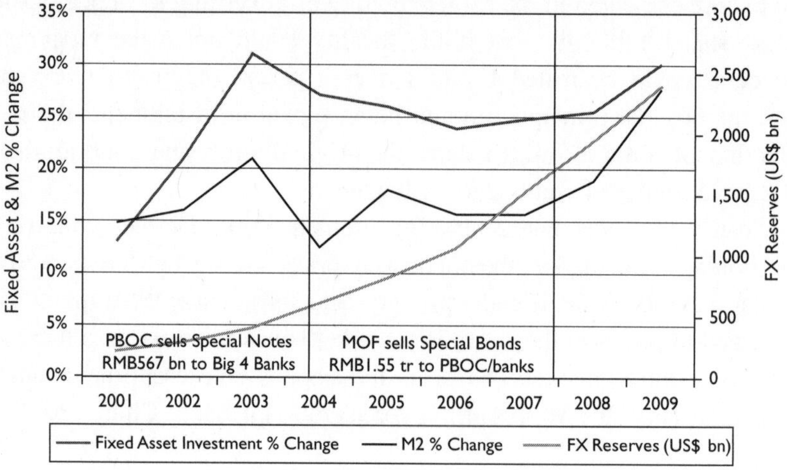

Source: PBOC, *Financial Stability Report*, various

Others also remembered 1993 and how Zhu Rongji had aggressively intervened in the economy using administrative orders to close off all channels to liquidity. Zhu simply shut off all bank lending, closing down the economy for almost three years until inflation that had peaked at over 20 percent in 1995 was finally beaten. The group favoring administrative intervention in 2002 argued that the economy was not overheating, only specific industrial sectors were and this could be dealt with using specific policy means. Their argument carried the day and bank credit to those sectors was cut off. By 2004, both efforts had reduced the growth of investment and M2 just in time to begin dealing with the flood of US dollars pouring into the country from China's booming trade surplus.

It was at this point in July 2005 that the PBOC succeeded in convincing the government to delink the RMB exchange rate from the US dollar and allow it to gradually appreciate. It was unfortunate that the predictability of the RMB's 20 percent appreciation led to huge inflows of hot money and even greater liquidity in the domestic markets, not to mention an explosion in the stock index and high-end real-estate speculation. That both sides could claim success in this earlier anti-inflation campaign complicated things significantly later on after the outbreak of the global financial crisis in September 2008, when market forces fell dramatically from political favor. Despite the PBOC's aggressive efforts to manage this flood of RMB, the data in Figure 5.7 suggest that the effectiveness of short-term notes began to decline after 2007. The growth in the money supply as measured by M2 had been stable at 16 percent, but it accelerated to 19 percent in 2008 and then 29 percent in 2009. For its part, the policy of appreciating the currency was canceled as soon as export growth turned negative in late 2008.

This is the macro economic background to the political struggle over China's financial framework that had been continuing since 2003. The struggle came to center on the establishment in 2007 of China Investment Corporation (CIC). It is ironic to consider that this sovereign-wealth fund, established to invest the country's FX reserves overseas, was in fact used to dramatically restructure China's own financial system. CIC is not the country's first sovereign-wealth fund. SAFE Investment Co. Ltd., a Hong Kong subsidiary of the State Administration of Foreign Exchange (SAFE), has been actively managing a portion of China's foreign-exchange

FIGURE 5.7   PBOC note issuance vs. growth in money supply (M2), 2001–2009

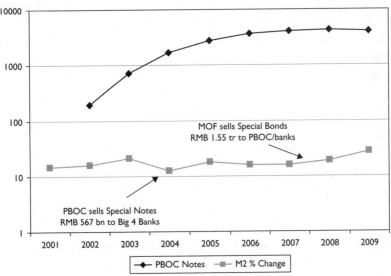

Source: PBOC *Financial Stability Report*, various; China Bond

reserves since 1997. So why establish a second fund? SAFE Investment is owned by the PBOC; CIC is owned by the MOF. Why would the MOF want to encroach on foreign exchange, which has clearly always been the legitimate turf of the PBOC? The answer seems to be that since the PBOC took over outright control of two of the four major state banks from the MOF, the MOF had the right to seek their recovery. In the end, the establishment of CIC is less about a sovereign-wealth fund than a battle over bureaucratic territory. The outcome of this particular round, moreover, is very clear: CIC is now the very lynchpin of the country's domestic financial system.

RMB sterilization and CIC

The story of CIC's capitalization shows that all institutional arrangements in China are impermanent; everything can be changed as a result of circumstances and the balance of political power. All institutions are in play, even the oldest and most important. The case of CIC also shows the extent to which China's financial markets have been distorted by the pressures created by the country's tremendous foreign-reserve imbalance. This distortion now extends beyond the domestic capital markets, both debt and equity, to the financial institutions that provide their foundation and beyond to the international equity markets and investors.

Since it was designed to invest reserves offshore, it might have been expected that CIC would receive its capital directly from foreign reserves, as had the state banks. China Construction Bank, Bank of China, Industrial and Commercial Bank of China and Agricultural Bank of China had each been at least partially capitalized from the foreign reserves by way of a PBOC-established entity called Central SAFE Investment, known commonly as Huijin. In 2007, a surging money supply threatened a major asset bubble and the debate about how to handle this—whether through monetary tools or outright administrative measures—became mixed up with the MOF/PBOC rivalry. The MOF claimed that the PBOC's management of reserves produced too low a return; from this it was a quick jump to the MOF asking for its own opportunity and then to a discussion of how to capitalize CIC. In the end, the Party agreed to allow the MOF a chance; after all, in 2007, there were plenty of reserves to be managed. But there was no direct infusion of

FIGURE 5.8 Step 1: MOF issues Special Bonds and drains market liquidity

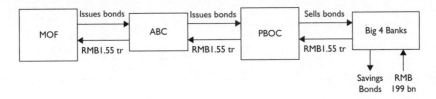

capital into CIC as had been the case with the banks. Instead, there was yet another MOF Special Treasury Bond.

This Special Bond was approved by the State Council in early 2007 and its size was a mammoth RMB1.55 trillion (about US$200 billion with 10- and 15-year tenors), as shown in Figure 5.8. Not only had the MOF accused it of poor reserve management, the PBOC also stood blamed for monetary growth that threatened an outbreak of inflation. The path these bonds took tells the tale of the PBOC's political weakness. The MOF sold the bonds to the PBOC in eight separate issues through the hands of Agricultural Bank of China. Direct dealings between the two had been prohibited by law since 1994 when the Central Bank Law was enacted; prior to this, the central bank had too often been forced to finance the state deficit directly. But this bond was not for deficit financing. The PBOC, for its part, bought the bonds from ABC and then, given their below-market interest coupons, forced them into the market, which consisted of the banks. This issue, therefore, drained a huge amount of liquidity from the banking system, an amount double what the PBOC had been able to achieve through its own short-term notes. This approach also relieved the PBOC of adding to a growing interest burden on its notes.

While this seemed like an innovative idea, nothing is without cost, as shown in Step 2 (see Figure 5.9). Considering the monetary objective, the MOF had done the PBOC a favor and the transaction could have stopped there. CIC could have been funded through a separate transaction with Huijin using foreign reserves, if the PBOC had been willing to go along. The MOF, however, was out to extract its final pound of flesh and used the RMB acquired from the bond issue to buy US$200 billion from the PBOC/SAFE, again via the services of ABC. The MOF then used these funds to capitalize CIC. Aside from its economic objectives, the institutional

FIGURE 5.9 Step 2: MOF buys US$ from the PBOC to capitalize CIC

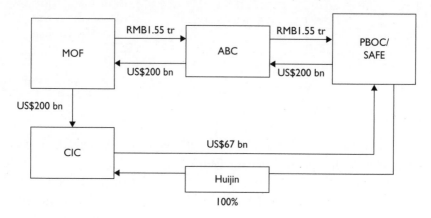

effect of this transaction was the restoration of the financial system to the pre-2003 status quo and a further weakening of the PBOC and the market-reform camp. But there was more.

After the money had changed hands, CIC for all intents belonged to the MOF. Although it reported directly to the State Council, its top senior management came from the MOF system. This was not necessarily a loss for the reform camp, since CIC was also staffed at senior levels with officials historically associated with market reform. But there was an awkward technical problem arising from the MOF's arrangement: how would interest be paid on its underlying Special Bonds? The cost involved amounted to around US$10 billion annually. The surprising answer was that CIC would pick up the interest. As the head of CIC dryly commented, the burden was about RMB300 million for each day CIC was open for business. How would CIC, a newly established entity not meant to be a short-term investor, have the immediate cash flow to cover such a huge obligation? The solution to this problem by itself has put an end to further hope of bank reform.

Careful calculation, however, had been given to this solution; it reveals how in 2007 the Party desired to organize China's financial system and goes to the heart of the PBOC's loss of institutional clout. Even before CIC received its new capital, the US$200 billion had been budgeted and spent, and only one-third of it related to its advertised mission as a sovereign-wealth fund. The other two-thirds, some US$134 billion, was to be spent on, first, a planned recapitalization of ABC, the CDB and other banks and financial institutions and, second, the outright acquisition of Central Huijin from the PBOC. In one stroke, CIC became China's financial SASAC.

One might ask why a sovereign-wealth fund would want to own or invest in domestic financial institutions already owned outright by the government: the money would just be going around in circles. But this is exactly what happens "inside the system." The attractive professional face its management presents internationally is belied by the reality that CIC is, at best, only a part-time sovereign-wealth fund. Its most important role is to serve as the lynchpin of China's financial system. That system has been restored to one inspired by the old Soviet model centered on the MOF and with a weak central bank.

The MOF is the obvious winner in this domestic game and it is a purely status-quo power. Its victory ultimately has significant negative implications for continued bank reform and can clearly be seen on referring back to Table 3.3, which shows the pre- and post-IPO controlling shareholders of China's major banks. From the very start of bank reform in 1998, the fundamental point of contention between the MOF and the PBOC has been over which entity owns the state banks on behalf of the state. Once reform entered its critical stages in 2003, the plans of Zhou Xiaochuan's group of reformers began to affect the economic and political interests of the MOF. When Huijin recapitalized CCB and BOC, it did so in a way that established direct economic ownership and, at the same time, used the MOF's equity interest to write off problem loans; no longer did these two banks "belong" to the MOF empire. In the years after Zhou's political defeat in 2005, the MOF won back control, starting with the ICBC and continuing through ABC, at least in part because of the PBOC's difficulties managing its primary responsibilities: inflation and the currency. But this was hardly the only reason.

A contributing part of the PBOC's political weakness during the crucial year of 2005 was the terminal illness suffered by Vice Premier Huang Ju, who was in charge of the financial sector. In early 2005, Huang stepped aside for treatment and the Premier assumed his portfolio. Consensus politics resumed and the consensus was that Zhou Xiaochuan had overreached.

Reform is not about consensus. It was an easy decision that rocked no boats to allow the MOF to retain as equity its 1998 capital contribution in ICBC. So Huijin, after injecting US$15 billion, received only 50 percent of ICBC and the MOF's 1998 contribution remained. The bureaucratic pendulum had begun its backward swing. By late 2007, with CIC's outright acquisition of Huijin, the status quo had been fully restored.

The argument in favor of this acquisition was simple: CIC was responsible for the interest on the Special Bonds. Acquiring the banks gave it access to their dividend stream.[11] Since it all belonged to the state anyway, what difference did it make? The fact is, it did make a difference and not just to the bureaucracies involved. If CIC were to acquire Huijin, then SAFE would want its original investment back. The US$67 billion price represented the original net-asset value of its investments in all three banks and a collection of bankrupt securities companies.[12] Since it would be simply a transfer of state-owned assets between state agencies, by government rules, there need be no premium paid. It was just a matter of accounting and the money going from one pocket to the other. The change in "owners," however, would have a huge impact on reform moving forward.

For CIC, the acquisition worked out very well. According to its first full-year financial report for FY2008, CIC carries at a market value of US$171 billion what it acquired from the PBOC for only US$67 billion. This increased in 2009 to over US$200 billion but, of course, included investments other than Huijin at that point. These investments by Huijin allowed CIC to claim a profit in its first year and so helped deter criticism of its controversial (and loss-making) investments in Blackstone and Morgan Stanley. But there was one small detail that had not been properly considered: three of the Big 4 banks were now internationally listed: the Party was no longer just playing "inside the system."

CIC squeezes its banks

Beyond its mark-to-market profit on its bank investment portfolio, CIC also relied on the banks for the cash flow to make its interest payments on the MOF bonds, not to mention to pay dividends to MOF that helped it meet its obligations on the IOUs given to ICBC and ABC. The Huijin arrangement designed by the PBOC team placed CIC in a position to receive dividends paid by the banks (see Chapter 7 for further details).

This rich source of cash had originally been designed to help offset the unrecoverable loans the PBOC had made to the AMCs in support of bank restructuring. The Huijin arrangement acted as a form of taxation that would, over time, have reduced the PBOC's credit losses and strengthened its balance sheet.

When CIC acquired Huijin in late 2007, it acquired direct economic control over China's major banks via their boards of directors and a decisive vote in the matter of their dividends. There would be no intervening levels of ownership, management, and powerful Party secretaries to muddy the issue (as was the case in the SASAC's state-owned enterprises). Huijin was controlled by the PBOC which, in turn, is controlled by the Finance Leadership Group at the very top of the Party hierarchy. In sum, now MOF was in a position to recommend, if not decide, how much was to be received by . . . itself.

This takes the story full circle back to the bank IPOs. The dividend payout ratio of around 50 percent for all three banks is not necessarily excessive by international standards for banks that are growing at a stable rate and in a normal business environment where bad loans and securities losses are not material. This, however, does not describe the situation faced by the Chinese banks. These banks drive national economic growth by increased lending typically at 20 percent a year and in certain years, such as 2009, much more. But from 2008, Huijin's new duty would be to pay interest on CIC's bond obligations to the MOF as well as help the MOF make good on its IOUs. Since the banks are publicly listed and audited by international accounting firms, cash dividends paid by them are transparent to all. To some extent, they might serve as a reliable indicator of how the government thinks about its banks.

In the early days of restructuring, as NPLs were being spun off to the AMCs and capital rebuilt, asset growth was tightly controlled (see Figure 3.7 for the years 2001–2005) and capital ratios were rapidly bolstered. After their respective listings, however, lending, profits and dividends for all three banks grew rapidly, particularly after CIC acquired Central Huijin in 2007. From that point, total dividends immediately increased to a level sufficient to cover CIC's interest obligations, leaving plenty left over to reduce the outstanding restructuring IOU due to ICBC from RMB143 billion (US$18 billion) to RMB62 billion (US$9 billion) (see Figure 5.10). Of course, to the extent that CIC and its banks were responsible for making such payments, the national budget was freed of the obligation.

These financial arrangements raise questions about the future path of China's bank reform. Given the experience of 2009, there is no question but that banks have reverted to their former business model as the Party's financial utility. But is it really possible that dividend policy is being set to meet the MOF's own parochial needs? The appearance certainly suggests that the listed banks have become cash cows subsidizing the MOF's efforts which, among other things, are aimed at sidetracking the institutional influence of the PBOC. Worse yet, it is outrageous that the full amount of cash dividends paid during this period has been funded by the IPOs of state banks (as discussed in Chapter 2). From a very simplistic point of view, international and domestic investors handed over US$42 billion in new capital to the banks and indirectly to the MOF, yet received in those years less than US$8 billion in dividends.

FIGURE 5.10   Big 4 bank IPOs, cash dividends paid and CIC, 2004–2009

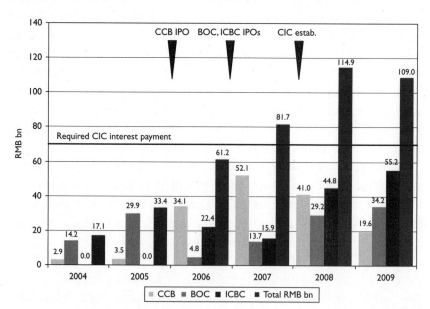

Source: Huijin; bank annual audited financial statements

Beyond that, is it possible that under pressure to maintain dividends, bank managements might easily be encouraged to increase lending? With fixed spreads over the cost of funding, more lending assures more earnings, higher dividends, better stock price and higher rankings on the *Fortune* Global 500. Then came the economic stimulus package, which provided all the excuse needed to do just that.

Not even a year later, in early 2010, however, the combination of 50 percent dividend payouts and binge lending have created huge challenges for the banks. Most challenged of all must be Bank of China, whose loan portfolio grew nearly 43 percent in 2009 while the other major banks hit levels over 20 percent. Given the high dividend payouts and asset growth, it is hardly surprising that the banks rapidly grew out of their capital base, with BOC and ICBC rapidly approaching capital ratios close to pre-IPO levels (see Table 5.2).

From that point, there was much government hand-wringing as to how bank capital could be increased. In early 2010, each of the banks announced record 2009 earnings and improved NPL ratios . . . and one after the other, each has announced plans to raise for a second time that US$40 billion chunk of capital they had raised from their IPOs and then paid out to the state (see Table 2.3). Of course, the state would be required to disgorge capital as well if it desired to maintain its shareholding. So it was not surprising when rumors emerged that Huijin, the direct majority shareholder of the major banks, was seeking approval for a large capital injection of up to US$50 billion to match its share of bank capital and maintain its equity position.[13] Even more interesting, CIC had requested an additional US$200 billion from the MOF. Both requests were

TABLE 5.2 Trends in core capital-adequacy ratio, 2004–1H 2010

%	2004	2005	2006	2007	2008	FY2009	1H 2010
CCB	8.6	11.08	9.92	10.37	10.17	9.31	9.27
BOC	8.48	8.08	11.44	10.67	10.81	9.07	9.33
ICBC	–	9.89	12.123	10.99	10.75	9.86	9.41
ABC	–	–	–	–	–	–	6.72

Source: bank annual and interim audited reports

subsequently cut back significantly, Huijin to an RMB190 billion (US$28 billion) bond issue and CIC to US$100 billion.

The dividends, the excessive lending and the scramble for new capital can all be ascribed, at least in part, to the MOF's acquisition of banking assets from the PBOC. Had China Investment Corporation been capitalized directly from China's foreign-exchange reserves, it could have remained a pure sovereign-wealth fund and the MOF would have had its own counterpoint to SAFE Investments. Had there really been the need to sterilize such a massive amount of RMB, the Special Bond could have been issued separately. But the MOF combined the two and the resulting structure twisted the heart of China's financial system into this awkward bureaucratic and economic position.

What to do with Huijin is perhaps the biggest topic on the agenda of the Fourth National Finance Work Conference in mid-2010. This is part of a much broader power grab by the MOF, which hopes to use Huijin as the basis of a "Financial SASAC" that would become, among other things, the Super Regulator for China's entire financial sector, replacing "one bank and three commissions."[14] Even if this were to happen and Huijin were to be freed of CIC, the arrangement with regard to the Special Bond would likely remain. Then there is the question of which state entity would pay CIC the US$67 billion it is nominally worth and where the money would come from. The point of this is that Huijin and its banks continue to be the object of a bureaucratic ping-pong game domestically that increasingly exposes the internationally listed banks to the valuation judgment of international investors precisely at the time that the government has actively desired to cut back foreign influence.

CYCLES IN THE FINANCIAL MARKETS

It is well recognized that China's currency policy of fixing the RMB exchange rate against the US dollar greatly limits flexibility in interest rates. This by itself means that real fixed-income markets cannot readily develop. There is another dimension to this problem. China's banks depend on Party-guaranteed profitability created by mandated minimum spreads between deposits and lending rates. The profit generated here from corporate borrowers subsidizes their "investment" in sub-market-priced government securities. This can work only so long as they operate in a protected domestic oligopoly well insulated from outside pressures. Foreign banks exist in China only to provide the suggestion of an open market. With profits guaranteed, banks have never had to be creative in competing for customer support. Nor have they had to worry about new capital or problem loans: these are the Party's problems, not those of bank management. So when the Party calls for development of the bond market, the banks follow, even though bonds are little more than disguised loans. The corporate-bond market stops there: there is no secondary market. But the fixed-income market is more than just corporate bonds.

In recent years, the flood of US dollars from a large trade surplus and inflows of hot money, the consequent creation of new RMB, the need to sterilize that RMB to prevent inflation and asset bubbles have combined to distort the very institutions on which the financial system is built. When in 2007 the MOF argued that PBOC notes were insufficient to offset excess RMB, the ensuing political solution attached itself to the wholly unrelated establishment of CIC. It was argued that CIC's capitalization solved two major problems: temporarily controlling money creation and putting to use a large portion of the country's foreign reserves. This was a clever *ad hoc* solution that became complicated by CIC's acquisition of Huijin.

Leveraging Huijin's bank investments to pay interest on the MOF's bonds may have seemed a good idea at the start; it appears that the Party mistakenly believes its own advertising about its banks being rich and strong. But it linked the stresses of China's domestic financial markets directly to the international financial markets. This has created an economic and political exposure contrary to the fundamental interests of the "system." An unconvertible currency, fixed exchange and interest rates and the need for strong bank lending to drive GDP growth create inevitable and predictable demand for huge amounts of new bank capital that, in turn, depends on international and domestic capital markets. With over US$70 billion in new capital to be raised, these markets will, in the end, be demanding and price sensitive, even if many friends of China internationally and domestically stepped up to make Agricultural Bank of China's US$20 billion IPO an apparent success as it was.

An economic stimulus package that in retrospect appears to have been excessive gave banks a free option to expand their lending. But stimulus or not, this is what the Party's banks do in any circumstances, as history has shown. With mandated loan spreads, RMB10 trillion (US$1.5 trillion) in new loans grew bank earnings dramatically. It is important to note as well that banks are happy to lend to local governments—at the behest, of course, of the local Party secretary—directly or through bonds. Can they go bankrupt? Are they lesser credit risks than SOEs? The interim announcements of the Big 4 banks in 2010 have been full of record profits and very high loan-loss reserves and, given rapid loan-portfolio growth, inevitably declining NPL ratios well below two percent. It is all a matter of simple mathematics and has nothing to do with strong management performance or value creation. There will be record dividend payouts and further improvements in their *Fortune* 500 rankings. But the lending explosion rapidly depleted bank capital. The first decade of the twenty-first century now appears to have ended, just as each of the last three decades of the twentieth century did, with China's major banks in desperate need of massive recapitalization.

This marks the completion of one full cycle of China's money machine; it has taken 10 years. But the fault lines, created playing by the rules "inside the system" while pretending to abide by international standards and regulatory requirements, have begun to be clear. The second cycle can now be reliably mapped out and illustrates why true reform of the system is unlikely. Mandated minimum loan-to-deposit spreads sustain bank profitability thereby guaranteeing that dividends can be paid out to investors, namely Huijin. Huijin, in turn, must meet the demands of CIC, which must meet the demands of the MOF Special Bond. In the cases of ICBC and ABC, too, the MOF must make repayments on its special IOU arrangements. Even if Huijin were separated from CIC, each year cash would flow up from the banks to the MOF and then from the MOF back to the banks. The banks will expand lending to borrowers to drive high GDP-growth numbers and generate greater profit as long as China's export and non-state sector remains weak.

How, then, can the Party allow the banks to be disintermediated by capital markets or real outside competition? Protectionist measures, controlled exchange rates and fixed lending spreads ensure the Party's control and the stability of the system, and virtually guarantee that the banks must raise new capital every few years to prime the cycle. Viewed from the outside, bank profits reassure retail depositors that their banks are sound and their deposits safe. International investors support bank shares since they are seen as proxies of a bank-driven GDP number. The banks use household deposits and new equity capital to fund new loans to drive GDP and to support the conceit that is China's debt-capital market, which sustains the appearance of overall convergence toward a Western-style market system.

Instead of removing the risk burden from the banks, China's backward bond markets create new risk. Making up around 30 percent of the total assets of the Big 4 banks, these "investment" portfolios enjoy negative interest spreads, leaving the banks exposed to significant market risk. In order to offset this weight, banks will inevitably lend more and increase credit risk. More asset bubbles, stock-market booms and problem loans are the inevitable product of this arrangement. The tools to deal with these problems, the AMCs, the MOF's IOUs and the PBOC's credit support, already exist. As has been shown with the first generation of bad loans, these measures have contained the problem and pushed the inevitable off into the future onto the agenda of the next Party leadership group and out of the memory of international observers. The cycles and the pressures that are building up "inside the system" can continue for a very long time. Where is the catalyst that will disrupt it? Even if the Emperor is ultimately seen to be naked, he is still the Emperor.

ENDNOTES

1   *The Economic Observer* 经济观察报, January 11, 2010: 1.

2   *The Economic Observer* 经济观察报, July 20, 2009: 41.

3   Zhu thwarted Chen's first attempt in 1995 to establish an investment bank in favor of Wang Qishan's joint venture with Morgan Stanley, CICC.

4   *The Economic Observer* 经济观察报, July 20, 2008: 41.

5   *The Economic Observer* 经济观察报, January 11, 2010: 1.

6   See Li Liming, "*Liangnian zhongguo jinrong shengtai gaibianle* 两年, 中国金融生态改变了 (In two years China's financial environment has changed)," *The Economic Observer* 经济观察报, August 29, 2005: 10. This failed effort at reform in 2005 was picked up again in the major article by Yang Kaisheng, ICBC's CEO, in early 2010, "*Wending woguo shangye yinhang ziben chongzu shuiping de jidian sikao* 稳定我国商业银行资本充足水平的几点思考 (Several thoughts on stabilizing the capital adequacy levels of our country's commercial banks," *21st Century Business Herald* 21世纪经济报导, April 13, 2010: 10.

7   It is confusing to translate "corporate bonds," as there are two types: one controlled by the NDRC and traded in the inter-bank market (*qiyezhai* 企业债), and one controlled by the CSRC and traded on the stock exchanges (*gongsizhai* 公司债). Zhou's loophole related to the NDRC regulations.

8   Zhou Xiaochuan, "Learn lessons from the past for the benefit of future endeavor," Speech at the China Bond Market Development Summit, Beijing, October 20, 2005, www.pbc.gov.cn/english/detail.asp?col=6500&ID=82

9   See Fang Huilei, Zhang Man, Yu Jing and Zhang Yuzhe, "Scary View from China's Financing Platforms,"*Caixin Magazine online,* February 5, 2010; and Victor Shih, "Big rock-candy mountain," *China Economic Quarterly* 14(2), June 2010.

10 *21st Century Business Herald* 21世纪经济报导, April 12, 2010: 6.

11 There is a second interesting attraction to using a bond and interest payments to channel money to the MOF: payment would not require any involvement of CIC's board of directors, it would simply be business as usual. As the cash flow came in as dividends from its subsidiary banks, CIC's CFO would simply pay interest when due to the MOF; no formal board decisions or minutes would need to be made. Contrast this with the SASAC.

12 Huijin paid US$22.5 billion each for BOC and CCB and US$15 billion for the ICBC, and US$7 billion for interests in a variety of securities companies. It carries these investments on its books at this same value, notwithstanding that the banks have all been listed and have a market value far above this number.

13 First rumored in November 2009 and then confirmed in April 2010. See Bloomberg, November 11, 2009; and *Caixin* 财新, April 23, 2010; *Asian Investor*, April 1, 2010.

14 This refers to the PBOC, the CSRC, the CBRC, and the China Insurance Regulatory Commission. For the background, see *The Economic Observer* 经济观察报, July 12, 2010: 2.

CHAPTER

6

Western Finance, SOE Reform and China's Stock Markets

"The debut price [of my IPO] was within expectations, but I am still a wee bit disappointed."

Chen Biting, Chairman, China Shenhua Energy
October 10, 2007

In capital-raising terms, China's stock markets pale in comparison to the bank loan and bond markets, but they have been instrumental in creating the country's companies and, at the same time, lending China the veneer of a modern capitalist economy. Without them, China would have remained for an even longer time without a truly national market for capital. More importantly, its ministries would not have learned at the knee of Goldman Sachs and Morgan Stanley how to use international corporate law and complex transfers of equity shares to build the National Team, a group of state-controlled enterprises of an economic scale never before seen in China. When in 2006 and 2007 these companies began to return home to the Shanghai market for secondary listings, they were able to use their great wealth to reward "friends and family", those other state enterprises and agencies closely associated with the Party and allowed to take profit from the listing as investors.

This explains the comment by Shenhua's chairman: his company's "poor" IPO performance was, perhaps, a disappointment to his supporters.

In these listings, company valuations deliberately set too low, biased lottery allocations[1] and the channeling of money among powerful state entities is clearly documented for all to see. It raises the question, however, of whether China is run, as people believe, by the Communist Party or whether the National Team has subsumed the Party and the government so that it can truly be said that "the business of China is business". China's stock markets are not really about money (that comes from the banks): they are about power.

CHINA'S STOCK MARKETS TODAY

On October 7, 1992, a small company that manufactured minibuses completed its IPO on the New York Stock Exchange (NYSE), raising $80 million. This would hardly have been a landmark event except that the company was Chinese and no Chinese company had ever listed its shares outside the country, much less on the NYSE.[2] Wildly oversubscribed, Brilliance China Automotive singlehandedly put China—and most certainly not the *People's Republic* of China—on the map of global capital. Since that time, the clamor surrounding China's stock markets makes it seem that New York and London have long since been eclipsed as the world's most significant markets for equity capital.

On their surface, China's stock markets are the biggest in Asia, with many of the world's largest companies, and more than 120 million separate accounts trading stocks in nearly 1,800 companies. Their capital-raising abilities are the stuff of legend (see Table 6.1). According to data from Bloomberg, since January 2006, half of the world's top 10 IPOs were Chinese companies raising over US$45 billion. It is not uncommon for new issues in Shanghai to be 500 times oversubscribed, with more than US$400 billion pledged for a single offering. The scale of China's companies since 1990 has increased exponentially. In 1996 the total market capitalization of the top 10 listed companies in Shanghai was US$17.9 billion; by year-end 1999, this was US$25.3 billion and, 10 years later, US$1.063 trillion! Like everything else about China, the simple scale of these offerings and the growth they represent at times seems staggering.

Of course, the scale of the profit involved can also be huge. In 2009, Chinese companies raised some US$100 billion, of which 75 percent

TABLE 6.1 Funds raised by Chinese companies, China and Hong Kong markets

US$ billion	A- and B-Shares			H-Shares		Red Chips	
Year	IPO	SPO	Rights	IPO	SPO/ Rights	IPO	SPO/ Rights
2010	59.94	36.54	8.72	12.06	5.84	0.23	3.77
2009	29.62	44.42	1.55	14.26	0.97	1.03	8.27
2008	15.24	34.08	2.22	3.8	0.6	0	28.88
2007	61.2	45.02	3.12	9.59	1.39	6.36	8.39
2006	21.03	13.19	0.06	37.3	1.77	0.36	6.17
2005	0.71	3.45	0.03	17.69	2.77	0.13	2.75
2004	4.27	1.93	1.27	5.15	2.47	1.87	1.52
2003	5.48	1.4	0.92	5.96	0.08	0.38	0.25
2002	6.25	1.96	0.68	2.16	0	2.69	4.07
2001	6.8	2.72	5.2	0.71	0.06	1.55	0.9
2000	10.53	2.06	6.16	6.63	0	5.65	32
1999	6.03	0.72	3.85	0.55	0	0.26	6.84
1998	5.04	0.37	4.16	0.27	0.19	0.02	2.22
1997	8.37	0	2.52	4.13	0.14	5.08	5.37
1996	3.05	0	0.8	0.88	0.13	0.44	2.01
1995	0.51	0	0.68	0.26	0.13	0.2	0.66
1994	0.72	0.09	0.61	1.28	0	0.2	1.51
1993	4.02	0	1.03	1.05	0	0.12	1.83
	248.81	187.95	43.58	123.73	16.54	26.57	117.41

Source: Wind Information and Hong Kong Stock Exchange to September 30, 2010
Note: US$ at prevailing rates; Hong Kong GEM listings not included; No B-share issuance since 2000.

was completed in their domestic markets of Shanghai and Shenzhen. Underwriting fees in China are around two percent, suggesting that China's investment banks (and only the top 10 at best participate in this lucrative business) earned fees totaling US$1.5 billion. This amount, as large as it, pales in comparison to the amount collected in brokerage fees. For example, on a single day, November 27, 2009, A-share trading on the Shanghai and Shenzhen markets reached a historic high of over RMB485 billion (US$70 billion) in value. For a market that doesn't allow intra-day trading, that turnover is truly impressive—more than double the rest of Asia, including Japan, combined. Brokerage fees for that one day alone totaled around US$210 million, spread between 103 securities companies. With all that money up for grabs (and a clear preference for domestic over foreign markets by Chinese companies) it is no wonder that there is so much noise surrounding China's stock markets—investment bankers anywhere are hardly known for being self-effacing and China's are no different.

Observers are also very impressed with the market's infrastructure. Like the inter-bank debt markets, the mechanics of the stock exchanges are state-of-the-art, with fully electronic trading platforms, efficient settlement and clearing systems and all the obvious metrics such as indices, disclosure, real-time price dissemination and corporate notices. The range of information provided on exchange websites is also impressive and completely accurate, but all of this is only a part of the picture. China's stock exchanges are not founded on the concept of private companies or private property; they are based solely on the interests of the Party. Consequently, despite the infrastructure, the data and all the money raised, China's stock markets are a triumph of form over substance. They give the country's economy the look of modernity, but like the debt-capital markets, the reality is they have failed to develop as a genuine market for the ownership of companies.

The engine at the heart of the debt markets is the valuation of risk and this is missing in China because the Party controls interest rates. Similarly, the heart of a stock market is the valuation of companies and this is also missing in China because the Party controls the ownership of listed companies. Private property is not the central organizing concept of the Chinese economy; rather, the central organizing concept is tied to control and ownership by the Communist Party. Given this basic premise, markets cannot be used as the means to allocate scarce resources and drive economic development. This role belongs to the Party which, to achieve its own ends, actively manipulates both the stock and debt markets. As shown in the previous two chapters, the debt market cycle takes place within a regime of controlled interest rates and suppressed risk valuations that are the corollary to the Party's control over the allocation of capital. The stock markets, in contrast, are vibrant, but do not trade securities that convey an ownership interest in companies. What these securities do represent is unclear, other than that they have a speculative quality that permits gains and losses from trading and IPOs.

In China, the stock and the real-estate markets have evolved into controlled outlets for surplus capital seeking a real return and, for the most part, this capital is controlled by agencies of the state. Stocks and real estate are the only two arenas in China that, although subject to frequent administrative interference, can produce rates of return greater than inflation. The huge run-up in the Shanghai Index in 2007 is an example of this (see Figure 6.1): the significant appreciation of the RMB that year drew in large volumes of "hot money" that was then parked in stocks, drawing the index ever higher. Like developed markets, China's stock markets operate rationally, but only within a framework shaped by the distorted and biased initial conditions set by the state. Their substance cannot and will not change unless these boundary conditions change. This would require outright and publicly accepted privatization—a highly unlikely prospect in any prognosticator's near- or medium-term futures.

FIGURE 6.1 Performance of the Shanghai Index, 1999–2009

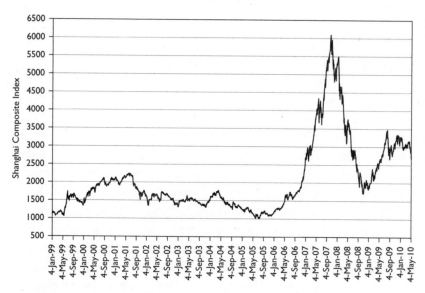

Source: Wind Information

WHY DOES CHINA HAVE STOCK MARKETS?

Why would China's government in 1990 of all times decide to create stock markets? The decision to open the Shanghai exchange was made in June 1990, just a year after Tiananmen, and it opened at year-end in the midst of malicious political mudslinging concerning whether the reforms of the 1980s belonged to what are commonly referred to in China as "Mr. Capitalism" or "Mr. Socialism." The markets were not needed from the viewpoint of capital allocation. Then, as now, the Big 4 banks provided all the funds the state-owned sector could possibly want. The reason for establishing stock markets was not related to political expediency or the capital requirements of SOEs. Rather, Beijing decided to establish stock markets in 1990 largely from an urge to control sources of social unrest and, in part, because of the inability of its SOEs to operate efficiently and competitively. The stock-market solution to both issues was purely fortuitous. If there had not been a small group of people sponsored by Zhu Rongji who had plans for stock markets already drawn up, China today could have been quite different. Moreover, had these people retained authority over market development into the new century, China could have been quite different in yet another way.

"Share fever" and social "unrest"

In the 1980s, China's stock markets arose for the same reasons as stock markets in Western private economies: small, private and state-owned companies were starved of capital and small household investors were seeking a return. The idea of using shares to raise money sprang up simultaneously in many parts of the country and, given the relaxed political atmosphere of the times, the ideas were allowed to take shape.[3] Despite Shanghai's raucous claims to be the country's financial center, there is no argument but that Shenzhen was the catalyst to all that has come after. Its proximity and cultural similarity to Hong Kong were major factors behind this. The key year was 1987, when five Shenzhen SOEs offered shares to the public. Shenzhen Development Bank (SDB), China's first financial institution (and first major SOE) limited by shares, led off in May and was followed in December by Vanke, now a leading property developer. Their IPOs were undersubscribed and drew no interest. The retail public's indifference to SDB's IPO even forced the Party organization in Shenzhen to mobilize its members to buy shares. Despite this support, only 50 percent of its issue was subscribed.

The fact is that after more than 30 years of central planning, near-civil war and state ownership, the understanding of what exactly an equity share was had been lost in the mists of pre-revolution history. Where securities called "shares" existed, investors thought of them as valuable only for the "dividends" paid; people bought them to hold for the cash flow. There was no awareness that shares might appreciate (or depreciate) in value, and so yield up a capital gain (or loss). So the market was understandably tepid for the bank's IPO and it was also unprepared for events that followed payment of the first dividend in early 1989.

The SDB's dividend announcement in early 1989 marked a major turning point in China's economic history and it should be recognized as such. The bank was very generous, awarding its shareholders—largely state and Party investors—a cash dividend of RMB10 per share and a two-for-one stock dividend. In the blink of an eye, those who had bought the bank's shares in 1988 for about RMB20 enjoyed a profit several times their original investment. Even so, a small number of shareholders failed to claim their stock dividends and the bank followed procedures to auction them off publicly. The story goes that when one individual suddenly appeared at the auction, offered RMB120 per share, and bought the whole lot, people got the point: shares were worth something more than simple face value. As this news spread in Shenzhen, a fire began to blaze. The bank's shares, as well as the few other stocks available, sky rocketed in wild street trading. SDB's shares jumped from a year-end price of RMB40 to RMB120 just before June 4, 1989, and despite the political trouble up north, ended the year at RMB90.

Armed with this new insight, China's retail investors set off a period of "share fever" centering on Shenzhen and gradually extending to Shanghai and other cities such as Chengdu, Wuhan and Shenyang where shares were traded. In the end, Beijing forced local governments to take steps to cool things down. Restrictions eventually took hold, leading to a market collapse in late 1990. Even so, investors had learned the lesson of equity investing: stocks can appreciate. But Beijing had also learned a lesson: stock trading could lead to social unrest. The decision to establish formal stock exchanges was made in the midst of "share fever" in June 1990 and the Shenzhen and Shanghai exchanges opened later the same year.

State-owned enterprise reform via incorporation

Of course, Beijing could simply have forbidden stocks and all associated activity, but it didn't. The reason for this can be found in a policy debate about the sources of dismal SOE performance. Despite the government's lavishing of resources and special policies of all kinds on SOEs during the 1980s, China's emerging private sector had left them in the dust.

The annual growth rates of private industry exceeded 16 percent as against only seven percent for the state sector (see Table 6.2). As a consequence, the private sector had increased its share of industrial output nationally from 22 percent to more than 43 percent during the decade. For the Party, this was simply not acceptable and, in fact, it is still not acceptable. Then (as now) the Party expected the state sector to dominate, and in the late 1980s, it desperately needed to find an effective way to strengthen the sector, if not to stimulate better SOE performance.

From 1985, a group of research students and staff at the State Committee for the Reform of the Economic System (SCRES) had developed a critique of state planning and state ownership of all aspects of industrial production. This group provides a clear insight into who among today's Party leadership belong to the market reformers. The SCRES group included Guo Shuqing (now Chairman of CCB), Lou Jiwei (now Chairman of CIC), Zhou Xiaochuan (now Governor of the PBOC), Li Jiange (now Chairman of CICC and previously Zhu Rongji's personal assistant) and Wu Jinglian (Zhu Rongji's favorite economist), all of whom today continue to make contributions to China's market-reform effort.

TABLE 6.2 Share of total industrial output by ownership

%		SOE	Total Non-State	Collective	Individual	Other
	1978	77.6	22.4	22.4	0.0	0.0
	1980	76.0	24.0	23.5	0.0	0.5
	1985	64.9	35.1	32.1	1.8	1.2
	1990	54.6	45.4	35.6	5.4	4.4
	1991	56.2	43.8	33.0	4.8	6.0

Source: *China Statistical Yearbook*, various

Based on their work, as well as on ideas brought back from New York by Gao Xiqing (now CEO of CIC), Wang Boming (Founder and Publisher of *Caijing* 财经 magazine) and others, by late 1988, the State Council and SCRES had initiated a project that would lead Beijing to co-opt the 1980s experiment with stocks for the benefit of SOEs.

At the historic Xizhimen Hotel Conference of December 1988, the framework for China's future stock markets was set. Discussion centered only on the question of how to improve the performance of SOEs and the recommendations related only to SOEs. The conference report concluded that the critical conditions to proceed with what was called the "share-holding system experiment" included: 1) avoidance of privatization; 2) avoidance of the loss of state assets; and 3) the guarantee of the primacy of the state-owned economy. If such objectives could be achieved, the conference concluded, the new form of companies limited by shares was attractive for two reasons. First, the corporate structure of a company limited by shares could address the perceived problem of excessive government involvement in enterprise management. Second, if properly managed, the sale of a minority stake in such a company could raise capital from sources other than the state budget and the PBOC printing press.

Efforts to obtain State Council approval of the conference's proposal prepared by the SCRES came to nothing in 1989, but a year later, the "social unrest" generated by a populace trying to get rich revived the reformers' suggestions. The government in Beijing saw exchanges as a way to close the street markets by moving them "inside the walls." In May 1990, the State Council approved an updated version of the SCRES recommendations that included: 1) no individual investors; only enterprise investment in the share capital of other enterprises; 2) no further sale of shares to employees; 3) development of OTC markets limited to Shanghai and Shenzhen alone; and 4) no new public offerings. On June 2, just a month later, the State Council gave the go-ahead to the formal establishment of the two securities exchanges.

So the opening of the Shanghai Stock Exchange in December 1990 and the Shenzhen Stock Exchange in July 1991 were highly symbolic historical events—but not for the reasons usually given. Outside observers saw them as signs that China had shrugged off the disaster of Tiananmen, picked up the torch of reform and was again embarking on the brave new world of capitalism when, in fact, the exchanges were opened to put an end to free private-capital markets. In their place, the exchanges and entire experiment were harnessed in support of the development of state enterprises only. What China got as a result, however, was of historical importance, but not in the way the Party had foreseen at the time.

WHAT STOCK MARKETS GAVE CHINA

Had it not been for two events in 1992, however, even this state-centric version of stock markets might not have eventuated and China might have developed in a very different direction. First, Deng Xiaoping in early 1992 affirmed the value of stock markets, which gave rise to the country's first huge equity boom. The political cover Deng gave for supporters of this experiment with modified capitalism was perhaps the critical political decision that led to the China we know today. But Zhu Rongji, then vice-premier in charge of banking and finance, also contributed greatly to China's future development when he agreed to open international markets and their limitless capital to China's SOEs. The first decision led to China's first truly national capital market; the second let in the ideas and financial technologies that created its great National Champions. Together, these decisions led to a centralization of financial power in Beijing that it had never had before, and changed—if not destroyed—old government institutions.

A national financial market and beyond

What did Beijing own in 1979? The answer is, everything and nothing. In some sense, it owned the entire economy, with an estimated official GDP that year of RMB406.2 billion (US$261 billion). The country's industrial landscape, however, was bare of anything resembling enterprises with economies of scale and China had extremely limited financial resources to invest. Over the course of the 1980s, neither the national budget nor the banking system could adequately support even the 22 major industrial projects designated in state plans as critical national investments. Given the dearth of state-supplied capital, it is no wonder that other ideas emerged.

Aside from the national budget, the banks were the primary providers of capital, but their capacity was very limited. Organized on the lines of the administrative hierarchy reaching to Beijing, the provincial branch bank was the key to this system and it operated independently of other provincial branches. Limited to a single province, its deposit base was geographically circumscribed, forcing it to rely either on a slowly growing national inter-bank market from 1986 and central budget grants, or on intra-provincial government, retail and SOE deposits. The central government for its part had limited taxable resources and also lacked the financial technology that would help it raise large amounts of capital by issuing bonds: a functioning bond market did not exist, nor was one permitted.

The Yizheng Chemical Fiber project in Jiangsu, one of the 22 key projects, is a case in point. This ambitious project became famous in 1980 when its sponsor, the Ministry of Textiles, approached China International Trust and Investment (CITIC) for funding it could not source elsewhere, either from banks or from the MOF. CITIC, led by Rong Yiren (its founder and the survivor of a successful pre-revolution Shanghai industrial family), proposed an international bond issue in Japan to raise 10 billion yen (US$50 million). This novel—many said counter-revolutionary—idea caused a political furor. Ultra-nationalists claimed it was a disgrace to rely on capitalist countries, much less Japan, to fund Chinese projects. It took an entire year for the political finger-pointing to die down and only after it had become clear that the money, in truth, could be found nowhere else in the country. The State Council approved the bond and it was successfully issued in 1981. The point is that such a small amount could not be sourced domestically even for a critically needed project. Yizheng was later one of the first nine candidates for overseas listing chosen by Zhu Rongji in 1993.

Several years later, the MOF was able to sell limited amounts of "special" bonds to fund similar industrial projects. For example, in 1987, it raised US$1.5 billion in support of new refinery projects at five centrally owned enterprises and, in 1988, another US$1 billion equivalent for projects at seven steel companies. Again the funds were limited in scale, especially given the capital intensity of such industries. The inability of central government, at this point 30 years into its revolution, to raise large amounts of capital is not unique to modern China. One scholar argues persuasively that the very absence of a national capital market and its ability to mobilize large amounts of money explains China's historical inability to develop economically beyond small-scale manufacturing.[4]

Given this dearth of capital, it is easy to understand why, despite ideological compunctions, local governments from the early 1980s were so attracted to the idea of stock markets. The image of Zhu Rongji finding the treasury bare on his appointment as Mayor of Shanghai in 1988 is priceless; he rapidly became the political godfather to the movement to establish formal stock exchanges. But like the banking system, the Shanghai and Shenzhen exchanges at their inception were geographically limited to listing local companies and relying on local retail investors. This changed rapidly, however, and by 1994, both had become markets open to issuers and investors on a national basis. This made it possible for provincial governments to raise incremental amounts of capital on top of what local banks and taxes could provide. Although small by international standards, the top 10 listed companies in Shanghai were by 1996 larger than any of their predecessors (see Table 6.3) and three years later larger still. It is noteworthy, in light of the discussion later in this chapter, that the top 10 companies in 2009 were all financial institutions and oil companies.

These companies, however, are the exception; the vast majority of companies listed on the domestic exchanges were tiny, with market capitalizations of under US$500 million. In the primary markets, as well, A-share IPOs on the whole remained small throughout the 1990s. With the exchanges operating only from 1992, one could hardly expect Chinese markets to reach their full size overnight or even by the end of their first 10 years. Nonetheless, the domestic markets would have remained side-shows for far longer had Zhu Rongji not permitted Chinese companies to list their shares on overseas markets.

This decision led to the dramatic growth of the Hong Kong Stock Exchange (HKSE) from its position as a small regional exchange in 1993 to a global giant in the twenty-first century. From its boast in 1993 of hosting IPOs of as much as US$100 million for local taipans within 10 years, thanks to Zhu, it was raising billions of dollars for Chinese SOEs. By approving the first batch of nine so-called H-share companies, Zhu changed Hong Kong's game entirely. His internationalism accounts for the huge capital raisings and market capitalizations of the top 10 listed companies in 2009. Of these companies, nine were also listed either in Hong Kong or New York. In the period 1993–2009, Chinese SOEs

TABLE 6.3 Top 10 Shanghai-listed companies: Then and now (US$ billion)

	12/1996	Market Cap	12/1999	Market Cap	11/2009	Market Cap
1	Shanghai Petrochemical	3.6*	Shanghai Pudong Dev Bank	7.2	PetroChina	319.5*
2	Lujiazui Finance & Trade Zone	3.0	Sichuan Changhong	3.4	ICBC	192.3*
3	Shenergy	2.5	Shenergy	2.4	Sinopec	124.6*
4	Sichuan Changhong	2.2	Luijiazui Fin & Trade Zone	2.2	BOC	107.3*
5	Maanshan Iron & Steel	2.0*	Shanghai Petrochemical	2.1*	China Life	93.3*
6	Yizheng Chemical	1.4*	Shanghai Oriental Pearl	1.8	China Shenhua	85.6*
7	Shanghai Outer Gaoqiao Free Trade Zone	0.9	Shanghai Automotive	1.6	Ping An	39.8*
8	Shanghai Raw Water	0.8	Hongqiao Airport	1.6	China Merchants Bank	39.7*
9	Shanghai Oriental Pearl	0.8	China Eastern Airlines	1.6*	BoComm	32.2*
10	Eastern Communications	0.7	Yizheng Chemical	1.5*	Shanghai Pudong Dev Bank	28.5
	Total Market Cap	17.9		25.4		1,062.8

Source: Shanghai Stock Exchange and Wind Information
Note: Capitalization calculated based on domestic market practice, which includes all domestic company shares but excludes overseas-listed shares; *denotes additional overseas listing in Hong Kong or New York.

raised US$262 billion in new capital from the international markets, with the year 2000 marking the turning point (see Table 6.4). For the first time in its history, China and its companies had access to the financial techniques and markets that enabled them to raise meaningful amounts of capital. They took these techniques and brought them back at last to Shanghai.

TABLE 6.4 Average IPO size per listing class

	Hong Kong-listed			China-listed		
(US$ million)	H-share	Red Chip	Pink Chip	Shanghai/ Shenzhen	SME	ChiNext
1991	–	–	–	6	–	–
1992	–	–	–	17	–	–
1993	214	185	–	42	–	–
1994	703	94	–	17	–	–
1995	60	42	17	12	–	–
1996	146	131	203	14	–	–
1997	260	504	9	37	–	–
1998	13	49	50	41	–	–
1999	229	62	16	61	–	–
2000	1,115	1,134	54	73	–	–
2001	110	476	18	94	–	–
2002	152	2,540	13	87	–	–
2003	339	132	21	85	–	–
2004	305	85	63	56	29	–
2005	1,473	33	82	146	30	–
2006	1,632	161	148	1,160	40	–
2007	1,596	911	587	2,372	54	–
2008	761	–	354	1,864	62	–
2009	2,455	517	643	2,036	115	83
Jan. 2010	–	–	–	685	119	105

Source: Wind Information and Hong Kong Stock Exchange

China Telecom: God's work by Goldman Sachs

How did China go from having small-scale companies that banks would hardly look at to ones raising billions of dollars in New York in just 10 years? If there is a single reason, it is the persistent enthusiasm for the China story among international money managers combined with their willingness to put vast amounts of money down on it. Their response to the tiny (and bankrupt) Brilliance China US$80 million IPO in 1992 was just as wild as that for China Telecom's US$4.2 billion IPO in 1997, but the scale of the two companies and the money couldn't have been more different. International markets introduced Chinese companies to world-class investment bankers, lawyers and accountants and brought their legal and financial technologies—the entire panoply of corporate finance, legal and accounting concepts and treatments that underpin international financial markets—to bear on China's SOE-reform effort. What happened when aggressive and highly motivated investment bankers and lawyers interacted with government officials at all levels up to and including the State Council altered the course of China's economic and political history and is the subject of a different book.

This technology transfer greatly strengthened Beijing's control over the money-raising process, but, strangely enough, in the end weakened the government by strengthening its companies. In 1993, at the start of China's IPO fever, Beijing was only one of many government entities owning companies competing for the right to raise capital overseas. There was a bureaucratic process at the center of which was the newly established China Securities Regulatory Commission. This heavily lobbied agency screened the listing applications of all local governments and central ministries to come up with an approved list of candidates for which foreign investment banks were allowed to compete for IPO mandates (see Table 6.5).

The early batches included what were then, in fact, China's best enterprises (for example, First Auto Works, Tsingtao Beer and Shandong Power). None, with the exception of the beer company, had any international brand recognition. The truth is that no one outside of China had ever

TABLE 6.5 Ownership of listing candidates for overseas IPOs

	Oct. 1993 1st Batch	Jan. 1994 2nd Batch	Sept. 1994 Special 7	Dec. 1996 4th Batch	Dec. 1999 5th Batch	Total	Completed	%
Central	3	10	1	9	0	23	15	65.22%
Local	6	12	6	30	9	63	32	50.79%

heard of these companies, knew what they did, or where they were located: China's SOEs were completely virgin territory for the world's investment banks. Had anyone ever heard of Beiren Printing, Dongfeng Auto or Panzhihua Steel? Not only were these companies unknown, there were not many of them. By the time calls went out for the fourth and fifth batches, provincial governments came up empty-handed; there simply were very few companies with the economic scale and profitability required for raising international capital. The fourth batch consisted largely of highway and other so-called infrastructure companies, while the fifth batch introduced farmland into the mix. Even Wall Street bankers could not find a way to list what was not even a working farm.

The fact of the matter was that there were few good IPO candidates. Enterprises owned by the central government had enjoyed access to the best financial and policy support since 1979 and this accounts for their reasonably high IPO completion rates. Even so, for the period from 1993 to 1999, they accounted for only one-third of the total of 86 candidates. There were very few that could, even with the best financial advice, meet the requirements of even the most enthusiastic international money managers and only 51 percent of the candidate companies succeeded in listing overseas. By 1996, China's effort to use stock-market listings to reform its SOEs seemed to have hit the wall. Then came the IPO of China Telecom (now known as China Mobile).

In October 1997, and despite the evolving Asian Financial Crisis, China Mobile (HK) Co. Ltd. completed its dual New York/Hong Kong IPO, raising US$4.5 billion—some 25 times the average size of the 47 overseas-listed companies that had gone before. This kind of money made everyone sit up and pay attention: underwriting fees alone were said to be over US$200 million. If China was, in fact, full of small companies, as the earlier international and domestic listings show, then where had this one come from? The answer is simple, yet complicated: China Mobile represented the consolidation of provincially owned and run industrial assets into what is now commonly called a "National Champion." This transaction demonstrated to Beijing how it could overcome the regional fragmentation of its industrial sector and, with huge amounts of cash raised internationally, create powerful companies with national markets.

The creation of such new companies out of the grist of the old SOEs would have been impossible without the legal concepts and financial constructs of international finance and corporate law that are the foundation of all modern corporations and the capitalist system itself. In fact, while the capital raised was important in building today's China, the most important thing of all was the organizational concept that permitted true centralization of ownership and control. The New China of the twenty-first century is a creation of the Goldman Sachs and Linklaters & Paines of the world, just as surely as the Cultural Revolution flowed from Chairman Mao's Little Red Book.

In the absence of new listing candidates and in the midst of the ongoing technological revolution in the US, Goldman Sachs aggressively lobbied Beijing using the very simple but powerful idea of creating a truly national telecommunications company. Such a company, it was argued, could raise sufficient capital to develop into a leading global telecommunications technology company. The ideas had already been used for the so-called Red Chips that were briefly all the rage among investment bankers in early 1997. Instead of creating holding companies owned by single municipal governments that held its breweries, ice-cream plants, auto companies and, in the famous instance of Beijing Enterprise, the Badaling section of the Great Wall of China, why not acquire and merge provincial telecom entities into a single company owned by the central government?

Given the strong centrifugal forces in the country, this required real political will and power that the imperious Minister of Posts and Telecommunications (MPT), Wu Jichuan, could supply in full. It also required the support of a central government that saw economic scale as a critically important building block to international competitiveness and that was also comfortable with the legal enforceability of shareholder rights (at least its own) in Western courts. China Mobile's wildly successful IPO catalyzed a series of blockbuster transactions that put Beijing front and center in the world's capital markets. If there is a single reason why the world is in awe of China's economic miracle today, it is because international bankers have worked so well to build its image so that minority stakes in its companies could be sold at high prices, with the Party and its friends and families profiting handsomely. The China Mobile transaction was the first big step in this direction.

How this historic US$4.5 billion IPO was put together is shown in Figure 6.2. Simply put, a series of shell companies were created under the MPT, the most important of which was China Mobile Hong Kong (CMHK). CMHK was the company that sold its shares to international investors, listed on the New York and Hong Kong stock exchanges, and used the capital plus bank loans to buy *from its own parent*, China Mobile (British Virgin Islands) Ltd. (CM BVI), telecom companies operating in six provinces.

FIGURE 6.2   China Mobile's 1997 IPO structure

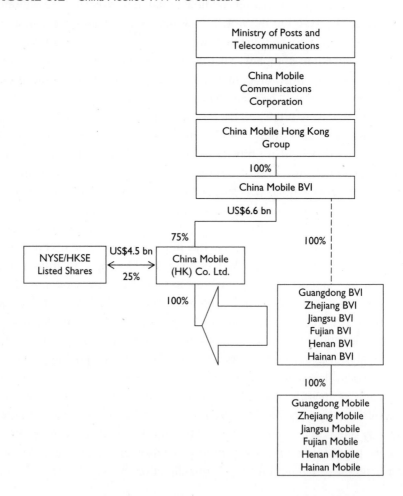

The key point that stands out in this transaction is that a subsidiary raised capital to acquire from its parent certain assets by leveraging the *future value* of those same assets as if the entire entity—subsidiary plus parent assets—existed and operated as a real company. The value of the provincial assets, as far as the IPO goes, was based on projected estimates of their future profitability as part of a notional company that was compared to the financial performance of existing national telecoms companies operating elsewhere in the world. In other words, the estimates were based on the assumption that CMHK was already a unitary operating company comparable to international telecom companies elsewhere. This most certainly was not the case in China: prior to its IPO, CMHK was a shell holding company that existed only on the spreadsheets of Goldman's bankers. The IPO, gave it the capital to acquire six independently operating, but as yet unmerged, subsidiaries. So even at this point, China Mobile could be said to exist only as a paper company, but with a very real bank account.

This was not the IPO of an existing company with a proven management team in place with a strategic plan to expand operations. It would be much closer to the truth to say that this was an IPO of the Ministry of Post and Telecommunications itself! But international investors loved it and two years later, in 2000, a similar transaction was carried out in which CMHK raised a total of $32.8 billion from a combination of share placement ($10.2 billion) and issuance of new shares ($22.6 billion). This massive injection of capital was used to acquire the MPT's telecom assets in a further seven provinces. As a result of these two transactions, China Mobile had reassembled the MPT's mobile communications business in 13 of China's most prosperous provinces in the form of a corporation that replaced a government agency. What happened to the US$37 billion raised after CMBVI was paid is unknowable since it is a so-called private unlisted entity and is not required to make public its financial statements.

The significance of this deal ripples down to this day over a decade later. First, as was the case for the original 86 H-share companies, the government could have simply incorporated each provincial telecom authority (PTA) and sought to do an IPO for each. This would no doubt have greatly benefited local interests and ended up creating many regional companies. The amount of money to be raised in aggregate, however, would in all probability have paled in comparison with China Mobile and there was no certainty that any local firm would have developed a national network. More importantly, the new structure conceptually enabled the potential consolidation of entire industries, making possible the creation of large-scale companies that might someday be globally competitive. Today, China Mobile is the largest mobile-phone operator in the world, with over 300 million subscribers and operating a network that is the envy of operators in developed markets.

Second, and equally important, the money raised was new money, not re-circulated Chinese money from the budget, the banks, or the domestic stock markets. Third, the creation of this structure made possible the raising of further massive amounts of capital simply by injecting new PTAs (or any other "asset"). The valuation of such assets was purely a matter of China's negotiating skills, flexible valuation methodologies employed by the investment banks and demand in the international capital market. In the case of the acquisition in 2000, foreign investors paid a premium of 40–101 times the projected *future value* of China Mobile Hong Kong's earnings and cash flow. This was truly pulling capital out of the air! Fourth, this new capital was without doubt paid back into the ultimate Chinese parent, CMCC, giving it vast amounts of new funding independent of budgets or banks. More importantly, the restructuring took what were relatively independent provincial telecom agencies originally invested in by a combination of national and local budgets and allowed China Mobile to monetize them by means of an IPO priced at a huge multiple of the original value. The ability to deploy such capital at once transformed CMCC into a potent force—political as well as economic.

Why wouldn't Beijing enthusiastically embrace these Western financial techniques when the foreigners were making the Party rich and China seem omnipotent? In the ensuing years, China's "National Team" was rapidly assembled (see Table 6.6) and a similar approach was used to restructure and recapitalize China's major banks, as described earlier. It need hardly be said that this list includes only central government-controlled companies: Beijing kept the goodies for itself.

None of this would have been possible if it had not been for international, particularly American, investment bankers. Over the period 1997–2006, bankers and professionals from a small number of international legal and accounting companies played major roles in the creation

TABLE 6.6   The National Team: Overseas IPOs, 1997–2006

Company	Industry	Lead Underwriter(s)	IPO Date	IPO Size (US$ billion)
China Mobile	Telecoms/ Mobile*	Goldman Sachs	10/23/97	4.5
PetroChina	Oil and gas	Goldman Sachs	7/7/00	2.9
China Unicom	Telecoms/ Mobile*	Morgan Stanley	6/22/00	5.1
Sinopec	Oil and gas*	Morgan Stanley	10/19/00	3.3
China National Offshore Oil	Oil and gas*	Merrill Lynch/ CSFB	2/28/01	1.4
Aluminum Corporation of China (Chalco)	Mining and processing*	Morgan Stanley	12/12/01	0.5
China Telecom	Telecoms/ fixed line*	Merrill Lynch/ Morgan Stanley	11/8/02	1.4
China Life Insurance	Insurance	Citi/CSFB/ Deutsche Bank	12/18/03	3.4
Ping An Insurance	Insurance	Goldman Sachs/HSBC/ Morgan Stanley	6/24/04	1.8
Air China	Airlines*	Merrill Lynch	6/15/05	1.2
China Shenhua Energy	Energy and Power*	Deutsche Bank/ Merrill Lynch	6/15/05	3.3
Bank of Communications	Banking	Goldman Sachs/ HSBC	6/23/05	2.2
China Construction Bank	Banking	CSFB/ Morgan Stanley	10/27/05	9.2
Bank of China	Banking	Goldman Sachs/UBS	6/1/06	11.1
ICBC	Banking	Merrill Lynch/ CSFB/Deutsche Bank	10/21/06	21.9
Total Capital Raised				**73.2**

Source: Wind Information

Note: * denotes company parent Chairman is on the central *nomenklatura* list of the Organization Department of the Communist Party of China.

of entire new companies. These companies were created out of industries that were fragmented, lacking economies of scale, or, in the case of the banks, even publicly acknowledged as being bankrupt. The investment banks put their reputations on the line by sponsoring these companies in the global capital markets, introducing them to money managers, pension funds and a myriad of other institutional investors. Supported by global sales forces, industry analysts, equity analysts and economists, the banks sold these companies for China. Sometimes investors were so excited they didn't even have to: for the first time, global investors had the opportunity to invest in true proxies of China's national economy.

Simply put, international financial, legal and accounting rules provided the creative catalyst for China's vaunted National Team. Even more important, their professional expertise and skills put Beijing and the Communist Party of China in the driver's seat for a strategic piece of the Chinese economy for the first time ever: the central government and the Party's Organization Department own the National Team.

ENDNOTES

1 Shares in the public offering are allocated to investors by means of a lottery process.
2 Of course, the authors are well aware that the Hong Kong Shanghai Bank and AIG are companies with deep Chinese roots, but they were not Chinese owned.
3 For more details on how the demand for capital gave rise to stock markets spontaneously in China during the early 1980s, see Walter and Howie 2006: Chapter 1.
4 See David Faure, *China and Capitalism: A history of business enterprise in modern China*. Hong Kong: Hong Kong University Press, 2006.

CHAPTER

7

The National Team and China's Government

"The source of crony capitalism in China is the unrestrained power held by certain factions that lets them intervene in economic activity and allocate resources. Supporters of the old economy want to increase SOE monopoly power and strengthen government's dictatorial power."

Wu Jinglian, *Caijing* 财经
September 28, 2009

There can be little doubt that the Chinese government's initial policy objective was to create a group of companies that could compete globally. However, the National Team created by government policy was, from its inception, more politically than economically competitive and, as a consequence, these oligopolies came to own the government. At the same time, that bankers were creating National Champions, Zhu Rongji was, perhaps inadvertently, making it possible for these huge corporations to displace the government. In 1998, Premier Zhu forcefully carried out a major streamlining of central government agencies that reduced their staffing by over 50 percent and eliminated the great industrial ministries that had been created to support the Soviet-inspired planned economy. These included the Ministry of Coal Industry, the Ministry of Machine-Building, the Ministry of Metallurgy, the Ministry of Petroleum, the Ministry of Chemicals, and the Ministry of Power, all of which became small bureaus that were meant to regulate the newly created companies in their sectors. The new companies and the bureaus were collected under the now long-forgotten State Economic and Trade Commission (SETC).[1]

The ministries disappeared, the SETC was again reorganized, but the companies remained. Then, in 2004, the State-owned Assets Supervision and Administration Commission (SASAC) was created to bring order to the ownership of state enterprises. The SASAC was meant to be the owner of the major central SOEs on behalf of the state, and was endorsed as such by the State Council. But it has largely been a failure precisely because it was based on Soviet-inspired, top-down, organizational principles. Because of the stock markets, China in the twenty-first century has progressed far beyond this to the point where Western notions of enterprise ownership are used to trump the interests of the state. To illustrate this point, the SASAC's relationship with its collection of central SOEs is contrasted to Central Huijin's investments in China's major financial institutions.

ZHU RONGJI'S GIFT: ORGANIZATIONAL STREAMLINING, 1998

The regulatory bureaus with which Zhu replaced the great ministries had far fewer staff than their predecessors. Even worse, their heads were not ministers, and lacked the seniority to speak directly to the chairmen and CEOs of the major corporations, who were, in many cases, the former ministry bosses of those left behind in the bureaus. In other words, by eliminating the industrial ministries and at the same time promoting the creation of the huge National Champions, Zhu Rongji effectively changed the ministries into Western-style corporations that were staffed by the same people at the top. However, he did not, or was unable to, change the substance.

That may have been because the former ministry officials now in charge of the new corporations successfully fought for the right to remain on the critical staffing hierarchy of the Chinese Communist Party. This would seem entirely natural given the Party's desire to ensure its control over the economy. However, had these new corporations been staffed by men who were outside of the Party's *nomenklatura*, things might have turned out differently and the political independence of the Party and government might have been preserved.

There was one crucial exception: in spite of all the financial clout they seem to wield, the Big 4 banks remain classified as only vice-ministerial entities. An entity is placed in the state organizational hierarchy based on the rank of its highest official; the chairmen/CEOs of these banks carry only a rank of vice-minister. The reason for this exception appears to be straightforward: the Party seems to have wanted to ensure that the banks remained subordinate entities, and not just to the State Council, but to the major SOEs as well. Banks were a mechanical financial facilitator in the Soviet system; the main focus of economic effort then was on the enterprises. Little has changed.

When transferring to these central SOEs (*yangqi* 央企) the former ministry officials were able to retain their positions on the Party list controlled by the central Organization Department. Today, 54 of the 100-plus central SOEs nominally managed by the SASAC are on what is called the central *nomenklatura* list. The chairmen/CEOs of these companies hold ministerial rank and are appointed directly by the Organization Department.[2] These men rank equally with provincial governors and all ministers on China's State Council, and many are members or alternates of the powerful Central Committee of the Communist Party of China (see Table 7.1). What would the chairman of China's largest bank do if the chairman of PetroChina asked for a loan? He would say: "Thank you very much, how much, and for how long?"

What then of the SASAC, the current entity charged with overseeing the central SOEs? The SASAC was established by the State Council in 2003 and had been created out of the SETC (see Endnote 1) and an agglomeration of other commissions and bureaus which previously had oversight of the central SOEs. It was created as a quasi-governmental entity (*shiye danwei* 事业单位) rather than a government ministry because such a powerful government entity would have attracted discussion at China's "highest organ of state power," the National People's Congress (NPC). This was particularly so since there was a line of argument in support of the NPC as the proper entity to own state assets. This argument held that since the NPC was, in fact, the legal representative of "the whole people" under the Constitution, it was better placed than the State Council to play this role. As a result, the entire process establishing the SASAC was rushed through just before the NPC convened in March 2003.

TABLE 7.1 The National Team: Representation on the Central Committee (2009)

Company	Name	Alternate Member	Full Member
China National Nuclear Group Co.	Kang Rixin		x
China Aerospace Science & Technology Group Co.	Yuan Jiajun	x	
China Aerospace Science & Industry Group Co.	Liu Shiquan	x	
China Aviation Industry 1st Group Co.	Lin Zuoming	x	
China Shipbuilding Industry Group Co.	Lin Changyin	x	
China North Industries Group Co.	Zhang Guoqing	x	
China National Petroleum Group Co.	Jiang Jiemin	x	
Sinopec	Su Shulin	x	
State Grid Corporation of China	Liu Zhenya	x	
China Telecom Corp.	Wang Xiaochu	x	
Anben Steel Group Co.	Zhang Xiaogang	x	
Baosteel Group Corp.	Xu Lejiang	x	
Aluminium Corporation of China (Chalco)	Xia Yaoqing	x	
China Commercial Aircraft Corp.	Zhang Qingwei		x
China Railway Construction Co. Ltd.	Shi Dahua	x	
China Investment Corp.	Lou Jiwei	x	
PetroChina, Daqing Oilfield Co. Ltd.	Wang Yupu	x	
Taiyuan Steel Group Co.	Chen Chuanping	x	
Haier Group Co.	Zhang Ruimin	x	
Total		17	2

Source: Kjeld Erik Brodsgaard, "Politics and business group formation in China," unpublished manuscript, April 2010

One of the greatest considerations surrounded the issue of the new commission's classification (*guige* 规格). For a moment it appeared that it would be similar to the Central Work Committee for Large Enterprises (*daqi gongwei* 大企工委), the other of the SASAC's two principal components, which was headed by a Party member at vice-premier level. The other choice was the arrangement at the SETC, with a ministry-level leader at the top. The final choice of the latter was a decision that weakened the SASAC almost fatally from the very beginning. Why should a major corporation owned by the Chinese central *government* be subject to the authority of what in the Chinese context is tantamount to a *non-government* organization (NGO) even if it was run by a minister? A vice-premier might have made the key difference.

Despite its weak position in the state hierarchy, the SASAC was charged by the State Council with very significant responsibilities: 1) representing the state *as owner* of those central SOEs that together constitute the "socialist pillars" of the economy; 2) carrying out a human-resource function for SOE senior management; and 3) deciding where to invest dividends received from the SOEs. In each of these areas, the SASAC has had great difficulty exercising its authority, not simply because it is a sort of NGO, but also because its organizational relationship to its nominal charges was inappropriate.

First of all, SASAC has been unable to address the simple fact that it was not the owner of these SOEs (see Figure 7.1). Previously, the industrial ministries could make such a claim since they were a component part of the government and, in fact, oversaw the investment process in their subordinate enterprises. After the strategic assets of these enterprise groups were spun off into listed companies, the remaining SOE group companies became, in fact, the direct state investors in the National Champions. In contrast, SASAC was tacked on after the old ministry systems were eliminated. Secondly, while SASAC could oversee the appointment of management at the vice-president and CFO levels, the Party's all-powerful

FIGURE 7.1 SASAC's "ownership" and supervisory lines over the National Team

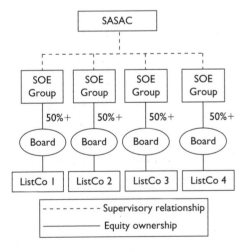

Organization Department appoints the chairmen/CEOs. How can even a governmental entity exercise authority over enterprises whose senior management has been appointed by the Organization Department? These chairmen/CEOs do not report to a government minister; they report directly on a solid line into the Party system.

Finally, the delicacy of the SASAC's position is well demonstrated by the fact that its "invested" companies have successfully resisted the payment of significant dividends, whether to the SASAC or the Ministry of Finance, despite a protracted struggle over the past few years. Even with a three-year "trial" compromise in place, reached in 2007 after years of wrangling, payments will be in the 5–10 percent range of post-tax profit, all of which has been used for projects that are equivalent to reinvesting into the SOEs. The profit made by these nominally state-owned enterprises is not small and in recent years has reached almost to 20 percent of China's national budget expenditures (see Figure 7.2). This is a vast amount of money that would be better redirected at the country's

FIGURE 7.2 Central SOE profit as a percentage of national budget expenditures

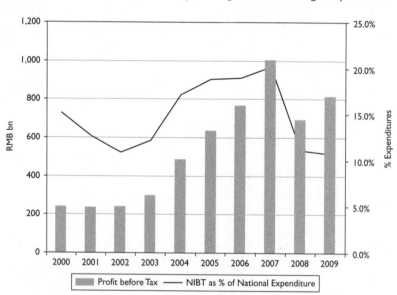

Source: 21st Century Business Herald 21 世纪经济报导, August 9, 2010: 11

burgeoning budget deficit. Instead, because of their political and economic power, coupled with the ingenuous argument that they continue to bear the burden of the state's social-welfare programs, the National Champions are able to retain the vast bulk of their earnings. The fact that the government is unable to access this capital is the best illustration of the power of these oligopolies.

The architecture of the entire SASAC arrangement bears the hallmarks of the Soviet-style ministry system abolished by Zhu Rongji in 1998. In that system, SOEs reported directly to their respective ministries and were administratively managed by them (*guikouguanli* 归口管理); the Party organization was their nerve system. The relationship between ministry and enterprise was all-encompassing, including investment, human resources and the deployment of capital and other assets. When the ministries were abolished, the line to the past was broken. The SASAC could not take their place, even though its structure was predicated on the thought that the old administrative management methods still worked. At best, the SASAC as presently constituted is rather like the State Council's Department of Compliance. China in the twenty-first century is no longer built on the Soviet model.

The SASAC model vs. the Huijin model: Who owns what?

In deliberate contrast to the SASAC and taking full advantage of the international corporate model, the PBOC team created Central SAFE Investments (or Huijin), as a limited-liability investment company rather than a government body of any kind. Huijin was to be the critical part of the project to restructure the banks and was designed for the express purpose of investing directly in equity of the Big 4 banks. But it became much more than that (see Table 7.2). In late 2003, Huijin made cash investments totaling US$45 billion in CCB and BOC, acquiring almost 100 percent of their equity. In 2005, it invested a further US$15 billion in ICBC for a 50 percent holding.

This direct holding was possible because of the "good" bank/ "bad" bank approach described in Chapter 2. For SOE restructurings, the parent or group SOE that remained behind was effectively the "bad" bank and, at the same time, the majority shareholder of the "good" bank. Consequently, whatever dividends were paid went directly into the group's

TABLE 7.2 Huijin investments, the financial SASAC, FY2009

Institution	Date of Investment	Amount	Original Holding (%)	Post-IPO Holding (%)
BOC	12/30/03	US$22.5 billion	100	67.53
CCB	12/30/03	US$22.5 billion	95*	48.23
China Jianyin Investment	4/4/04	US$2.5 billion	100	NA
ICBC	4/22/05	US$15 billion	50	35.4
China Galaxy Securities	7/14/05	RMB5.5 billion	100	78.57
Shenyin Wanguo Securities	9/21/05	RMB4.0 billion	100	37.23
Guotai Junan Securities	10/14/05	RMB2.5 billion	100	21.28
China Reinsurance	4/11/07	RMB30.9 billion	85.5	–
CDB	12/31/07	RMB146.1 billion	48.7	–
ABC	10/29/08	US$19.1 billion	50	40.93
Under China Jianyin Investment				
China International Capital Corp	9/17/04	RMB350 million	43.35	–

Note: * includes China Jianyin Investment; China Jianyin was formed to hold those CCB assets not included in the IPO entity. These assets included CICC. From 2004, however, the PBOC began a takeover of failed securities companies and China Jianyin held a number of medium-size and small entities that were later sold off; Huijin invested directly in the big ones. For more, see Walter and Howie 2006: Chapter 9.

coffers as the agency of the state. Removing non-performing assets to an entity owned by a nominal third party avoided this situation of having to create a holding company with the result that the state held direct equity interests in the banks. By 2005, Huijin had become the controlling shareholder on behalf of the state and enjoyed majority representation on the boards of directors of CCB and BOC and, together with the MOF, of ICBC, CDB, ABC and a host of other financial institutions.

In short, even after its acquisition by CIC in 2007 and no matter how it may be disposed of in 2010, it is in a position to directly control the decisions of these banks by a simple vote of its appointed directors at bank board meetings: senior bank management, having only vice-ministerial rank, had no excuses to prevaricate (see Figure 7.3). Of course, this all assumed that the Party agreed to Huijin's positions, but, as Huijin's continued operations over the years indicates, the structure has been viewed positively by the Party.

National Champions: The new government or the new Party?

The Party is able to ensure its control over China's most powerful business groups by having the power to appoint their top management. Allowing the senior management of SOEs to retain their respective ranks within the Party *nomenklatura* after the dissolution of the ministries, however, created a fissure within the Party and government along business and political lines. In some sense, this was a pre-existing split in that families and friends of senior leaders had actively engaged in their own businesses since at least the early 1990s. But it is no longer simply a case of the sons and daughters of the rich and famous being out in the market selling influence. With access to huge cash flows, broad patronage systems and, in many cases, significant international networks, the senior executives of the National Champions can expect to succeed in lobbying the government

FIGURE 7.3 Huijin's pre-IPO ownership and board control of the state banks

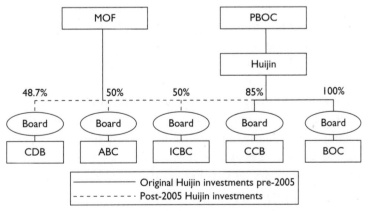

for beneficial policies or even to set the policy agenda from the start. The sons, daughters and families now have institutional backing outside of the Party itself and this gives rise to questions over whether these business interests have, over the past decade, replaced the government apparatus or eroded the government from within. How accurate is the statement that "The business of China is business" and is this beneficial in a system of communist-style capitalism?

The case of Shandong Power

The notorious case of Shandong Power (*Luneng*) illustrates the consequences of Zhu Rongji's elimination of the industrial ministries. In 2006, news was leaked out by *Caijing* 财经 magazine that the state-owned electric utility in Shandong province and a number of its major adjunct enterprises had been completely privatized.[3] The company, a subsidiary of the State Power Corporation, was the largest enterprise in the province ahead of PetroChina's subsidiary, Shengli Oil, Yanzhou Coal, and the well-known Haier Group. Its total assets of RMB73.8 billion (US$10 billion) and a total installed power-generating capacity of 360 gigawatts (second only to China Huaneng Group) had been acquired by two Beijing companies of uncertain background for a modest RMB3.7 billion (US$540 million). The name of the person behind the "acquisition" was well-known to market insiders and was (and remains) the president of a central-government enterprise group under SASAC, as well as an alternate member of the Central Committee. *Caijing* 财经, of course, did not reveal his name; there was no need.

The transaction took place over a 10-year period and it was clear to the central government early on that a true privatization was in progress. In early 2003, an article in the *21st Century Business Herald* gave rise to questions about an ongoing employee buy-out at Shandong Power and led to an enquiry being made at the State Council. In August that year, SASAC, the NDRC and the MOF jointly issued an emergency notice requiring that all transfers of ownership of power-related companies come to an immediate halt; apparently the same thing was happening all over the country. This notice referenced a State Council document of October 2000 that also had clearly called for a halt to any transfers of ownership in the power sector unless approved by the State Council. Neither of these documents had the least impact on the situation at Shandong Power; it is unclear what may have happened elsewhere.

By mid-2006 the two Beijing companies had acquired a 100 percent interest in Shandong Power from entities purportedly representing the company's employees and staff including the company's trade union. Representatives of the new shareholder were able to produce legal opinions claiming that the transaction was perfectly legitimate. Meanwhile, *Caijing* reported a senior official at the SASAC as saying: "We did not know a thing about this. Who would have thought that such a large transaction involving state assets would not be reported to the SASAC for approval?" This comment must be seen as extremely disingenuous or entirely facetious. Throughout 2004 and 2005 the SASAC had been actively investigating management buy-outs of SOEs across the country and had released notices seeking to standardize oversight procedures.

More realistic is the assessment of a former deputy head of the State Planning Commission who commented, as follows:

> SASAC had once deliberated producing a document on how to deal with manage-ment buy-outs. In this document, there was a proposal suggesting that employees holding shares in power companies choose either to stay in the company and give up their shares or leave the enterprise (and keep their shares). In the end SASAC feared that the impact would be too large and it (the document) was unable to come out officially.[4]

In other words, the SASAC was afraid to create waves, even when it knew that state assets for which it was nominally responsible were actually being privatized. Was it afraid of the employees who were acquiring shares in Shandong Power? Certainly, there may have been some consideration of possible "social unrest" if staff were required to return any shares acquired. But the real fear related to the persons behind such transactions. When the sponsor of an activity is sufficiently senior in the central *nomenklatura*, there are few ways to stop them.

HOW THE NATIONAL TEAM, ITS FAMILIES AND FRIENDS BENEFIT

Even if parts of the government retain their independence of business interests, there is no doubt that the National Champions call the shots in the domestic and Hong Kong stock markets and, of course, at the CSRC.

The workings of the stock markets confirm that the business of the National Champions is business in their own self-interest.

Jumbo investors in jumbo listings

Between mid-2001 and mid-2005, China experienced a severe bear market as a result of reformers tinkering with the system's framework. By 2005, a solution acceptable to all major stakeholders—that is, all the major state shareholders—was found that enabled business to pick up where things had left off in June 2001.[5] In 18 months, the Shanghai index then miraculously surged from just below 1,000 points to 3,000 at year-end 2006. The proximate key to this boom was China's entry into the WTO process and the certainty shared among foreign and domestic investors alike that the country was open for business. But the real key to the surge was the certainty among all domestic players that the huge overhang of non-tradable shares would not come on the market until after the Beijing Olympics in 2008. With this worry put aside, all the talk was about round-trip listings (listing on the Hong Kong exchange and then returning to list in Shanghai) of the National Champions and, especially, bank listings. Then, to add jet fuel to the fire, came the gradual appreciation of the renminbi.

The confluence of these events made a hero of Shang Fulin, Chairman of the CSRC. Appointed in 2002, Shang had previously been the chairman of the Agricultural Bank of China and was firmly protectionist to the extent of removing nearly all overseas returnees from the CSRC on his arrival. He had been responsible for arresting and reversing the collapse of the domestic stock exchanges and the concurrent bankruptcy of China's securities industry. In his attempts, he had employed every possible political and economic measure traditionally used to prop up the markets, and all had failed. In late 2004, he was provided with a workable solution by Zhou Xiaochuan's reform group. After claiming full credit for this, Shang oversaw its implementation just as the RMB began its ascent against the dollar (see Figure 7.4). The great stock market boom of 2006 and 2007 strengthened Shang's political position and thus put the seal to the opening of the country's stock markets to meaningful foreign participation.

At this same moment, the restructuring of the Big 3 Banks (minus ABC) was completed and their long-awaited IPOs in Hong Kong

FIGURE 7.4 Shanghai Index and RMB appreciation, 2005–2010

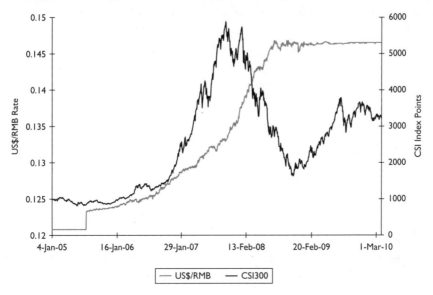

Source: Bloomberg

had begun. CCB listed to great fanfare in late 2005 with an H-share offering; Bank of China re-opened the domestic markets with a simultaneous Hong Kong/Shanghai IPO in June 2006; and the ICBC IPO came in October the same year with a dual Hong Kong/Shanghai listing. This period was characterized by super-large offerings; BOC's Shanghai IPO raised RMB20 billion (US$2.4 billion) and ICBC's offering was for a mammoth RMB46.6 billion. How did such huge amounts become available so soon after the market had tested historic lows? The friends of the family had stepped up to help out.

The prevalence of "strategic" investors in these major deals is an important factor in explaining how the market was able to get up off its knees. In similarly stagnant market conditions in 1999, the CSRC had created this third category of "strategic" IPO investors when the traditional retail and professional institutional investors failed to step up.[6] What was the incentive for this new category of "strategic" investors? Until 1999, all prospective IPO investors, retail and institutional, were required to submit an application for IPO shares in a nationwide lottery. In contrast to a similar lottery system in Hong Kong, however, the submission of an application did not guarantee receipt of even a minimum lot of shares. In China, the success ratio of the lottery is applied against the number of applications submitted.

For example, a deal that is a thousand times oversubscribed means an investor has a 0.1 percent chance of having his application selected. He can enhance his odds, however, by submitting as many separate applications as he can afford, placing a full deposit with his broker to back up each bid. This is the arrangement that has led to the market's characteristically wild oversubscriptions. To ensure even a small allocation, it is not unusual to see investors producing enough money to subscribe for the entire offering! The system is clearly biased against the small investor and in favor of big institutions with lots of money, whether borrowed from banks or their own.

The system did not work well during the stagflation of the late 1990s, so the CSRC created this category of "real strategic" investors, which was broadly defined to include everything in the Chinese economic land-scape including, most certainly, listed SOEs and their parent groups. Such "strategic" investors would agree to buy a block of shares at issue price before a deal was formally launched. Although subject to a lock-up period of, generally one year, they received a full allocation of their order. In contrast, as regular investors, whether offline or online, they were not assured of receiving any allocation, much less a full one, no matter how many forms they had submitted.

In 2006, recovering markets that had hosted no IPOs in over a year faced a potential flood of listings from the National Champions, which meant that strategic investors were once again in demand. Of the 24 Shanghai listings completed between June 2006 and June 2007, 14 benefited from the support of strategic investors, even when the amounts raised in the open lotteries were many times the IPO proceeds (see Table 7.3). For example, for ICBC's massive IPO, 23 "strategic" investors (including a couple of the AMCs) contributed RMB18 billion (US$2.2 billion) to ensure the bank's success (see Table 7.4). All of these investors were central government enterprises. They were given full allocations and their subscriptions represented 38 percent of total funds raised. Everyone else put in RMB781 billion for an IPO which, even though it was 17 times oversubscribed, only jumped in price by an unsatisfying five percent on the first day, showing just how weak primary markets were then and just how important, there-fore, strategic investors were to completing the IPO.

TABLE 7.3 Strategic investors in Shanghai IPOs, June 2006–June 2007, July 2010

Stock	Listing Date	IPO Funds Raised (RMB million)	Gross Subscriptions (RMB million)	Times Oversubscribed	Allocation to Strategic Investors (%)
Bank of China	7/5/06	20,000	670,355	33.5	19.8
Daqin Railway	8/1/06	15,000	552,675	36.9	30.0
Air China*	8/18/06	4,589	44,586	9.7	21.4
Beijing North Star*	10/16/06	3,600	242,055	67.2	36.7
ICBC	10/27/06	46,644	781,031	16.8	38.6
China Merchants Energy Shipping	12/1/06	4,452	381,135	84.7	28.8
Datang International Power*	12/20/06	3,340	303,841	91.8	39.4
Guangshen Railway*	12/22/06	10,332	450,682	43.7	33.9
China Life*	1/9/07	28,320	832,541	29.4	40.0
Industrial Bank	2/5/07	15,996	1,163,348	72.7	30.0
Ping An Insurance*	3/1/07	38,870	1,093,573	28.1	30.0
China CITIC Bank	4/27/07	13,351	1,402,178	105.4	22.5
Bank of Communications*	5/15/07	25,204	1,454,352	57.7	30.0
China COSCO*	6/26/07	15,127	1,629,048	107.2	30.0
Agricultural Bank of China	7/15/10	59.591	480,253	8.1	40.0

Source: Wind Information and author calculations

Note: * denotes overseas returnee listing

TABLE 7.4 Strategic investors in ICBC's A-share IPO

	Name	Value of shares allocated (RMB billion)
1	China Life Insurance (Group) Co.	2.0
2	China Life Insurance Co. Ltd.	2.0
3	China Pacific Life Insurance Co. Ltd.	2.0
4	China Huarong Asset Management Co.	1.5
5	Ping An Life Insurance Co. Ltd.	1.1
6	China Huaneng Group Co.	1.0
7	China Guangdong Nuclear Group Co. Ltd.	0.9
8	COFCO Group Co. Ltd.	0.8
9	BaoGang Group Co. Ltd.	0.5
10	Dongfeng Motors Co.	0.5
11	State Development Investment Co.	0.5
12	Capital Airport Group Co.	0.5
13	Taikang Life Insurance Co. Ltd.	0.5
14	Pacific Life Insurance Co. Ltd.	0.5
15	Minmetals Investment Development Co. Ltd.	0.5
16	Xinhua Life Insurance Co. Ltd.	0.5
17	China Eastern Asset Management Co.	0.5
18	China Offshore Oil General Co.	0.5
19	China Re-insurance Group Co.	0.5
20	China Yangtze Power Co. Ltd	0.4
21	China Machinery Industry Group Co.	0.4
22	China Nuclear Industry Group Co.	0.3
23	Huatai Property Insurance Co. Ltd.	0.2
	Total	18.0

Source: ICBC public notice, October 17, 2006

Once the market picked up, however, strategic investors were no longer needed until, that is, the huge Agricultural Bank of China IPO in July 2010, which the government sought to make the world's largest. It was able to achieve its goal of raising nearly US$9 billion in Shanghai only by relying on a group of 27 strategic investors for 40 percent of an offering that received a very weak reception and was only a little over eight times oversubscribed. This time, 50 percent of strategic allocations were subject to an 18-month lock-up period, indicating again just how weak the reception for the ABC IPO was. By comparison, CCB's IPO raised US$1 billion less in its Shanghai offering but attracted RMB1.7 trillion (US$210 billion) in lottery applications. Then there was China Railway Group, with some US$400 billion in applications (see Table 7.6).

This arrangement served all the important parties well. It meant that the larger deals were about a third sold before they had even been announced, so the downside risk was well covered. But, most importantly, the major investors were able to access huge blocks of otherwise unobtainable shares in the "strategic" group. They were able to hedge these shares, which were by regulation locked up, by massively participating in the open online lottery, in which there was no lock-up period and which, in normal circumstances, guaranteed them eye-popping IPO returns, as discussed in the next section. The lucrative involvement of "family and friends" in an SOE's IPO ensures that it will receive support from the same group if and when they are called upon: a favor received means a favor returned at a later date.

An example of who such friends were in the case of ABC's IPO can be seen in Table 7.5. The biggest investors included China's major life-insurance companies and the finance subsidiaries of several National Champions. Further down the list of 173 investors were the proprietary trading accounts of almost the entire list of the SASAC's National Team as well as asset-management companies and the always profit-oriented Military Weapons Equipment Group Company. These offline friends accounted for 20 percent of the offering. In short, some 60 percent of ABC's Shanghai listing was supported by the government acting through its National Team. These investors, despite the policy reason for their participation, could not have been heartened by ABC's modest performance. The first day after listing, its shares rose only one percent, as compared to an average jump of 69 percent even in 2010's weak market.

ABC's IPO came in the aftermath of the Great Shanghai Bubble of 2007. From June of that year, the market entered the final stage of its heroic bubble, rising 50 percent in four months to nearly 6,100 points. Many people, caught up in the euphoria, believed the index would easily break 10,000 by year-end. During this period, 17 more companies listed on the Shanghai exchange, including PetroChina, China Shenhua Energy and

TABLE 7.5 Top 20 offline investors in the Agricultural Bank of China A-share IPO

	Name	Value of shares allocated (RMB million)
1	Ping An Life Insurance designated accounts	1,668.6
2	CNOOC Finance Co. proprietary account	1,195.4
2	Shengming Life Insurance Co. designated account	1,195.4
3	People's Insurance Co. managed accounts	929.3
4	Ping An Insurance Co. proprietary account	896.6
5	China Pacific Insurance Co. managed account	650.5
6	Taikang Life Insurance Co. managed accounts	525.3
7	China Power Finance Co. proprietary account	448.3
8	Xinhua Life Insurance designated account	366.1
8	NSSF designated accounts	335.9
9	CITIC Trust designated account	278.8
10	China Aviation Engineering Finance Co. proprietary account	149.4
10	Deutsche Bank QFII account	149.4
11	Jiashi Top 300 Index Fund	97.6
12	Daiya Bay Nuclear Power Finance Co. proprietary account	92.2
12	Red Tower Securities Co. proprietary account	92.2
13	Boshi Stable Value Fund	83.4
14	Yifang Top 50 Fund	72.2
15	Fuguo Tianyi Value Fund	55.8
15	Jingshun Growth Equity Fund	55.3

Source: ABC public notice, July 8, 2010

CCB, and none used the formal strategic-investor route (see Table 7.6). The reason for this is simple: there was no longer any need; the market was full of liquidity and listing success was guaranteed.

This is not to say that these IPOs did not attract the small investor. But in almost any market circumstance, the average deposit required to secure an application was far beyond the reach of any normal retail investor.

TABLE 7.6   IPOs in the closing days of the Great Shanghai Bubble, 2006–2007

Name	Listing date	IPO funds raised (RMB million)	Gross subscriptions (RMB million)
Western Mining	7/12/07	6,201	1,513,153
Bank of Nanjing	7/19/07	6,930	1,038,148
Bank of Beijing	9/19/07	15,000	1,895,082
CCB	9/25/07	58,050	2,260,607
China Oilfield Services	9/28/07	6,740	2,172,919
China Shenhua Energy	10/9/07	66,582	2,667,983
PetroChina	11/5/07	66,800	3,377,823
China Railway Group	12/3/07	22,440	3,388,054
SDIC Xinji Energy	12/19/07	2,070	543,604
China Shipping Container	12/12/07	15,468	2,642,019
Liaoning Publishing	12/21/07	650	196,639
China Pacific Insurance	12/25/07	30,000	2,830,185
China Coal	2/11/08	25,671	3,124,485
China Railway Construction	3/10/08	22,246	3,126,496
Jinduisheng Molybdenum	4/17/08	8,915	2,257,595
Zijin Mining	4/25/08	9,982	2,149,420
China South Locomotive	8/18/08	6,540	2,269,547

Source: Wind Information and author calculations

During the mid-2006 to mid-2007 period, the average online "retail" bid was nearly RMB700,000; in the second half of 2007, when strategic investors were no longer needed, it rose to RMB1.2 million *on average*. During this period, there were more than a million online investors per IPO; PetroChina attracted over four million. So while small investors most certainly came out to help boost the number of applications, they did not account for the bulk of the money put down online: institutions did.

As for the offline tranche, the amounts of money involved could be staggering. For example, in PetroChina's Shanghai IPO, 484 institutional investors successfully bid for allocations in an offline tranche that accounted for 25 percent of the entire share offer. The smallest successful bid was made by the appliance-maker Haier, which received 2,089 shares and was refunded RMB1.64 million from its lottery deposit. The largest was Ping An Life, which received a total of 119 million shares in a handful of separate accounts and got back RMB93.2 billion (US$11.4 billion) in excess bid deposits. Not far behind was China Life, with over 100 million shares and deposits worth RMB78.5 billion (about US$10 billion) returned. Reviewing the 400-plus names reveals a *Who's Who* of China's top financial and industrial companies, including even the Military Weapons Equipment Group Company (*Bingwu Gongsi*) of the People's Liberation Army.

If one of the original goals of creating stock exchanges was, as stated, to ensure the primacy of a socialist economy overseen by the Party, then China's experience with stocks has succeeded far beyond any reasonable expectation.

Keeping everyone happy: Primary-market performance

In addition to the lottery arrangements that create mass feeding frenzies, the share valuation mechanism set by the CSRC explains the popularity of IPOs in China. Simply put, prices are knowingly set artificially low while demand is set high, with the result that big price jumps on listing day are virtually guaranteed (see Table 7.7). This approach also eliminates underwriting risk so that securities firms need not be concerned that their underwriting fees are so thin. But this all comes at a cost. The pricing process eliminates the need for investors to understand companies and the industries in which they operate to arrive at a judgment as to valuation.

Since the process is dumbed down to a formula, underwriters have never learned how to value companies and price risk. Even worse, the investor population, in whatever category, never became educated as to the values of different companies, the prospects for their shares, or the risks associated with investing. Over time, the result has been that companies became commodities and getting an allocation of shares, any shares, became the sole objective and wildly oversubscribed IPOs were the result. From another angle, what these valuations of China's National Champions are most certainly not revealing is Chinese management skill, technical innovation, entrepreneurial flair, or the growth of genuine companies.

TABLE 7.7 A-share listing-day price performance

Year	Number of Listings	Average first-day jump (%)	Average first-day turnover* (%)
2010	127	47	69
2009	99	74	79
2008	77	115	80
2007	126	193	65
2006	66	84	70
2005	14	48	58
2004	100	70	55
2003	67	72	52
2002	68	134	62
2001	77	138	64
2000	135	152	59
1999	93	113	60
1998	92	149	62

Source: Wind Information; author's calculations; 2010 data through March 31
Note: * represents the amount of shares sold as a percentage of what was allowed to be sold on the first day.

What they do show is the state's confidence in its own ability that, when push comes to shove, it can manage the market index so that it will go up and the state's holdings will increase in value. Chinese investors refer to their stock markets as "policy" markets for this very reason: they move on the expectation of government policy changes and not on news of company performance. The fundamental value-creation proposition in China is the government, not its enterprises.

In spite of this, prices play a huge role, although not in valuing the risk related to the business prospects of companies. As mentioned, the CSRC formulas uniformly result in share valuations well below prevailing market demand so that double-digit and triple-digit first-day jumps in prices become par for the course. Put another way, the regulator requires that companies and their underwriters price shares in a completely opposite way to market practice in Western markets. Forced by their ultimate state owner, companies effectively sell their two-yuan shares for one yuan.

FIGURE 7.5   Money left on the table

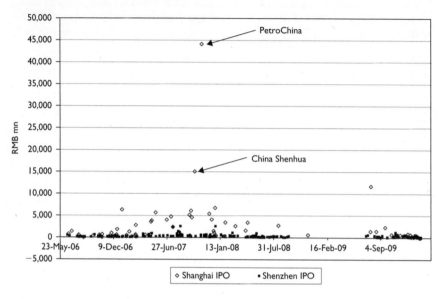

Source: Wind Information and authors' calculations

From an international perspective, the losses to companies arising from this practice are enormous. As an extreme example, take PetroChina. The company raised RMB67 billion (US$9.2 billion) in its Shanghai IPO and received RMB3.4 trillion (US$462 billion) in subscription deposits. The difference between its actual share price and a market-clearing price based on actual demand is shown in Figure 7.5. As indicated, PetroChina's cheap pricing meant that it had left RMB45 billion (US$6.2 billion) on the table. Not surprisingly, on its listing, PetroChina's shares jumped nearly 200 percent, giving it, albeit briefly, a market capitalization of more than US$1 trillion. From a developed-market viewpoint, this was a complete crime. It should have been an even bigger crime in the SASAC's eyes, given the cheap sell-out of state assets. From the company's viewpoint, an astute chairman would have wondered why he had just sold 10 percent of his company at half the value attributed to it by the secondary market. To put it another way, he had sold US$16.8 billion of stock for just US$8.9 billion. In an international market, he would, no doubt, have fired his investment bankers outright and then been fired by his board.

But this money, as shown previously, was hardly lost to the state: it had just been given to those state-owned institutions, the group of "family and friends" that had participated in the prearranged lottery. From this, it seems that IPOs function as a means to redistribute capital among state entities with, possibly, some leakage into the hands of retail investors and mutual-fund holders to smooth things out.

The looking-glass culture of these markets creates figures such as the chairman of China Shenhua Energy, Chen Biting, who could say without a trace of irony: "The debut price was within expectations, but I am still a wee bit disappointed."[7] His lament was that on the first day of Shenhua's IPO, its shares jumped only 87 percent, leaving just RMB15 billion on the table for his friends. Such generosity characterized the highs of the 2007 stock bubble and Chen was no doubt looking for a doubling of his company's share price. If he had been running PetroChina, he would have been much happier, it seems. After all, PetroChina's chairman, Jiang Jiemin, could look his buddies straight in the eyes, knowing that he had delivered for them and the Party that backed them all up. More importantly, he knew that he could now count on their continued support should he need it.

For those in the central *nomenklatura* of the Party, there are no independent institutions, only the Party organization and it is indifferent as to which box does what. On the other hand, just think how relieved the two AMC investors in ICBC's Shanghai IPO must have felt, knowing they had made enough quick money to pay interest on the PBOC and bank bonds.

Whose hot money?: The trading market

The stock market money-machine works best when IPO prices are cheap and there is huge liquidity in the trading market. This environment drives up the prices of "strategic" investments locked up in the hands of the state investor pool. As is the case in the IPO market, this money does not come from retail investors, as the state would have us believe. From roughly 1995 until the present day, the Chinese secondary markets have been dominated by institutional traders; that is, SOEs and state agencies. Their investment decisions move the market index. While much of the evidence is anecdotal, it has been estimated that anywhere up to 20 percent of corporate profits came from stock trading in 2007. The authors themselves once received a call from a recently listed company asking for advice on how to set up an equity trading desk now that management had some cash in hand. Given the ability to achieve a return greater than the bank deposit rate and the ease with which trading can be disguised, why wouldn't a corporate treasurer look to make some easy money while the market is running hot?

Based though it is on sparse public information, Table 7.8 provides a rough breakdown by types of investors in Chinese A-shares at the end of 2006, just as the market was beginning its historic boom. The market reforms of 2005 notwithstanding, shares owned in various ways by the original state investors remain locked up. As a result, the tradable market capitalization is a known figure and at FY2006 totaled US$405 billion. The figure for domestic mutual funds is published quarterly. The retail number is based on the assumption that half of retail investors invest through mutual funds and half invest directly. If accurate, this would mean that retail investors account for nearly 30 percent of the traded

TABLE 7.8 Investors in China's stock markets, December 31, 2006

	US$ billion	% of Total
Total A-share market capitalization	1,318	100.0
Less: capitalization under three-year lock-up	913	69.3
Tradable market capitalization	405	100.0
Total identifiable institutional investors including:	100	24.7
- Domestic funds (actual number)	60	14.8
- QFII (100% of existing total approved quota)	20	4.9
- Securities companies estimate	10	2.5
- NSSF (100% of approved limit)	5	1.2
- Insurance companies (100% of approved limit)	5	1.2
Estimated retail investors	60	14.8
Estimated other investors including:	245	60.5
- State agencies	115	28.4
- State enterprises	65	16.0
- Large-scale private investors	65	16.0

Source: *China Economic Quarterly* 2007 Q1, p. 11

market; this is considered to be a high estimate. The size of total Qualified Foreign Institutional Investor (QFII) quotas is publicly known, although the investment mix is not, and the NSSF and insurance companies at this time had known restrictions as to how much they could invest in shares. The assumption in each of these three cases is that 100 percent of their approved quotas was placed in equities; this yields a US$30 billion estimate. Netting all of these knowable fund sources out of the tradable market means that some *60 percent*, or US$245 billion, of the A-share float as of year-end 2006 cannot be linked to identifiable categories of investor.

Who are these unknown investors that own the majority of the A-share float? Almost certainly, they include many overseas Chinese tycoons who have the wherewithal to evade the prohibition on foreign individual investments in A-shares. More interestingly, during the market ramp-up in 2006, many domestic financial reporters believed the market rumor that China's army and police forces alone had brought onshore upward of US$120 billion and committed it all to stock investments. While this figure is outlandish, it may have been possible that a smaller amount had been repatriated and invested just as the market began its upward move in 2006, resulting in this much higher value. But there can be no doubt that SOEs and government agencies between them must have held some US$180 billion in *tradable* shares in addition to shares they held subject to a lock-up.

A CASINO OR A SUCCESS, OR BOTH?

It has been nearly two decades since the Shanghai and Shenzhen exchanges were established. Why, if they are still regarded as casinos, have they been so successful? How have they come to be seen as beacons of China's economic reform and attained such central roles in the country's economic model? The answer is simple: you can make money from them. These markets are driven by liquidity and speculative forces, given the almost-arbitrary business decisions made by companies influenced more by politics than profit. How can this not be the case when companies are the property of the Party and its families?

Such a market may seem daunting to investors from developed markets, but the Chinese are long accustomed to operating in a No Man's Land of political interference and contradictory signals. None of this stops them from playing or being played by the market: if you buy a share at RMB10 and sell at RMB15, you do make RMB5. Putting money on deposit with banks or playing the bond market is hardly worth the effort; interest rates are set in favor of state borrowers, not lenders, so they do not provide a real return over the rate of inflation.

In China, the only two ways to make this real return are property and the stock markets. Of the two, the stock markets are preferable since they are more flexible than the property market (not that those with the means cannot play both). The investment measure in stocks may be smaller, but liquidity is substantially better than the property market. In contrast to interest rates, the equity market equivalent, the price-to-earnings (PE) ratio, is free to run as high as the market will take it. In the glory days of the Golden Bull Market from 2006 to 2007, the overall Shanghai PE multiple rallied from 15 to nearly 50 times. With that sort of valuation expansion, the upside is very large indeed.

The Chinese market simply doesn't have natural stock investors: every body is a speculator. Chinese history and bitter experience teach that life is too volatile and uncertain to take the long-term view. The natural result of this is a market dominated by short-term traders, all dreaming of a quick return. The one natural investor is the state itself and it already owns the National Champions. In contrast, ownership in developed markets is far more diversified; large companies simply do not have dominant share-holders owning more than 50 percent of their shares. For example, the largest shareholder of Switzerland's biggest banking group, UBS, is the Government Investment Company of Singapore, with less than a seven percent holding. Contrast that with Bank of China: even after its IPO the bank's largest shareholder, Huijin, still controlled 67.5 percent of the bank's stock.

Since China's stock markets, which include Hong Kong, are not places that decide corporate control, the pricing of shares carries little weight when thinking about the whole company simply because it is never for sale. This is why there is no true M&A business in China and most definitely none involving non-state or private enterprises acquiring listed SOEs. Instead, market consolidation is driven by government fiat and is accomplished by mixing listed and unlisted assets at arbitrary valuations. This leaves share prices to simply reflect market liquidity and demand at any given time. The high trading volumes in the market are its most misleading characteristic since they give outside observers the impression that it is a proper market. High volumes lend credibility to the idea that prices are sending a signal about the economy or a company's prospects. In fact, in China, all that the volume represents is excess liquidity.

All markets are driven by a mixture of factors, including liquidity (how much money is in the system); speculation (the belief in making a profit from market volatility); and economic fundamentals (the underlying business prospects and performance of listed companies). Chinese markets are often seen to be decoupled from the actual economic fundamentals of the country. A rough comparison of simple GDP growth and market performance would certainly show minimal correlation between the two. As long as Chinese A-shares ignore economic fundamentals, the market will always be thought of as a casino and too risky for most investors. Chinese investors, however, instinctively know what they are buying because they think the share price is going up, not because the company that issued the shares is having a great quarter or the economy is having a record year.

Much of the effort over the 1990s to develop the markets was aimed at strengthening this fundamental component by creating or introducing more long-term institutional investors, as in developed markets. The entire domestic mutual-fund business was created by the CSRC in the late 1990s with this in mind. The introduction of foreign investors in 2002 via the QFII facility was another step in this direction. The growing volume of company and economic research from local and foreign brokerage houses is all based on the belief that China's markets are becoming, or will become, more fundamental and driven from the bottom up.

This entire effort is misdirected. It isn't the absence of equity research that makes the market a casino. It is the absence of genuinely accountable companies subject to market and investor discipline. If the chairmen/CEOs of China's major companies care little about the SASAC, they care still less about the Shanghai stock exchange or the legion of domestic equity analysts. The CEO knows full well that his company possesses the resources to assure the performance of its own shares. The National Champions dominate China's stock markets, accounting for the lion's share of market capitalization, value traded and funds raised.

The growing number of private (non-state) companies listed on Shenzhen's SME and ChiNext boards is encouraging, but most of these companies, with few exceptions, are tiny in the broader market context. Perhaps investors can look at the SME or ChiNext market and apply the usual investment analysis used in the international markets, but how can an investor look at PetroChina and compare it with ExxonMobil when it is nearly 85 percent controlled by the state and will remain so as long as the Party remains in power? It is the same with China Mobile or China Unicom; can they really be compared with Vodafone, T-Mobile, or BhartiAirtel? The fact that foreign telecommunication providers are barred from China's domestic market means that China Mobile and China Unicom have a comfortable duopoly. Their privileged positions are simply not subject to the same regulatory or market checks and balances that their global peers face.

The fact that the National Champions are all jumping at the chance to invest in China's suddenly undercapitalized banks surely flags the question of whether National Champions can be looked upon as genuine companies or simple extensions of the government. How else to view China Mobile's acquisition of a 20 percent "strategic" stake valued at US$5.8 billion in the Shanghai Pudong Development Bank, or China Unicom's investment in the Bank of Communications, or Alibaba.com's (China's Google) investment in China Minsheng Bank?

IMPLICATIONS

Hovering over all this activity are the CSRC and the state in general. The state is involved at every stage of the market as the regulator, the policymaker, the investor, the parent company, the listed company, the broker, the bank and the banker. In short, the state acts as the staff for China's major SOEs. With the National Team formed and with its senior management being coterminous with the very center of political power, can there be any true reform of corporate governance? Is it likely that they would accept the creation of a Super Regulator with real authority over the market and their own conduct? With the existing regulator already on their side, ensuring that the market is tuned in their favor, why would they want foreigners with their own ideas of how markets operate to have significant influence? So, no meaningful opening to foreign participation can be expected. In fact, the scope of foreign influence can be expected to be cut back even further as Chinese securities companies, law firms and auditors assert themselves and Chinese-style regulation is extended from Shanghai to Hong Kong.

In late 2009, the first material step in this direction took place when the Hong Kong Stock Exchange indicated it would accept Chinese firms as auditors for Chinese companies listed on the Hong Kong exchange subject to their vetting by the MOF or the CSRC. Ostensibly, this was done to make Hong Kong more competitive with Shanghai, since Chinese auditors are far less costly than major international firms. Since the quality and reliability of disclosure is what this is all about, can international investors expect local firms charging one-third the price to produce meaningful financial reports of increasingly complex national companies? As for vetting by the MOF or the CSRC, one might expect a handful of firms to receive approval and that these firms would be quite attentive to the needs of the National Team and their staff. If foreign investment banks and others are now struggling to establish a presence in China's domestic markets, it can only be because they know that their days in the lucrative Hong Kong market are numbered.

Since China Life's IPO on the New York Stock Exchange in 2003 was investigated for a possible Sarbanes-Oxley violation (there was none), no other members of the National Team have listed there. Instead, Hong Kong became the venue of choice. Now the overseas "returnees" are moving back to Shanghai where things, as one SOE chairman put it, are "a bit easier to manage". This trend of events is quite ironic if it is considered in the context of why China opened its border to international share offerings. When Zhu Rongji gave the go-ahead for overseas listings in 1993, one of the key reasons was that the more professional and demanding standards of the Hong Kong regulators and international legal and accounting standards would upgrade the management capacity of China's enterprises. Would Zhu now believe that after less than 20 years, his goals for China's SOEs and their management have been achieved?

ENDNOTES

1 The NDRC's predecessor was the State Planning Commission (SPC), which was founded in 1952. The SPC was renamed the State Development Planning Commission (SDPC) in 1998. After merging with the State Council Office for Restructuring the Economic System (SCORES) and part of the State Economic and Trade Commission (SETC) in 2003, the SDPC was restructured into the NDRC.

2 See Kjeld Erik Brodsgaard, "Politics and business group formation in China—the Party in control?" unpublished manuscript, April 2010.

3　If it can be found, see *Caijing* 财经 176, January 8, 2007: 28–44. The issue was pulled from the market the day it was published.

4　*Ibid.*: 42.

5　See Walter and Howie 2006: Chapters 9 and 10.

6　There are two major investor categories at present: 1) the "strategic investor" (*zhanlue touzizhe* 战略投资者) who participates prior to the formal announcement of the transaction, gets a full allocation, but is subject to a one-year lock-up; and 2) those investors participating after the formal announcement, of which there are two types: a) the "offline" "regular legal person investor" (*yiban faren touzizhe* 一般法人投资者), who is subject to a three-month lock-up; and b) the "online" investor, which includes retail and any other investor desiring to participate, who is not subject to any lock-up. In this last category, investors participate in the lottery and orders are subject to allocation.

7　"Shenhua soars 87 percent but chief still not happy," *South China Morning Post*, October 10, 2007.

CHAPTER

8

The Forbidden City

A huge vermillion compound filled with immense golden-roofed palaces, moats, hidden gardens and carved dragons, the Forbidden City is the heart of China's capital. It is a masterpiece that belongs to both China and the world, for surely by now half the world must have walked through its spaces. Perhaps the significance of its structural layout exceeds even the riches left by the Yuan, Ming and Qing Dynasties and goes to the heart of Chinese organizational culture.

Entering the palace through the Meridian Gate, one is struck with the great spaces enveloped by looming outer walls. Once through these massive walls, the visitor walks across marble bridges spanning the Golden Waters toward the Gate of Supreme Harmony. This is another, even broader, space, overwhelming in its grandeur, its walls receding into the distance. The courtyard's overall design is awe-inspiring; it seems to encompass both heaven and earth. As one penetrates more deeply into the palace, however, spaces become smaller, and long, narrow corridors are punctuated here and there by small entrances. The huge walls close in, progressively blocking off all lines of sight.

Even before finally entering the Imperial Garden, with its constricted space, rock gardens and towering Hall of Imperial Peace, the visitor comes to the realization that, like the gardens and the trees, he too is boxed in by the design. The great spaces at the Palace entrance are mere illusions because, in truth, there is just one way to look beyond the walls and that is to look up. Only the Emperor in his palaces atop the walls could see into the courtyards both large and small; those below were constrained to act within their allotted space. Cut off by walls from other courtyards and, indeed, the rest of the Palace, within their own space people were free to pursue the activities assigned to them. Only the Emperor had the authority to intervene and only he could understand the larger design of their work.

The workings of the Forbidden City in Imperial times serve as a metaphor for China's government and political practice today. At the center lies Beijing, a complex labyrinth of separate power centers, each with just a single reporting line that extends up to the party secretary general (although nominally through the State Council, the premier and the National People's Congress). Coordination or integrated action across multiple bureaucracies is difficult and time-consuming unless it is ordered by the party secretary general. Without a strong leader, each bureaucracy proceeds within its own scope of authority and jealously guards the entrance to its courtyard. The only way to join the "emperor" in his palaces a top the walls is either through lineage, or by maximizing achievements within one's own narrow grounds, or both. Then, of course, there may be some who prefer to stay within their own courtyards, pursuing their own interests.

As the China Development Bank's attempt to replace the Ministry of Finance in the bond markets and the tug-of-war between the MOF and the People's Bank of China over control of the major banks have shown, there is a great deal of predatory behavior exhibited within the walls of this monumental edifice. There is also much copycat behavior. The China Securities Regulatory Commission (CSRC) has its securities companies and stock markets in one courtyard; in another, the China Banking Regulatory Commission (CBRC) has its own investment-banking platform, the trust companies, and access to the debt markets. And how else to explain the SASAC's belated press release that it has created its own domestic sovereign-wealth fund in replication of China Investment Corporation; or to explain Huijin, which itself replicates SAFE Investments? It would be easy, of course, to go beyond these relatively specialized entities to include the large SOEs. When PetroChina acquires companies overseas on behalf of the government, isn't it also a sovereign-wealth fund? All this demands the simple question: What in China isn't a sovereign-wealth fund?

Only a strong premier or party secretary can coordinate such activity to ensure it is in line with the Party's general goals; only they can channel the energies of government and Party leaders and minimize costs. The absence of a strong leader is a weakness that allows the special-interest groups to take advantage. A vice-premier in charge of finance may understand his remit, but unless he has the ear of the general secretary, it is to no avail. A central bank governor may know clearly the critical issues across the financial maze, but unless he is supported, political compromise will trump all else. On the other hand, for the National Team, the less scrutiny there is, the better.

THE EMPEROR OF FINANCE

This perspective suggests just how great an achievement the securities markets, no matter how flawed, really are. From 1992, for the first time in its long history, China had a national market and it was a market for capital, and that capital could flow without hindrance across all government jurisdictions. Not only that, at the start these markets had a single "emperor" overseeing them, the People's Bank of China. The PBOC (or, more accurately, its powerful provincial branches, together with the local Party) was the great force behind market development during the late 1980s. Liu Hongru, a PBOC vice-governor at the time, is commonly recognized by all participants as the "godfather" of the stock markets. The central bank oversaw the establishment of China's first 34 securities companies in 1988. From 1985, its Shenzhen branch played a critical role in developing market infrastructure and regulations, while the PBOC head office played the key coordination role among government-market stakeholders. Without the PBOC's initiative and support, China's experiment with shares and stock markets would have been stillborn. Moreover, the PBOC's sponsorship opened the international markets to Chinese IPOs, as was resoundingly demonstrated in October 1992 with the first-ever listing of a Chinese SOE on the New York Stock Exchange. This sort of daring would never have been possible with consensus leadership.

Over the course of the 1990s a fragmented regulatory environment began to take shape, particularly after 1997 when Zhu Rongji moved the government-bond market from the securities exchanges and the CSRC's oversight to the inter-bank market under the supervision of the PBOC. This was just the beginning. By 2003, seven regulators were responsible for the four major categories of bond products, and equity and commodities had also been parceled out. Each regulator had its favored group of financial institutions or markets—the PBOC had the debt markets; the CSRC and the NDRC had the securities companies and commodities brokers; the

MOF had the banks; the CBRC had the trust companies; and the CIRC had insurance companies and private-equity funds. Now even the NDRC is looking for that special vehicle that can give it access to the financial markets. The capital markets are thus divided up into small areas of special interest and members of that group are thereby guaranteed a slice of the action with the help of their own patrons (see Figure 8.1).

This is not to say that a single Super Regulator is necessarily the answer to coordination across China's capital markets. There are good reasons for different regulators for different sectors; stock broking is not banking, and vice versa. The trouble is that in China, the different regulators have over the past few years created so-called "independent kingdoms"; effective coordination across these fiefdoms has been difficult in the apparent absence of strong political leadership.

The lack of a unitary market regulator may have been less important in the 1990s when banks were almost the sole source of capital in the

FIGURE 8.1 Capital-market products by regulator and business beneficiary, FY2009

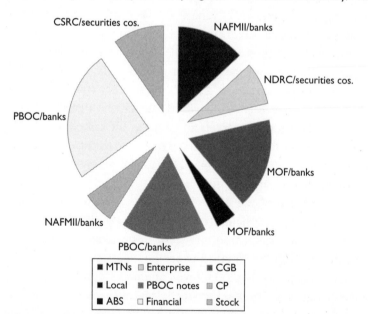

Source: Wind Information

economy. But after the Asian Financial Crisis, Zhu Rongji's plans to radically restructure the Big 4 banks required a far more integrated approach. Recapitalizing the banks was only one part of a larger plan designed to address the problem of systemic risk. But an integrated solution required the coordination and active support of a wide variety of government agencies including the MOF, the SPC/NDRC, the CSRC and the PBOC. Who would lead? Zhu Rongji was both willing and able to drive financial reform forward until the end of his term in 2003; the momentum that had built up from 1998 carried through until 2005. But, in his absence, when the PBOC sought to institutionalize these reforms in 2005, with itself as the Super Financial Regulator, supporters of the status quo, led by the MOF, pushed back hard enough to stop the consolidation of an integrated approach to financial markets.

As outlined in earlier chapters, when the MOF took back control of the banks from the PBOC, China's financial system incurred a high cost for its bureaucratic revenge. Foreign investors made a down payment through their participation in IPOs that were, in fact, a prepayment of cash dividends used to make good the interest payments on the MOF's Special Bond. For their part, China's major banks became simple channels for this interest, as well as for payments on the special "receivables" the MOF used to restructure Industrial and Commercial Bank of China and Agricultural Bank of China. It would seem that with the MOF's interest being paid by the banks, the national budget did not need to bear the expense. Perhaps this explains why this Special Bond is no longer recorded in the PBOC's central depository; after December 31, 2007, these bonds simply disappeared. In addition, the major banks are now in search of another US$42 billion to fill an equivalent gap in their capital created by dividend payments. Even more ungainly, the new sovereign-wealth fund suddenly found itself to be the heart of the entire banking system.

These are the costs to the system when complexity reigns and there is no "Emperor of Finance". Since 2005, there has been some talk of a unitary financial regulatory body, but there has been little of any substance to emerge except, perhaps, the idea of a "Super Coordinating Commission" that would include all stakeholders. However, just such an agency had existed before, in the late 1980s, and had proved a failure. Who would lead such a commission when even previous coordinating meetings between these regulatory agencies had lapsed into disuse because of "scheduling difficulties"?

BEHIND THE VERMILLION WALLS

So, without a strong champion for change, the status quo asserted itself; each of the major stakeholders in the system settled back inside its own "courtyard" and pursued their own interests including, especially, seeking access to increasing amounts of bank money. This poorly coordinated chase for funding has rapidly led to significant growth in China's public-debt burden. The data in Table 8.1 illustrate the various stakeholders who have contributed to China's stock of public obligations. For simplicity, the only changes in the projection for 2011 from 2009 are in the estimates of local-government obligations and non-performing loans, the two areas with potentially the greatest variability. These estimates are meant to be conservative and serve simply to show the scale of debt that has already been built up. To be clear, these numbers represent debt obligations; this does not imply that there is no value to the assets or services or other activities that such debt finances. But at a certain point, the cost of these liabilities adds up to a critical mass, becomes burdensome for an economy, and begins to inhibit economic growth. The international standard for such a red line is 60 percent of GDP, beyond which growth may suffer as a government spends more on managing its debt burden than on investing in growth-creating programs.

The table shows that if only the obligations of the MOF (as representative of the sovereign) are used to define central-government debt, then China's debt ratio is less than 20 percent of GDP, well below the international standard. This is the commonly held view, but it ignores how Beijing has structured its finances over the past decade. The MOF once funded a national budget that included major investments in infrastructure and other fixed assets. Today, such projects are outside the budget and are the responsibility of the policy banks and an aggressive Ministry of Railways (MOR). The obligations of these near-sovereign (if not fully sovereign) entities should be included as part of China's public debt: would the Party allow any of the policy banks to fail? Such sovereign entities include the MOR, the policy banks, the subordinate debt of the major state banks, as well as any known contingent obligations incurred by the MOF itself

TABLE 8.1 China public-debt obligations, 2009 and 2011

RMB million	FY2009A	% GDP	FY2011P	% GDP
GDP 2009 Actual, 2011 Projected	**33,535.3**		**42,066.7**	
A) Central Government Obligations				
Central government	6,471.0	19.3%	6,471.0	15.4%
Ministry of Finance receivable, ICBC and ABC	807.9	2.4%	807.9	1.9%
Ministry of Finance 1998 + 2007 Special Bonds	1,820.0	5.4%	1,820.0	4.3%
China Development Bank bonds	3,200.6	9.5%	3,200.6	7.6%
Agriculture Development Bank bonds	438.3	1.3%	438.3	1.0%
Export-Import Bank bonds	810.9	2.4%	810.9	1.9%
Ministry of Railways (MOR) bonds	396.0	1.2%	396.0	0.9%
Big 4 Bank subordinated debt	345.1	1.0%	345.1	0.8%
Sub-total: Central Obligations	14,289.8	42.6%	14,289.8	34.0%
B) Local Government Obligations				
a. Current o/s local debt FY2009	7,800.0	23.3%		
b. Assume new local debt of RMB4 trillion			11,800.0	28.1%
Sub-total: Local Obligations + Central	7,800.0	23.3%	11,800.0	28.1%
C) NPLs				
a. Asset-management company outstanding obligations	2,730.0	8.1%	2,730.0	6.5%
b. 20% NPL rate on 2009–2010 non-local loans	0.0	0.0%	3,200.0	7.6%
c. Existing NPLs as of FY2009	504.0	1.5%	504.0	1.2%
Sub-total: NPLs	3,234.0	9.6%	6,434.0	15.3%
Public debt to GDP		75.5%		77.3%

Notes: a) GDP grows 12 percent per annum; b) central government, 2009 NPC budget report; c) Policy bonds from China Bond; MOR from Wind Information; d) current local government debt, *Wall Street Journal*, May 4, 2010; e) incremental local government debt, *The Economic Observer* 经济观察报, May 10, 2010: 3; f) AMC obligations, Table 2.5; g) future NPLs based on 20 percent of total 2009 plus estimated 2010 non-local government loans of RMB19.56 trillion; h) Existing NPLs 2009, CBRC.

(those IOUs plus the 1998 and 2007 Special Bonds). When these obligations are included, public debt almost doubles, to 43 percent.

To this must be added the obligations of local governments, which are without doubt a part of the China sovereign. Beijing historically has been aware of this debt and that it is substantial; a quick look at the finance section of any *China Statistical Yearbook* illustrates this point. The Party, however, is conflicted: Does it really want to know the exact picture? Most successful Party leaders must at some point in their careers serve in the localities. Since local budgets are severely constrained, creative funding solutions—many of which would not withstand outside scrutiny—are the only choice open to the ambitious Party leader. Consequently, the best choice is not to arouse such scrutiny. Local governments comprise more than 8,000 entities at four distinct administrative levels. What is known is that the stock of local debt increased enormously after the announcement of the stimulus package in late 2008. Beijing required local governments to contribute at least two-thirds of the publicly announced total of RMB4 trillion.

This discussion is not meant to suggest that all these figures are exact and correct; it is enough to know the approximate scale of such obligations. In early 2010, Beijing publicly admitted to a figure for total local debt of RMB7.8 trillion—23 percent of GDP and likely to increase over the next few years, if only to complete projects already under way. One estimate of such additional funding needs is RMB4 trillion. There will undoubtedly be additional credit extended but, given the creative financing possibilities offered by the interaction of governments, banks, trust companies and finance companies, no one can know how much. For the purposes of this discussion, it is simply assumed that only RMB4 trillion is spent, so that by 2012, total local debt will be close to RMB12 trillion, or 28 percent of estimated GDP. While no one knows the true amount of local-government debt in China (the banking regulator most certainly does not), if the Hainan and GITIC experiences can be used as reference points, the scale of such debt is as vast as the country it finances.

Not to be forgotten in all of this are the non-performing loans, both current and those obligations yet to be written off from the 1990s. For the upcoming crop of NPLs that will derive from the stimulus-package lending of 2009 and follow-on loans of 2010, a total of about RMB20 trillion (US$2.9 trillion) is assumed.[1] Of this, 20 percent is assumed to have gone to local governments, while the other 80 percent relates to typical SOE or project lending for which new NPLs are estimated, based on a 20 percent rate that begins to be seen in 2011. For the obligations left over from the earlier bank restructuring, the total of RMB3.2 billion is a hard figure derived from audited financial statements and the bank regulator. Together, these old and forecast NPL numbers yield a total of RMB6.4 trillion or over 15 percent of estimated GDP for 2011.

Adding all this up suggests that as of year-end 2009, China's stock of public debt stood at nearly 76 percent of GDP, well above the international standard. This burden can only increase, given China's practice of generating a significant portion of GDP growth through fixed-asset investment. Others will arrive at different estimates. The point is simply that in the past few years, China has quickly built up significant levels of public debt, and that is without taking the value of contingent liabilities, such as social security obligations, into consideration.

AN EMPIRE APART

What if this debt buildup is not just the result of a weak hand at the financial tiller? It may also be accurate to say that these increases are the result of the government deliberately leveraging China's domestic balance sheet to achieve its policy goal of high GDP growth. The economics are simple and well understood: borrow expensive RMB now to build projects the state believes it needs, and make repayment at some point in the distant future using inevitably cheaper RMB.

Figure 8.2 shows the growth of outstanding central-government debt, here defined narrowly as that of the MOF plus the three policy banks and the Ministry of Railways only, as against the public debt of four developed economies, including the US. These developed economies have issued debt for a century; at times, as in the case of England in the late 1940s, national debt has been more than 200 percent of GDP. At times, these governments have even defaulted on their debt, as Germany did after World War II. These developed economies have extensive experience in managing public debt, both positive and negative. What is interesting about this chart is how in just a few years, China's narrowly defined stock of debt seems to be catching up with the levels of developed countries, some with a GDP many times larger than China's.

This picture of government borrowing is also illustrated by the amount of the annual national budget financed by new debt net of that issued to

FIGURE 8.2   Trends in outstanding public debt: US, Europe and China, 1990–2009

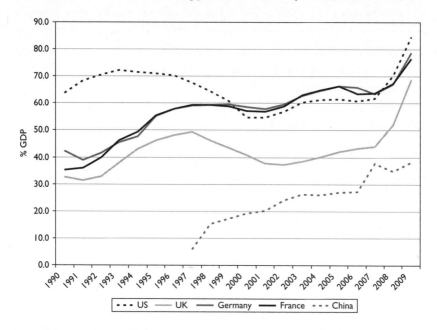

Source: China Bond and International Monetary Fund
Note: China's public debt includes only the MOF, the three policy banks, and the MOR. The Special MOF bonds of 1998 and 2007 are included.

repay maturing bonds (see Table 8.2). Such debt issuance represents new money and finances new budgetary spending and, of course, it will add to the stock of a country's obligations. In 2009, for example, net new bond issues from the MOF and the policy banks supported 22 percent of national expenditures, while new CGB issues alone financed 57 percent of central-government expenditures.[2] Similar to other Asian countries, China's national budgets seem to be dependent on increasing amounts of debt.

The budgetary dependence on debt can also be seen in the rapidly increasing amount of maturing central- and policy-bank debt. Over the period 2003–2009, the value of maturing MOF and policy-bank bonds grew at an annual compounded rate of 26.5 percent. These bonds were all refinanced; that is, rolled over into the future (see Figure 8.3). Net new debt plus debt issued to repay (and roll over) maturing debt equals the total amount of debt issued by China each year. Both add to the stock of China's outstanding public debt.

TABLE 8.2 Net new-debt issuance as proportion of government expenditure, 1997–2009

RMB million	National budgetary expenditures	Central budgetary expenditures	% National expenditures CGB + PB	% Central expenditures CGBs
1997	923	253	51%	46%
1998	1,080	313	52	128
1999	1,319	415	20	38
2000	1,589	552	19	44
2001	1,890	577	15	32
2002	2,205	677	31	79
2003	2,465	742	27	63
2004	2,849	789	19	40
2005	3,393	878	20	33
2006	4,042	999	18	20
2007	4,978	1,144	46	150
2008	6,259	1,334	17	19
2009	7,600	1,528	22	57

Source: *China Statistical Yearbook*, China Bond; author's calculation
Note: 2007 might be considered an anomaly given MOF's RMB1.55 trillion Special Bond.

FIGURE 8.3 Amount of MOF plus policy-bank debt rolled over, 1997–2009

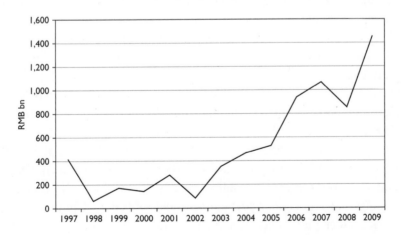

Source: China Bond
Note: Retired debt is calculated as a function of year-end depository balances and annual new debt issuance.

It might be the case that this debt machine is not fully understood by China's most senior leaders or they may be aware only of the more narrowly defined levels reported in the media. China's public-debt figure is typically presented as only MOF obligations, its most narrow definition. It is unlikely to be a coincidence that of the total of China's domestic debt obligations, only one percent is held directly by the end-investor: savings bonds. Aside from a minimal amount held by foreign banks and QFII funds, all else is either held or managed by state-controlled entities, from banks to fund-management companies. As the CEO of ICBC explained, China relies on "indirect" financing to achieve its economic growth goals. This means that banks decide on behalf of depositors how, to whom and under what conditions to lend deposits out. In a capital-market model, there is less room for such an intermediary; the end-investor is independent of the debt or equity issuer and makes investment or divestment decisions based on considerations independent of the interests of the issuer or borrower. In China, this is not the case: the Party controls the banks and the banks lend, as directed, to state-owned entities.

This is precisely where China differs from Mexico of 1994, Argentina of 1999 and Greece and Spain today. Aside from trade finance, China does not borrow money overseas and, because of the non-convertibility of the RMB, offshore investors are overwhelmingly excluded from the domestic capital markets. Nor are foreign banks competitive in the domestic loan and bond markets, given their need to make an adequate return on capital. As a result, foreign banks rarely contribute more than two percent to total financial assets in China; after the lending binge of 2009, they now stand at 1.7 percent. The only other major entry point into the system, QFII, is a CSRC product that is directed at the stock markets rather than bond markets. In any event, the current total quota allocated is, at US$17.1 billion, a relatively small amount. Even if fully invested in bonds, this would still pale by comparison with outstanding bond obligations of US$1.87 trillion. There is simply no way that offshore speculators, investors, hedge funds or others can get at China's domestic debt obligations and challenge the Party's valuation of these obligations. In short, the closed nature of China's financial markets suggests a deliberate government strategy based on a particular understanding of past international debt crises. China's financial system is an empire set apart from the world.

CRACKS IN THE WALLS

The fact that it is well-insulated from outside markets does not mean that China's finances are crisis-proof. The system can be disrupted by purely internal factors, as it clearly has been in the past. Take, for example, household savings, pension obligations and interest-rate exposure. Household savings are the foundation of the banks' capacity to lend. The heroic savings capacity of the Chinese people is virtually the only source of non-state money in the game. Since 2004, China's banks have enthusiastically expanded their consumer businesses to include mortgages, credit and debit cards and auto loans. What would happen to bank funding if the Chinese people learned how to borrow and spend with the same enthusiasm as consumers in the United States? Over the long term, this might be good for the economy and even for the banks. But in the short-to-medium term, it seems unlikely that the government will actively encourage American-style consumerism outside of the rich cities of the eastern seaboard. This, in itself, may be a source of great social instability as the more numerous relatives in the hinterlands become envious of leveraged lifestyles.

The overall demographic is pushing in the same direction. By 2050, *XinhuaNews* has stated, one out of four Chinese will be over the age of 65, but the actual number of retirees will be far greater (see Table 8.3). As the population ages, savings will be spent on old-age and health care. If the government continues to pursue growth through borrowing, the possibility

TABLE 8.3   China's ageing population

	Population (billion)	0–14 years	15–64 years	65+ years
1995	1.21	327	808	76
2000	1.26	328	845	87
2010	1.35	293	956	104
2020	1.43	287	989	214
2030	1.48	278	989	214
2040	1.49	287	950	252
2050	1.47	211	962	300

Source: World Bank, *Wall Street Journal Asia*, June 15–17, 2001: M1

of developing an economy based more on domestic consumption than export growth would seem low.

This also suggests that full funding for any national social-security program is a reform whose time is unlikely to come. Despite a strong beginning in 1997, the government continues to face difficulties in creating a standardized national program, on the one hand, and, on the other, sufficiently funding the programs it does have. Moreover, the funds it has under management lack suitable investment opportunities that can, with acceptable risk, yield returns higher than the rate of inflation. As noted earlier, at present only stocks and real estate, both highly speculative in nature, can potentially provide such a return. This harks once more back to the issue of China's stunted capital markets. As the workforce ages, it appears likely that Beijing may have to fund any gap in such obligations largely through debt issuance.[3] The Ministry of Labor and Social Security has estimated this contingent liability to be only RMB2.5 trillion, whereas in 2005, the World Bank arrived at an estimate of RMB13.6 trillion. This puts the range at somewhere between 10 to 40 percent of China's GDP; a very large obligation.

China's debt strategy is also vulnerable to increases in interest. At some point, a heavy interest burden arising from increasing amounts of debt will limit the government's ability to invest in new projects and grow the economy. Very rough estimates suggest that, as of FY2009, total interest expenditure on central- and local-government debt represents 12 percent of national budget revenues and may grow over the next two years to 15 percent (see Table 8.4). Inflation also poses a threat since it would both increase these government borrowing costs and put pressure on the valuation of bonds held on the banks' books as long-term investments; valuation provisions would have to be made. This is why the PBOC finds it so difficult to raise interest rates, thus limiting the range of tools at its disposal to deal with inflation. Raising bank lending rates affect enterprise performance and have a knock-on effect in the bond markets. It also raises expectations of currency appreciation and, therefore, can encourage inflows of hot money. The PBOC last changed lending rates (downward) in late 2008 and has since relied solely on the previously little-used deposit-reserve requirement.

This reserve tool was first established in 1985. Used only four times prior to 2003, it has been employed 28 times since. It limits a bank's capacity

TABLE 8.4 Estimated interest expense of central and local debt, 2009–2011

RMB billion	2009A	2010P	2011P
Amount			
Central-government debt	6,471.0	7,442.0	8,558.0
Policy banks plus MOR	4,845.8	5,577.0	6,414.0
MOF Special Bonds + receivables	2,628.0	2,628.0	2,628.0
Total central-government debt	*13,944.8*	*15,647.0*	*17,600.0*
Local-government debt	7,800.0	9,800.0	11,800.0
Interest Rate			
Central Government	0.0215	0.0215	0.0215
Policy banks plus MOR	0.0338	0.0338	0.0338
MOF Special bonds & receivables	0.0225	0.0225	0.0225
Local government debt	0.0625	0.0625	0.0625
Total annual interest	849.5	1,020.1	1,197.4
National revenues	6,847.7	7,395.5	7,987.2
Central revenues	3,589.6	3,876.8	4,186.9
Total interest expense as % national revenues	12.4%	13.8%	14.9%
Central interest expense as % central revenues	10.1%	10.5%	11.0%

Note: Assumes revenues grow eight percent annually; interest rates for central-government bonds reflect data in the ICBC FY2009 performance review; local-government debt interest rate assumed four percent over one-year deposit rate. Interest rates remain unchanged through 2011.

to make loans by removing a proportion of bank deposits: no funding, no loan. Currently the reserve ratio stands at 17 percent, which is close to its historic high of 17.5 percent; that is, 17 percent of all bank deposits sit in the PBOC's accounts. Using this policy tool and making massive sales of short-term notes into the inter-bank market are all the PBOC can do to manage China's money supply. It is little wonder that the central bank is vulnerable to political conservatives touting the efficacy of Soviet-style administrative intervention.

None of this means that China is in danger of default or even of a slowing in economic growth. If properly managed, there is no reason why China's use of debt can't continue for a long time. Witness the ongoing debt crisis in Europe, which has been a decade in the making. In the case of Greece, it appears likely that its financial accounts were managed to meet the requirements of entry into European Economic Community from the start. Yet it is only today, more than a decade later, that problems have emerged in public and markets have focused on them. Greece is an open economy with a thriving democracy. Think how long things may be obscured within China's still-opaque economic and political system.

Given China's geographical size and huge population, it is unlikely that its economy will grind to a halt in the way that Japan's did after its magnificent run in the 1980s. Unlike the Japanese banks then, China's banks are not deregulated nor are they near being sufficiently international to consider "going out," even if the Party would allow them to do so. To this can be added the very big lesson China's government appears to have learned from Japan: keep a tight lid on currency appreciation. China knows well that when Japan freed up the yen to appreciate and deregulated its financial markets, it was entering the last stage of its wild asset bubble. The Party will perhaps allow the RMB to appreciate a little to defuse diplomatic tensions, but it will never make the currency freely convertible. All of the talk around the internationalization of the RMB has proven its weight in gold diplomatically, but it cannot be any more than that unless holders of the RMB are able to use it freely offshore like any other currency. Until then, "internationalization" of the yuan is simply another form of barter trade.

In sum, China's growing dependence on debt to drive GDP growth implies that there will be no meaningful reform of interest rates, exchange rates or material foreign involvement in the domestic financial markets for the foreseeable future. Nor will there be any further meaningful reform or internationalization of the major banks, although future recapitalizations will inevitably take place. The events of the fall of 2008 have put an additional seal on this outcome. "Don't show me any failed models," is the refrain of Chinese officials these days. But is its own financial system a model for the world to study? Can China be thought of as an economic superpower, either now or in the future, with such a system?

IMPERIAL ORNAMENTS

Against this background, the question has to be asked: why go to the trouble of building debt and stock markets when the banks stand behind everything? Why don't the banks simply lend directly to the MOF or the CDB, just as they do to the local governments and their projects? What is the advantage of creating such a complex and difficult-to-manage financial system?

The answer to such questions is complicated and has many aspects. These include that the system serves as: i) an important catalyst for corporate transformation; ii), a mechanism allowing money to flow among various groups; and iii) a familiar surface for local business and politics that attracts foreign support and admiration. First of all, in the late 1980s as it considered SOE and other economic reforms, the Party wanted to make use of the most advanced economic practice available. The Western financial model, involving shareholding and capital markets, seemed to offer this. With strong support from Deng Xiaoping, a consensus formed around the active pursuit of equity-capital markets and SOE IPOs as channeled by Western legal, accounting and regulatory practices. In just a few short years, experimentation with international listings led to the creation of perhaps the largest Chinese enterprises in history: the National Team began to form.

This can only have been seen by the Party as a great success, but the National Team was also, in many ways, the gamechanger in China's political economy. Endowed with great economic and political power, why should these huge state enterprises want a domestic (or international) regulator or any other government agency to have a significant influence over their operations? Would such corporations want China's stock markets, including Hong Kong, to develop toward international best-practice standards? The answer at this point appears to be "No." The National Champions have the clout to slow, if not halt, market development if it is not in their interest. This explains why China presents such a mixed picture to international observers. Its markets have all the trappings of Western finance: B-shares, H-shares, locally incorporated bank subsidiaries, local-currency derivatives, QFII, QDII, securities, mutual fund and commodities joint ventures—all have been tried, some with great success, but they remain small extensions to the vast grounds of the Forbidden City.

There has been talk of an international board on the Shanghai Exchange since at least 1996 when Mercedes Benz sought a listing in Shanghai. In the debt markets, only the Asian Development Bank and the International Finance Corporation have been allowed to issue bonds, and only within the existing interest and investor framework and to fund state-approved projects. China's lively and important non-state sector has been allowed access to the Shenzhen stock market since 2004, but of the 400 companies listed, only four have made it to China's Top 100 by market capitalization and altogether they account for just 2.2 percent of total capitalization. In addition, the non-state companies are to be found in such areas as consumer, food, certain areas of hi-tech, pharmaceutical and other light industrial sectors in which the Party historically has had little stake. In short, the non-state sector, no matter how important to China's exports and employment, has not been allowed to develop into a challenge to the National Team.

The second aspect to answering this question is that it suits China's powerful interest groups to have a complex yet primitive financial system in which money frequently changes hands. Multiple products, regulators, markets and rules all disguise the origin and destination of China's massive cash flows. In this business environment, the National Champions, their family associates and other retainers plunder the country's large domestic markets and amass huge profits. With nationwide monopolies or, at worst, oligopolies, these business groups do not want change, nor do they believe that foreign participation is needed. How can China use its Anti-Monopoly Law when the Party owns the monopolies? The addition of foreign participants simply makes things more complicated than a simple consideration of the possible value they might add; why share the wealth? If Zhu Rongji's intention in signing China up to the World Trade Organization was to open it up to foreign competition and, therefore, economic change, after 2008, this goal seems to have faded from sight.

Can it be fairly said that these business interests are, in fact, China's government? Is it simply that, lacking a strong leader, the government presently cannot set its own agenda if it is in conflict with that of the National Team? The answer may well be "Yes." As far as the financial sector goes, the collapse of Lehman Brothers in September 2008 undermined the influence of those in the Party who sought a policy of greater openness and international engagement. The global financial crisis eliminated the political consensus in support of the Western financial model that had been in place since 1992. This has allowed the pre-reform economic vision of an egalitarian socialist planned economy to re-emerge. There are many in the Party and the government who never supported Red Capitalism in the first place. Like the old cadre quoted at the start of Chapter 1, these people have always wondered what the revolution had been for if it simply meant a return to the pre-revolution era of the 1930s and 1940s, with all its excesses. They see today the re-emergence of the same issues that led to the revolution in the first place. What they misunderstand is that without Western finance and open markets, China would not have achieved the extraordinary rise of which they are so justly proud.

There has been a great cost to China as a result of the Party's support for the National Team but the entire intention of creating National Champions should be understood against the backdrop of the globalization of industries taking place in the late 1990s.[4] In almost every industrial sector, China was beginning to face international competitors of a scale, expertise and economic clout that its own companies simply did not possess. The success of the US$4.5 billion China Mobile IPO in 1997 showed a way forward. The goal of placing companies on the *Fortune* 500 list for Zhu Rongji became the equivalent of America's Apollo moon program. Ironically, however, the new National Champions were born with too much political power—the Party should never have allowed their chairmen and CEOs to remain on the *nomenklatura* and enjoy such great political influence. As a result, these companies grew fat, wealthy and untouchable as they developed China's own domestic markets and always with the unquestioning support of a complaisant financial system.

Since they are so comfortable in a domestic market closed to meaningful foreign competition, the National Team faces great difficulties developing into an International Team. If China's banks are the strongest in the world, where were they when Western commercial and investment banks were on the ropes, ready to be bought for a song? It is entirely disingenuous to say, as a major Chinese banker has said, that the developed markets do not present significant profit opportunities for China. Rather, the government appears to be far happier working in weak economies, where its mix of economics and politics is quite effective. But this still demands the question: where is China's International Team?

There is a third aspect to China's mixed financial scene and involves a picture that outside observers, whether political, business or academic, feel comfortable with since it makes China resemble other emerging markets. In this regard, the infrastructure is the thing. Over the past 18 years, China has developed stock and debt-capital markets, a mutual-funds industry, pension funds, sovereign-wealth funds, currency markets, foreign participation, an internationalist central bank, home loans and credit cards, a burgeoning car industry and a handful of brilliant cities. As it looks like the West, international investors easily accept what they see; they are excited by it because it is at once so familiar and so unexpected. There is the feeling that all can be understood, measured and valued. They would not feel this way if China explicitly relied on a Soviet-inspired financial system even though, in truth, this is largely what China remains.

The Chinese commonly explain the complexity of their system saying: "Our economy is different from the West, so our markets work differently than those in the West." It turns out that this is a simple statement of the truth. China is an economy that, from the outside, appears as a huge growth story; one extraordinary boom that has continued over the last 10 years. This is just the surface. China has been a series of booms and busts within its overall growth story; it deserves and repays far closer scrutiny from all sides including the Chinese themselves, but especially from those in the West. One cannot simply assume that words such as "stocks" or "bonds" or "capital" or "yield curves" or "markets" have the same meaning in China's economic and political context. To do so reflects a lack of curiosity and seriousness that can rapidly lead to misunderstanding and wasted opportunity. It is a luxury that neither China nor its foreign partners can afford. The prolonged efforts of the Party and government to mix Western capital markets with state planning have produced spectacular change in a short period. This has obscured the fact that all able bodies are desperately engaged in "the primitive accumulation of capital" in an unprecedented social experiment. If Karl Marx were alive today, he would without doubt find plenty of material for a new version of his masterpiece which he might call *Das Kapital with Chinese characteristics*.

ENDNOTES

1   This is derived as follows: 2009, RMB9.56 trillion actual; 2010, RMB10 trillion based on annualized 1Q 2010 actual lending.

2   Bond issues are accounted for as revenue in China's budget accounting. Since 2000, interest expense has been included in expenditure budgets, but repayment of maturing bond debt is not included as an expenditure item.

3   Since 2008, the government has adopted the old 2001 policy of paying 10 percent of the shares of listing companies into the National Social Security Fund. Even so, the fund continues to be seriously underfunded.

4   See Nolan 2001 for an extensive discussion of SOE reform in the context of the global consolidation of industry.

Appendix

Central Government Organization of Major Financial System Participants

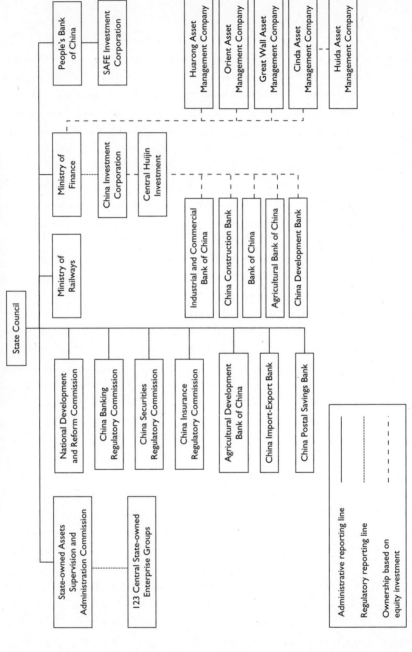

Ministry of Finance Off-Balance Sheet Debt Obligations in Co-managed Accounts

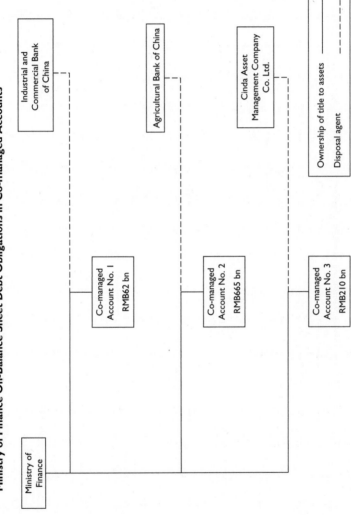

Typical Local Government Financing-related Entities

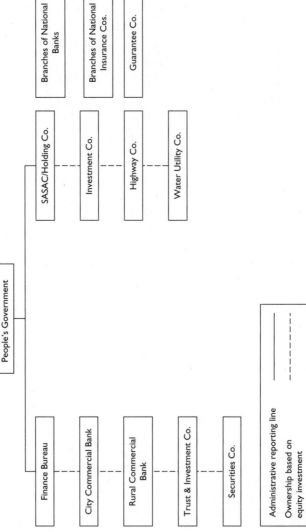

Select Bibliography

Newspapers and periodicals

21st Century Business Herald 21世纪经济报导
Caijing 财经
Financial Times
The Economic Observer 经济观察报
Wall Street Journal

Websites and Information Systems

Bloomberg
Caixin 财新   www.caing.com
China Bond   www.chinabond.com.cn
NAFMII   www.nafmii.org.cn
People's Bank of China   www.pbc.gov.cn
US-China Business Council   www.uschina.org
Wind Information   www.wind.com.cn

Publications

Yearbooks or annuals

Agricultural Bank of China, annual reports, 2007–2008
Agricultural Bank of China, H-share prospectus, 2010
Bank of China, annual reports, 2003–2009
China Development Bank, Prospectus, US$600 million notes due 2014
Construction Bank of China, annual reports, 2003–2009
Industrial and Commercial Bank of China, annual reports, 2003–2008
State Statistical Bureau, *China Statistical Yearbook* 中国统计年鉴, *various years* (Beijing: China Statistics Press 中国统计出版社)
People's Bank of China, *Financial Stability Report*, 2005–2009, www.pbc.gov.cn
Su Ning, Chief Editor, 1948–2005 *China Financial Statistics* 中国金融统计, two volumes (Beijing: Zhongguo jinrong chubanshe 中国金融出版社, 2007)

Books, articles and monographs

Brodsgaard, Kjeld Erik, "Politics and business group formation in China," unpublished manuscript, April 2010.
Curry, Timothy, and Shibut, Lynn, "The cost of the savings and loan crisis: truth and consequences," *FDIC Banking Review* 13(2), December 2000: 26–35.
Demirguc-Kunt, Asli, and Levine, Ross, *Financial Structure and Economic Growth*. Cambridge: MIT Press, 2004.

Faure, David, *China and Capitalism: a history of business enterprise in modern China*. Hong Kong: Hong Kong University Press, 2006.

Gao, Jian, *China's Debt Capital Markets*. Singapore: John Wiley & Sons, 2007.

Gao, Jian, *Zhongguo guozhai* 中国国债 (China Bonds). Bejing: Economic Science Press 经济科学出版社, 1995.

Nolan, Peter, *China and the Global Economy*. Palgrave: MacMillan, 2001.

Shih, Victor, "Big Rock Candy Mountain," *China Economic Quarterly* 14(2), June 2010.

Walter, Carl E. and Howie, Fraser J.T., *Privatizing China: inside China's stock markets* (2nd edition). Singapore: John Wiley & Sons, 2006.

Wang, Nianyong, *Fusu yu qibu*: 1980–1991 *nian Zhongguo zhengquan shichang jianshi* 复苏与起步: 1980–1991 年中国证券市场简史 (Recovery and Rise: a brief history of China's securities markets from 1980–1991). Beijing: China Financial & Economic Publishing House 中国财政经济出版社, 2004.

Wu, Jinglian, *Zhongguo jingji 60 nian* 中国经济60年 (60 years of China's economy), *Caijing* 财经, September 28, 2009, p. 98 ff.

Xing, Ziling, *Qianqiu gongzui Mao Zedong* 千秋功罪毛泽东 (Mao Zedong: merits and crimes of the century). Hong Kong: Shuzuofang chubanshe 书作坊出版社, 2007.

Yang, Kaisheng, "Wending woguo shangye yinhang ziben chongzu de jidian sikao 稳定我国商业银行资本充足的几点思考" (Several thoughts about stabilizing the capital adequacy levels of our commercial banks.). *21st Century Business Herald* 21世纪经济报导, April 13, 2010:10.

Zhou, Xiaochuan, "Learn lessons from the past for the benefit of future endeavor," Speech at the China Bond Market Development Summit, Beijing, October 20, 2005, www.pbc.gov.cn/english/detail.asp?col=6500&ID=82

Index